Jurgen's book is practical and fun, but most of all, it's subversive. If you care enough to get started, you'll discover that these tools will transform everything about your organization.

Seth Godin

Author of *The Icarus Deception*

Brilliant, counterintuitive, and creative approach to management. Very insightful and humanistic. Highly recommended!

Derek Sivers

Founder of CD Baby, TED speaker, author of *Anything You Want*

Managing for Happiness is the best walkabout in a constantly evolving landscape of management.

Tomas Rybing

Director Project Management at Aptilo Networks

In our always-on, real-time world, the nature of work has changed, potentially for the better. While people can be more autonomous and more productive, they can also self-destruct easier. Jurgen tackles these important changes in his fun and interesting book.

David Meerman Scott

Bestselling author of *The New Rules of Marketing and PR*

Don't wait for managers to fix management problems around you. Be the manager of your own fate and take action instead! This insightful book will not only help you get on the right track, but will also teach you how to enable people around you so that you can create a better working environment for yourself.

Kamil Posiadała

Agile Software Developer

Engage people, improve work, and delight clients: These are the tenets of this amazing book, which will show you how to transform the entire layer of management in your organization into a wellspring of creativity, productivity, and engagement. Excellent!

Marshall Goldsmith

A Thinkers Top 50 Expert, Top Ten Global Business Thinker, and top-ranked Executive Coach

---

Today, all managers are marketers. You need to sell your ideas, your plans, and your solutions. *Managing for Happiness* sets you on a path to success in a world where we are each responsible for managing our own career and our own contribution to the world.

Penelope Trunk

Author of *Brazen Careerist: The New Rules for Success*

How do you become one of the best managers in the world? Sports professionals would hire a good coach and exercise daily. *Managing for Happiness* from Jurgen Appelo is your personal coach who gives you tons of exercises and practical advice for the modern manager. The only thing you need to add is the daily exercising.

Tobias Leisgang

Systems Engineering Manager at Texas Instruments

In a rapidly changing world where predictable Newtonian doctrine is no longer up to the challenges being placed on managers, Jurgen Appelo's timely book provides an incredibly accessible leap into the thinking that is likely to define the manager of tomorrow.

Deane Sloan

Chief Technology Officer at Equinox IT

Want to know what the next stage of management may look like? Do yourself a favor and take a look at *Managing for Happiness* by Jurgen Appelo. Chock full of management nuggets as well as exercises and activities, *Managing for Happiness* provides insights into how to engage the next-generation workforce.

John Baldoni

Author of MOXIE: *The Secret to Bold and Gutsy Leadership*, Chair of Leadership Development at N2Growth

Do you want a feel-good book about management? Enjoy reading *Managing for Happiness*. Every chapter is full of aha! moments. I read it in public transport, and I reached the office with a smile and great ideas to improve the workplace.

Jeanne Estelle Thebault
President of Montreal IIBA Chapter

Steering a software factory team of 700 people, I'm confronted every day with the challenge to unleash the best out of our people and our teams in order for happy customers to receive high-quality software every two weeks. This book provides our teams with insights, tools, stories, games . . . to keep our people doing the right thing right, with passion.

Johan Lybaert
Director of Applications Europe at Cegeka

Do you dream of a management more adapted to the complexity of our world? Great news, this is a reality! *Managing for Happiness* by Jurgen Appelo is the toolbox of the agile gardener who promotes collaboration, builds the team around common values, grows skills, and motivates his coworkers. You now have the keys to change the world. Like me, read this inspiring book and cultivate happiness in your organization.

Loïc Leofold
AGILE and Management Consultant at Astrakhan

Leadership is hard to get right, but with a decent set of tools and exercises, the job is immeasurably easier. This book offers those tools, exercises, and above all, insight into how a twenty-first century manager behaves. Work and the workforce are fundamentally different compared to how they were even a decade ago, and Jurgen's book helps engage and enthuse the reader to become a better manager and lead their team to success.

Mike Pearce
Development Manager at MOO.com

If management is too important to leave it to managers only, then the agile management practices described by Jurgen Appelo in this book are way too valuable to apply them only to the IT environment. Motivated, nimble, and versatile teams are a pillar of success in today's world of financial services. You will find out how to build them from this book!

Tomasz Sitkowski
Acting CRO at mBank CZ/SK

As the current generation enjoys work-life integration, people will look and respond to "lean forward" management. *Managing for Happiness* will provide a complete guide to step out of the office and contribute to a culture of success as a goal while having fun as your journey.

Sebastián Diéguez
Agile Coach and Evangelist

Many authors make claims, but Jurgen Appelo delivers on them. He offers a combination of crisp, articulate thoughts in an easy, engaging read. If you're looking for actionable advice that will help you build a better, stronger, and more productive relationship with those you lead, then I'd highly recommend you read Jurgen's book.

Mike Myatt
Author of *Hacking Leadership*, a *Forbes* leadership columnist, and founder at N2Growth

There's another way to envision management. In this book, Jurgen Appelo is offering practices and exercises you can easily try, to change your own environment. While developing your management talent, you will say, like me: Thank you, Jurgen!

Alexis Monville
Chief Agility Officer at eNovance, Cofounder of Ayeba

Cover design: Linda Hirzmann

This book is printed on acid-free paper.

Published by John Wiley & Sons, Inc., Hoboken, New Jersey.
Published simultaneously in Canada.

For general information about our other products and services, please contact our Customer Care Department within the United States at (800) 762-2974, outside the United States at (317) 572-3993 or fax (317) 572-4002.

Wiley publishes in a variety of print and electronic formats and by print-on-demand. Some material included with standard print versions of this book may not be included in e-books or in print-on-demand. If this book refers to media such as a CD or DVD that is not included in the version you purchased, you may download this material at http://booksupport.wiley.com. For more information about Wiley products, visit www.wiley.com.

ISBN 978-1-119-26868-0 (cloth); ISBN 978-1-119-26900-7 (ePDF); ISBN 978-1-119-26901-4 (ePub)

Printed in the United States of America

10 9 8 7 6 5 4

Managing for Happiness

Games, Tools, and Practices to Motivate Any Team

Jurgen Appelo

WILEY

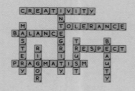

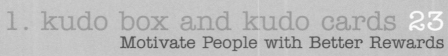

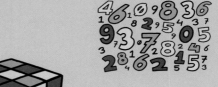

Preface: Better Management for Everyone

> Good ideas are not adopted automatically. They must be driven into practice with courageous patience.
>
> Hyman Rickover,
> American admiral
> (1900–1986)

I once tried to motivate an employee to improve his performance and productivity by giving him a smaller raise than his peers on the team. It didn't work. The situation actually got worse, and in a typical example of the-universe-hates-all-my-best-intentions, ultimately the whole team was affected by demotivation and resentment.

In my defense, the work this employee had produced was terrible. As his manager, I had to deal with the complaints, threats, and abuse by customers over the quality of our services—or lack thereof—and I was feeling quite desperate. I had to do something! So I did, but it was the wrong approach. And because nothing ever worked, I hated being a manager.

That was 20 years ago.

As a manager, you have to make choices. You cannot just let demotivation among your team members run its course. You have to do something! This book will help you to do things. It contains a number of great practices and exercises for teams and managers in the twenty-first century. Most are borrowed from other people who often did a much better job at motivating their colleagues than I ever could, and they became great managers of teams. Fortunately, I dared to run some experiments of my own and had a couple of small successes too. Therefore, some of the ideas presented here are my own simple inventions.

I started loving management when I decided to stop inflicting bad management practices upon my coworkers. I manage the worldwide Happy Melly business network, the global Management 3.0 licensing program, my speaking engagements, and everyone who is somehow involved with my articles, books, and courseware. I don't pay any of these people an annual bonus in order to get things done; I don't have vacation policies, flextime policies, or open-door policies; and none of my contacts need to fear that I will require an annual performance appraisal. Interestingly enough, the Management 3.0 facilitators, Happy Melly members, and many others I work with are highly engaged, love improving their work, and are eager to learn how to delight their clients. How is that possible without organizing regular one-on-ones in my private office with each and every one of them?

Last year, one of the members of my current team said to me, "You are the first manager I've had who doesn't suck." She meant that as a compliment. This was 20 years after I made a complete mess of team motivation. Now I am proud to say that my current team members are happy, motivated, and quite productive. And as their manager, I don't suck. That's a relief.

This is a management book for everyone: developers, artists, writers, team leaders, middle managers, designers, project managers, product managers, human resource managers, marketers, testers, coaches, mentors, consultants, trainers, facilitators, entrepreneurs, and freelancers. Everyone is, to some degree, responsible for management activities. This book tells you how you can implement better management, possibly with fewer managers, by looking at what other companies in the world have been doing. They have paved the way for the rest of us!

Read this book and squeeze 20 years of struggle for me into a few days of learning for you. I will show you how you can get a happier organization thanks to great practices and plenty of management activities that, in many cases, don't even require managers.

And maybe it will take me another 20 years of running management experiments to actually become really, really good. I hope you will join me on that journey.

Jurgen Appelo, December 2015
jurgen@noop.nl

No managers were harmed while writing this book.

introduction

What Is Management 3.0?

> Contrary to what I believed as a little girl, being the boss almost never involves marching around, waving your arms, and chanting, "I am the boss! I am the boss!"
>
> Tina Fey,
> American comedian
> (1970-)

When an organization's culture is bad, don't just blame the managers. Happiness in an organization is everyone's responsibility. Better management means engaging people, improving the whole system, and increasing value for clients. For most people, however, these principles are not enough. They need concrete practices or, in other words, regular exercises.

Management is too important to leave to the managers. I have come to this conclusion after 20 years of being a manager, writing two management books, giving 80 management courses in 30 countries, and speaking at almost 100 conferences worldwide, some of them about management. I've noticed that most leaders don't know how to solve their management problems and most knowledge workers, such as engineers, teachers, consultants, and designers, don't realize that they are also (to some extent) responsible for management stuff. I firmly believe that, like keeping the noise down, the files organized, the meeting room tidy, and the customers happy, management is *everyone's job*. At one time or another, we all fit the description of manager.[1]

I am pleased to say that, of all the participants in my public workshops, fewer than 20 percent considered themselves to be managers. The other 80 percent were usually developers, coaches, consultants, entrepreneurs, team leaders, and other kinds of **creative workers** (see sidebar). This wide diversity of participants shows one of two things: Either management is an activity that is relevant to many more workers than just managers, or I am extremely bad at targeting the correct audience for my courses. I prefer the former interpretation!

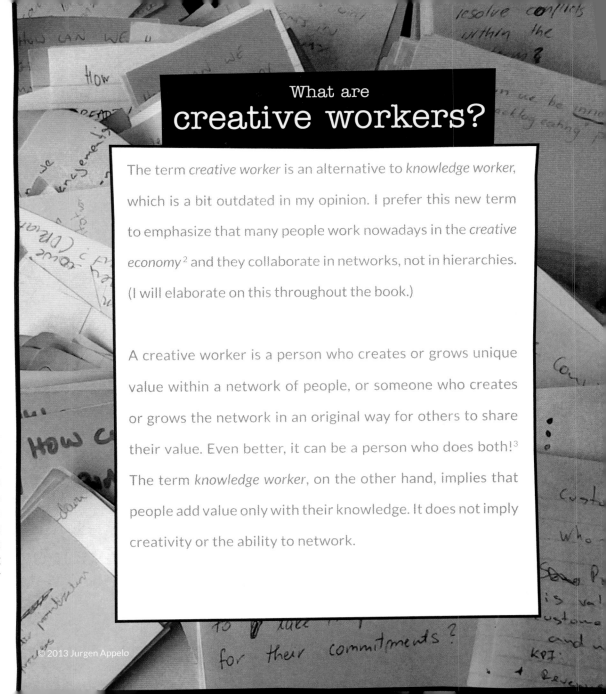

What are creative workers?

The term *creative worker* is an alternative to *knowledge worker*, which is a bit outdated in my opinion. I prefer this new term to emphasize that many people work nowadays in the *creative economy*[2] and they collaborate in networks, not in hierarchies. (I will elaborate on this throughout the book.)

A creative worker is a person who creates or grows unique value within a network of people, or someone who creates or grows the network in an original way for others to share their value. Even better, it can be a person who does both![3] The term *knowledge worker*, on the other hand, implies that people add value only with their knowledge. It does not imply creativity or the ability to network.

For two years, I kept track of the questions that participants from all over the world asked me during these management workshops. I have a box with nearly 2,000 colorful sticky notes expressing an equal number of colorful and sticky problems. Many issues in the box are the same or similar and were reported to me almost everywhere I went. These are the questions I encountered most often:

- How can we motivate our workers?
- How can we change the organization's culture?
- How can we change the mindset of managers?
- How can we get teams to take responsibility?
- How can we improve teamwork and collaboration?
- How can we get managers to trust their teams?
- How can we develop people's competencies?
- How can we be agile when the organization is not?

Notice that *all* these questions, except the last one, are asking, "How can we change *other* people?" This attitude is a reflection of the traditional approach to management: one person manipulating the behaviors of others. But what if all these management problems were simply the outcome of an incorrect interpretation of management? When everyone is trying to manipulate everyone else, should we be surprised that problems never go away and that new ones keep popping up? When people don't focus on improving *themselves*, is it any wonder they're always complaining about *each other*?

I often ask audiences if they have heard about global movements, improvement methods, or innovative management practices, and usually only a few hands go up. But when I ask them if their organization's culture needs to change, almost everyone says yes! It seems that few people learn, but most find fault in how their colleagues work. Perhaps they could change the culture together if they just start learning what has already been tried successfully elsewhere. Maybe they could stop reporting problems when they stop manipulating each other and instead start to improve themselves.

The focus of this book

The improvement of a person's approach to management is my focus in this book. I want to show all creative workers, including designers, middle managers, project managers, mentors, trainers, freelancers, and others, what they can do to change the way their collaborative work is managed. You don't have to solve all the problems mentioned earlier. If you choose to have a different view of management, the problems can resolve themselves. And you don't need to wait for permission from the managers. Change yourself, inspire others, and enjoy the book!

© 2013 FaceMePLS, Creative Commons 2.0
https://www.flickr.com/photos/faceme/8345123691

If your best experiences in life are all vacations, then maybe you shouldn't return to work tomorrow.

The misery of workers worldwide (managers included) is personified by the fictional character of Melly Shum, who has hated her job for almost 25 years. Melly is depicted on a huge billboard in my hometown of Rotterdam, the Netherlands. She sits in her office, looks into the camera with a thin smile, and has not stopped working since 1990 (except for a brief vacation in 2013 due to office maintenance, after which she returned to work on another floor). Melly Shum, imagined and realized by artist and photographer Ken Lum, is for me *the* symbol for all workers who feel disengaged and unhappy about their organizations but who don't feel ready to quit their jobs. According to several studies, this situation accounts for about two-thirds of the global workforce.[4,5,6]

The happiness of managers and other workers is crucial because happy people are more productive.[7] I firmly believe we can only improve worker happiness when everyone feels responsible for management and learns to manage the system instead of managing each other. The only reason people suffer from bad organizations is that they don't stand up to say, "I'm not taking this any longer; go boss yourself!" It troubles me that, when I ask people for their favorite moments in life, they usually only list things that happened in their personal time. But if your best experiences are all vacations, then maybe you shouldn't return to work tomorrow.

Doing the Wrong Thing

The reason I travel a lot is that I give presentations and workshops on almost every continent about modern management in the twenty-first century. Some people have said that the advice and practices I share are simply common sense, and I might even agree. Unfortunately, as many before me have observed, common sense is not common practice. Common practice for me is eating giant bags of M&Ms while watching a movie; common sense would be to watch my health and eat only the green ones. For organizations, common practice is that they are managed like machines, with their workers treated as gears and levers. I call this **Management 1.0**. In this style of management, people assume the organization consists of parts and that improvement of the whole requires monitoring, repairing, and replacing those parts. We can find Management 1.0 everywhere around us.

For example, some writers suggest that "winner-take-all" organizations should rank employees using measurements of individual achievements and give more work to the organization's "best performers" while getting rid of the bad ones.[8] These writers seem to assume that the community of employees is better served with competition and politics than with collaboration and a shared purpose.

Other writers suggest that employees have a tendency to "slack off" when the boss is on vacation. After all, "When the cat's away the mice will play!" Therefore, the boss should return to the office regularly to peek around the corner and check which of the mice are laboriously sweating on the treadmill and which ones are partying with the cheese.[9] It seems the assumption here is that work-life balance is bad and that nobody is needed to check the "work" of the cats.

Further extending this idea, other writers suggest that bosses should continuously monitor whether people are actually using office tools to do work and not for Skyping with friends, Facebooking diary entries, or Photoshopping baby pictures. The crucial and ethical part of this practice, it is claimed, is to let everyone know that they're being watched.[10] In this case, the assumption is that managers can keep everyone's trust only when they are honest about not trusting anyone.

sigh

It is interesting to note that these examples were all delivered to my online news reader on *one single day*. Imagine the volume of nonsense that floods workers over the span of a year, or during a lifetime! For me, such articles are a clear sign that treating employees like adult human beings might be common sense, but it is not common practice. On the other hand, it is a great opportunity for anyone who tries to make the world of work a better place. There's obviously plenty to do!

> Treating employees like adult human beings might be common sense, but it is not common practice.

Doing the Right Thing Wrong

Fortunately, some people have learned to do better. In a **Management 2.0** organization, everyone recognizes that "people are the most valuable assets" and that managers have to become "servant leaders" while steering the organization from "good to great." These are certainly interesting ideas, but sadly, managers often use the wrong approach. They correctly understand that improvement of the whole organization is not achieved by merely improving the parts but, at the same time, they prefer to stick to the hierarchy and have a tendency to forget that human beings don't respond well to top-down control and mandated "improvements."

One of these good ideas is that managers should have regular **one-on-ones** with employees.[11] It's an idea I feel positive about—it acknowledges that management is about human beings and that managers must seek ways to help people find their true calling and achieve great results together. Unfortunately, many managers don't see that they should manage the system around the people, not the people directly, and that they should leave micromanagement to the teams. Instead, they use one-on-ones for individual goal-setting, and they follow up later by asking people for status updates—both of which only *reinforce* the superior-subordinate relationship that is typical in all command-and-control organizations.

The suggestion to organize **360-degree feedback** is also quite reasonable.[12] The issue is that managers are not independent observers. They cannot objectively assess the performance of individual people, and therefore evaluations should be provided from multiple perspectives. Unfortunately, some people don't realize that the method they use to evaluate performance will influence that performance. And thus HR departments install electronic performance appraisal tools that require people to give anonymous feedback about each other. Trust breaks down completely because managers are allowed to know more about employees than employees are allowed to know about each other, which emphasizes that managers are more important than nonmanagers.

There's also not much wrong with the idea behind **balanced scorecards**.[13] The problem with measurements is that one metric easily leads to sub-optimization (improving one part of the work while diminishing another part), and therefore you need multiple perspectives to have a more holistic view of the organization's performance.

> Managers are allowed to know more about employees than employees are allowed to know about each other.

Unfortunately, when managers continue to view the organization as a hierarchy, they usually try to impose goals and metrics on every part of the system. But in complex systems, performance is usually found in the relationships between the parts, and proper goals and metrics can only emerge from intelligent local interaction, not as part of a top-down target-setting framework.

I could go on and on discussing the positive ideas behind *servant leadership*, *total quality management*, the *theory of constraints*, and many more management models. All of them have undoubtedly helped organizations move away from Management 1.0, which is good. Management 2.0 organizations are at least *trying* to do the right thing. But they do some of those things the wrong way because they're still stuck with a hierarchical view of organizations. They adopt good ideas but force-fit them onto a bad architecture. This is primarily why the good ideas rarely stick and why fads and fashions fail to deliver on their promises and will always be replaced one after the other.[14] The only effect consistently achieved across all ideas implemented by bosses is that they *reinforce the position of the boss*.

> The essential flaw of TQM [total quality management] is that, when implemented, it tends to reinforce the mechanistic and hierarchical models that are consistent with the mental maps of most managers.
>
> Chris Argyris,
> *Flawed Advice and the Management Trap*, loc:359

© 2012 Jurgen Appelo

No Control

Do managers need to be smarter than nonmanagers? Recently, I got involved in an interesting e-mail discussion about the question of whether management work requires smarter people. It is a regularly occurring topic. The reasoning is usually that managers have a higher role than other workers, overseeing a bigger part of the organization, and therefore their work involves more complexity. The increased responsibility suggests the need for them to be smarter than nonmanagers.

It sounds reasonable. It's also nonsense.

Scientists seem to agree that the human brain is one of the most complex systems in the universe. Together with the complexity of the rest of the human body, this makes each human being very, very complex. The *law of requisite variety*, probably the most famous law among complexity thinkers (see sidebar), says:

> **If a system is to be stable, the number of states of its control mechanism must be greater than or equal to the number of states in the system being controlled.**

Wikipedia, "Variety (Cybernetics)"

What are complexity thinkers?

The study of *complexity science* investigates how relationships between parts of a complex system (such as an ecosystem or an economy) give rise to the collective behaviors of that system, and how the whole system in turn influences the parts. The term *systems thinking* represents the process of understanding how human systems (including people, teams, and organizations) behave, interact with their environment, and influence each other. A *complexity thinker* applies both: insights from scientific research into complex systems and understanding of the workings of social systems.

Some people claim that the law of requisite variety is as important to managers as the Laws of Relativity are to physicists.[15] The Law of Requisite Variety requires that anything that controls a system must be *at least as complex* as the system being controlled. When we translate this to management work, it means the manager of a system must operate at a similar or higher level of complexity than the system, in order to *fully control* it.

That idea makes sense, but there's a caveat. When I am the manager of a group of people, I can never have more complexity than this complex system of human beings (which includes all their complex interactions). It's just impossible!

The problem here is the word *control*. We shouldn't use it in a social context. People are not thermostats! Instead, we should use terms such as *lead*, *coach*, *inspire*, *motivate*, *constrain*, *govern*, and *help*. By using these words we work our way around the law of requisite variety because we choose to ignore part of the system's complexity.

For example, a surgeon treating a human heart chooses to ignore a significant part of the complexity of the human body. He focuses only on the heart. Not the hands, not the brain, not the tonsils, and not the hemorrhoids—just the heart. That's his job. In fact, during an operation the surgeon might ignore so much complexity of the human body that his job could be called merely difficult, but not complex. However, the nurses who handle the patient before and after the operation focus on the patient's well-being, which is definitely a complex matter. But they ignore the details of the heart. That's what the surgeon is for.

Now, what about the hospital director? Does she have a "higher role"? Is her work "more complex" because her scope of concern is the entire hospital, including lots of surgeons, doctors, nurses, and patients? Does the role of the director require a smarter brain?

Not at all!

With hundreds of patients and workers in the hospital, the complexity is astounding. Nobody can ever claim to "control" the hospital, because *indeed* the law of requisite variety would demand that there be at least as much complexity in the director's brain as the complexity of everyone else combined! Obviously, this is not a reasonable requirement. With a complex system, there is no such thing as central control. The director ignores a tremendous amount of complexity and only focuses on the things she considers important. The rest is all delegated to smart creative workers. In fact, the work of the director could be *less* complex than that of a nurse!

> With a complex system there is no such thing as central control.

Delegation of control is the only way to manage complex systems. There is no other option. If we didn't have delegation, the president of the United States would have to be the person with the highest mental processing ability in the entire country! Obviously, the United States has performed quite well without usually having such a person in the Oval Office.

The idea that management work is "more complex" and that the management role requires "higher mental abilities" is, frankly, nonsense. However, I understand it is an easy mistake to make with a limited understanding of systems theories. It is no surprise that many managers love this kind of thinking! Who doesn't want to hear they are smarter than others? Who doesn't want to see confirmation that their work is hard and requires much higher pay? Who doesn't want to be acknowledged as "the boss"? Any book confirming that bosses are "leaders" who are destined to lead their organizations to greatness is sure to be consumed like cake at a children's party. In fact, it follows logically that Management 1.0 and Management 2.0 literature sells quite well to upper management layers!

> I see this classic image of "the boss" as a total anachronism. It may work in certain connotations like "organized crime boss," "union boss," or "pit boss," but being bossy per se is not an attribute that I have ever seen as desirable in a manager or anyone else for that matter.

Richard Branson, *Like a Virgin*, loc:2400

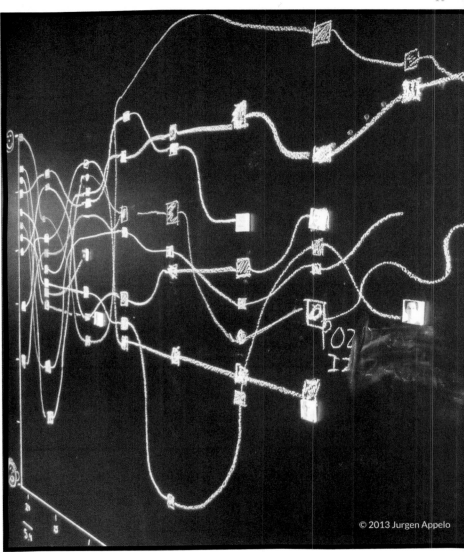

© 2013 Jurgen Appelo

Why Do We Need Management?

In the last decade or two, we have witnessed the emergence of a good number of big ideas, including agile, lean, scrum, kanban, beyond budgeting, lean startup, delivering happiness, design thinking, real options, scenario planning, conscious capitalism, and many more. What all these manifestos, methods, and movements have in common is that they promote better ways of working while borrowing a thing or two from science. 🦋 I often say they're like a family. They all share the same DNA, which they received from their parents: **systems thinking** and **complexity theory**. And sometimes the family members quarrel and fight, just like in any other normal family.

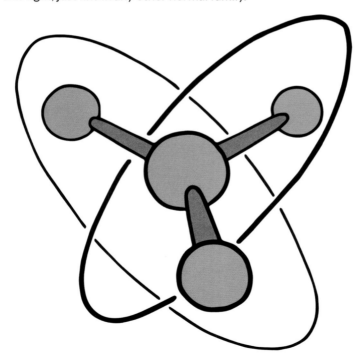

Unfortunately, many creative workers find it hard to implement such big ideas in their organizations because they always encounter obstacles. The barriers most often mentioned are organizational culture, organizational structure, change management, people management, command-and-control hierarchies, and other topics usually directly associated with management.[16] In fact, all around the world, the cultures and practices of Management 1.0 and 2.0 are the main obstacles. They prevent people from upgrading their work processes to more modern and sensible approaches.

This should come as no surprise to anyone who has ever read the work of management expert Peter F. Drucker, since he convincingly argued decades ago that "management is about human beings, and management is the critical, determining factor."[17] You can optimize all you want in development, design, testing, finance, marketing, human resources, or anywhere else. Ultimately, management always needs to change as well, or else your improvement efforts will run into a wall.

Management always needs to change as well.

Interestingly enough, Drucker referred to the work of *management* as being critical, not the job of the *managers*. I usually compare it to the work of *testing* versus the job of *testers*. Obviously, it's crucial that you test your products, but it may not be crucial for you to work with full-time testers. The availability of dedicated testers depends on the size of the organization, the need for specialization, and various other factors. But no matter whether you have testers or not, *everyone* should feel responsible for testing the products they are working on. And when the product is bad, I hope nobody blames only the testers.

Likewise, *management* of the work is a crucial activity, but this could be done with or without full-time managers. Again, having dedicated managers depends on the size of the organization, the availability of mahogany desks, and plenty of other things. However, no matter whether there are managers or not, *everyone* should feel responsible for management. When the organization sucks, don't blame just the managers!

As I said in the beginning, I strongly believe management is too important to leave to the managers. Management is everyone's job.

> No matter whether there are managers or not, everyone should feel responsible for management.

Do we <u>really</u> need managers?

The same discussion emerges again and again. "Can we do business without managers?" "Can we get rid of all the management layers?"[18, 19, 20]

When you translate it to testing or marketing, you will see how silly the discussion is. "Can we make products without testers?" "Can we get rid of all the marketers?" As if only design and development make a viable business. Dream on! Obviously, your business will require work that we typically categorize as testing, marketing, or management activities. Whether or not you have people who *specialize* in these activities is beside the point. The work is crucial and needs to be done, one way or another. Sure, fire all the managers. But someone needs to define the purpose of the business, which people get hired, how everyone gets paid, and how much to spend on coffee. This book is for those who care about their organization, not about the titles on their business cards.

Management 3.0 Principles

I have claimed that Management 1.0 is doing the wrong thing and that Management 2.0 is doing the right thing in the wrong way. Now you probably expect me to say that Management 3.0 is doing the right thing (or maybe doing the wrong thing right). But what is "doing the right thing" when it comes to management? To answer that question, I need to answer another one first.

The great thing about traveling to many countries and meeting people at lots of companies and conferences is that I get to hear very interesting questions, like I did recently in Gothenburg, Sweden:

> **What if we did everything that the <insert method here> experts tell us to do, including all the practices, but the products we make are still bad, and the organization still sucks? What then? What can we do when <insert method here> is not enough?**

Well, I think that's easy. Principles rarely change, but practices always depend on context. Therefore, it depends on how you interpret <insert method here>. If you associate the method with a collection of principles, you can always keep inventing new practices, as long as they adhere to the principles. But if you associate <insert method here> with a specific set of practices, you're doomed. You're going to need a new fashionable word very soon.

Some of my friends prefer organic food over factory food. I respect their opinion that consuming organic food is, for them, the right thing to do. Choosing better food over mass-processed food is not a method. It's not a framework. It's not a religion. It's a way of life. It's what my friends believe is right. Doing "the right thing" means acting in a way that is consistent with a core belief.

My core belief for management is that organizations are complex, adaptive systems and that good management means taking care of the system instead of manipulating people. I believe that improving the environment so that it keeps workers engaged and happy is one of the main responsibilities of management; otherwise the organization fails to generate value. I believe that management should continuously optimize the whole system or else, at some point, atrophy of the organization will surely follow. And I believe that management should take care that it maximizes value across all clients (see sidebar "Clients and Stakeholders (or Involvees)"); otherwise the organization becomes dysfunctional. In other words, a management practice is a good practice when:

1. it engages people and their interactions;

2. it enables them to improve the system;

3. it helps to delight all clients.

For example, I consider *management by walking around* (see Chapter 2, "Personal Maps") a good practice because it requires management to interact with the teams who are doing actual production work. The goal is to find out how to help improve the system in which the people are doing their work. And it is done in order to understand how value is delivered to customers and other stakeholders.

Clients and stakeholders
(or Involvees)

In this book, I use the terms *clients* and *stakeholders* interchangeably. A stakeholder is anyone who has a stake in what an organization is doing. A client is anyone who is served by whatever value the organization provides. Broadly speaking, it comes down to the same thing and includes customers, shareholders, employees, suppliers, communities, and many more.

Sadly, stakeholders are often confused with shareholders, and clients are usually mistaken for customers. For lack of a better word, I've decided to mix the words *clients* and *stakeholders* throughout this book. Just remember that I do not mean only customers or only shareholders. I mean *everyone* who is somehow involved in and cares about the business. (And I vote that *involvee* be added to the English dictionary.)

Everyone can come up with useful new practices that satisfy the three principles. Management 3.0 is not *defined* by concrete activities, such as the delegation board, the kudo box, moving motivators, or feedback wraps (see later chapters). These practices and exercises are just *examples* of things management can do to increase the health of the organization. Merely drinking ecological coffee does not make someone an "organic-minded" person, and neither do we expect all organic food lovers to be coffee drinkers. Ecological coffee is not part of a framework or method but a simple practice that certainly fits well with the organic food mindset.

Likewise, Management 3.0 is neither a framework nor a method. It is a way of looking at work systems, and it has a few timeless principles. Having a merit money system, exploration days, a salary formula, or a happiness door fits nicely in the Management 3.0 mindset. None of these practices are *required*, but you could definitely *consider* them. Or even better, maybe you can invent your own Management 3.0 practices.

And yes, I believe Management 3.0 is "the right thing" to do.

Management 3.0 Practices

When experts discuss work approaches for certain groups of people, they often come up with collections of "best practices." I agree with those who say there is no such thing as *best* practices, only *good* practices, but I also think that *not* offering any practices is worse. In principle, it is good practice to offer both principles *and* practices. Project managers, software developers, and creative workers in other disciplines have access to plenty of practices they can borrow in their daily work. But what are the good practices for management?

> In principle, it is good practice
>
> to offer both
>
> principles and practices.

Strangely enough, when I ask employees for examples of good management practices, they only seem to come up with principles, such as "delight the customer," "have a shared purpose," and "trust the team." I believe these suggestions are sound, and well meant, but they are not *concrete*. By concrete I mean specific practices that can be explained to a novice so the novice knows exactly what to do on a Monday morning. "Be a servant leader" is abstract. "Bring the team some coffee" is concrete. "Make yourself dispensable" is abstract. "Take a six-month vacation" is concrete.

When it comes to management, most people are novices. They need concrete advice and step-by-step guidance in answer to their "how" questions.

- *How* do we measure performance?
- *How* do we replace performance appraisals?
- *How* do we decide on salaries and bonuses?
- *How* do we offer career paths and promotions?
- *How* do we motivate our employees?

When people learn to drive a car, it is not enough to tell them, "The general principle is to arrive at a certain place without hurting or killing anyone. Good luck!" Novice drivers need a bit more guidance than that. (I certainly did!) They need concrete tips on how to sit in the seat, how to hold the steering wheel, how to look at the road, and how to use the headlights and the turn indicators. In Europe new drivers learn how to use the gears, and in the United States they learn how to use the cup holders. Novice drivers will understand the principles soon enough, but only if they survive practicing the rules. It is the instructor's job to explain that all the rules are merely suggested good practices that help to keep everyone safe.

Regrettably, as soon as you give people concrete practices, you run into the danger that some of them will follow the advice to the letter instead of trying to understand the principles. For example, a team needs to understand that the purpose of a standup meeting is to keep communication brief and effective. However, I was told of one team that cut off team members after 15 minutes because the practice was called the "15-minute daily standup." Another team was reported to have difficulty accepting a person in a wheelchair in their standup meetings because the person couldn't stand up! The mindless adherence to rules, combined with a steady loss of principles, is always a prelude to bureaucracy.

When I offer good Management 3.0 practices, I create the danger of similar dogmatic and bureaucratic tendencies. For example, when I suggest that people give each other kudo cards as tokens of appreciation, I sometimes get questions such as "Should this be anonymous or public?" "Should I give them personally or should I put the cards in a box?" "Should this be on paper or can we do this electronically?" It's as if I tell them to bring the team coffee in the morning, and they ask *me* if the team needs milk and sugar, and if it's OK to add a cookie, and if it should be a cookie with chocolate or a healthy one; and what about that one person who only drinks tea? I refuse to be too specific because the danger is that people will make a checklist and do exactly as I say! The *principle* behind bringing the team coffee is that you're trying to be a servant leader, so act like one.

Great Management

This chapter began with a number of depressing stories of misman-agement. I don't want to end this chapter without offering you some more uplifting examples. Fortunately, I have plenty of good stories to choose from. For example, here are some that deal with the use of office space by employees:

At VI Company, a software company in Rotterdam, the Netherlands, management has turned some of the office walls into big black chalkboards, and they made colorful markers available so that the employees can create their own useful office decoration. One time, a team decided to publicly plot their happiness index  and different team members drew colored lines all over the wall. The chalk walls didn't just make the office look more colorful; they also supported the team's need for experimentation, learning, and improvement.

At Cisco Systems Norway, in Oslo, the employees love playing with their foosball table in the lunch area. However, it's not just *any* foos-ball table, it's a *special* one! The technical guys have upgraded the table with a few technical modifications of their own. For example, the two goals have laser beams installed in them, and the table has a digital counter so that it can count the goals that are being scored. The table also has a security card reader attached so that the players can identify themselves to the table. The employees made these upgrades because experimenting with technologies helps them to be innovative, and management allows them to spend as much time as they want on that foosball table.

Future Processing in Gliwice, Poland, has walls full of photographs and names of all its employees. It is a tradition at this company to take a picture of every new employee and to hang those pictures in the lunch area. They also plot the rapid growth of the company over the years with a graph made out of people's names. This is how the company acknowledges that it owes everything to the people who are working there, and it instills a sense of pride among the workers.

At InfoJobs, a company in Barcelona, Spain, which has been recognized as a "best place to work," the employees decided to give their meeting rooms names that correspond to the company's values and to use and decorate those rooms accordingly. For example, the *Alegría* ("happiness") room has nice pillows, blankets, flowers, books, and yoga mats. It is the room where people can express themselves and experience a bit of happiness. Oh, and the Human Resource department renamed itself to People Development Support because its employees thought the new name better reflects what they do.

CCP Games, an online gaming company in Reykjavík, Iceland, makes vast virtual worlds and universes, full of battleships and aliens. What I found interesting was that two teams discovered a useful way to have different styles of task boards living side-by-side. A "scrum" board (a visual board depicting requirements and tasks) is used to manage the iterative flow of their product releases, and a "kanban" board (another style of workflow visualization) is used for the continuous development of spaceships. The teams proudly showed me the pictures of their spaceships flying from one task board to the other!

At Spotify, the online music company in Stockholm, Sweden, management delegated the design of the new offices to their employees. One particular solution the workers and coaches came up with is to separate open work spaces from corridors by using a mesh of wires, instead of using glass or walls. This solution gives people both a sense of transparency *and* privacy at the same time.

Another company with a very modern office space is Wooga, an online gaming business in Berlin, Germany. The employees at this company have been running contests against each other for the best designed office space. I admit that it was easily one of the most colorful offices I have ever visited.

Yes, I visited all these companies myself. (Did I tell you that I travel a lot?) Granted, tweaks in the use of office space can sometimes be purely cosmetic. But I believe the examples I witnessed were indicators of good management, which often doesn't require a lot of money or effort. In fact, the things I mentioned here are simple, cheap, and not very spectacular. But they work! I witnessed the happiness and pride of workers. I also saw people not waiting for managers to improve their work and taking responsibility for management in their own hands. Creative workers choose to boss themselves.

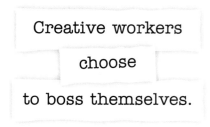

Creative workers choose to boss themselves.

It's good to see that some people do know how to motivate employees, improve the system, and increase value for stakeholders at the same time. And it's good to see that smart knowledge workers and creative workers don't wait for permission from the boss to start changing things. Hopefully, there will be many more stories like these in the future.

I understand people's need for more concrete management practices, but I've always argued against the definition of "One Management Method." The inevitable result would be a series of conferences about the One Management Method, accreditation of One Management Method trainers, official One Management Method tools, One Management Method maturity level assessments, and online tests validating whether people understand and apply the One Management Method correctly. Learning would come to a standstill. This would be at odds with complexity science and incompatible with systems thinking. Offering a method or framework inspired by science is a contradiction in terms.

I sometimes like using the workout metaphor. Everyone understands that yoga and Pilates are just names for endless collections of ~~painful~~ useful practices based on guiding principles. They're not methods or frameworks. We all know that doing twenty push-ups per day is healthy, but it's not required. It's perfectly fine to replace this good practice with something else. In fact, as your personal trainer knows, every now and then you should! Likewise, you could play moving motivators (see Chapter 10, "Moving Motivators") until you are tired of it. You can ask people the yay questions until they get bored. You could try the personal maps practice until it loses its value. And you can't go wrong making delegation boards until you don't need them anymore.

Are you an artist, developer, tester, doctor, manager, leader, coach, facilitator, public servant, or entrepreneur? Would you like to help your organization become fit and happy?

© 2013 Jurgen Appelo

In this book, I offer you a collection of concrete management practices because everyone should learn how to manage the system, not the people. These are practices for *all* workers so that they can introduce better management, with fewer managers. These serious games and modern tools will help you change your organization's culture, step-by-step, beginning tomorrow.

Start working out; make the system healthy, and have fun!

Introduce better management,

with fewer managers.

1

kudo box and
kudo cards

Motivate People with Better Rewards

There are many wrong ways to reward employees. A simple but effective approach is to install a kudo box, which enables people to give each other a small reward. The kudo box fulfills the six rules for rewards and works much better than bonuses and other forms of financial motivation.

Anything that has real and lasting value is always a gift from within.

Franz Kafka,
Austro-Hungarian author
(1883–1924)

> It may come as a shock to many to learn that a large and growing body of evidence suggests that in many circumstances, paying for results can actually make people perform badly, and that the more you pay, the worse they perform.

Nic Fleming, "The Bonus Myth"[3]

In 2001, Enron, an American energy and services company, collapsed into bankruptcy because its managers liked their bonuses more than they liked the truth. They incentivized themselves to maximize their own paychecks, not the success of the organization. Similar creative financial practices occurred at Parmalat, WorldCom, Bernard L. Madoff, AIG, Barings, and many other companies. Corporate history is littered with the remains of organizations that allowed individual greed and egos to outgrow the solvency of the company. And bonus systems are still implemented all around the world "to incentivize performance," despite the fact that experts have known for decades that there's no proven correlation between bonuses and performance.[1]

Indeed, excessive greed might be the biggest problem in free markets. Bankers in the United States and Europe have been so focused on their personal results that they collectively plunged the world into one of the deepest recessions we have ever seen.[2]

Excessive greed
might be the biggest problem
in free markets.

Extrinsic Motivation

Extrinsic motivation is defined as behavior that is driven by external rewards (given by others), such as money, grades, and praise. Rewards are among the trickiest and least understood tools in management. When applied in the right way they can generate significant results. Unfortunately, a common assumption among managers is that nothing works like money when you want to make people work harder, longer, or more effectively. Also, it is often assumed that extrinsic motivation works quite well when implemented as a financial bonus. These assumptions are both wrong.

> Money is as important to knowledge workers as to anybody else, but they do not accept it as the ultimate yardstick, nor do they consider money as a substitute for professional performance and achievement. In sharp contrast to yesterday's workers, to whom a job was first of all a living, most knowledge workers see their job as a life.

Peter F. Drucker, *Management*.[4]

Scientific research has revealed that incentives for performance actually work the other way around.[5] The anticipation of a reward (either money or something else) works counterproductively, since it kills people's intrinsic motivation. The incentives ensure that people stop doing things just for the joy of the work. It is called the **overjustification effect**.[6] Instead of expecting and feeling enjoyment, people expect a reward.

> Incentives ensure
> that people stop doing things
> just for the joy of the work.

Another problem is that rewards based on outcomes increase the risk of cheating, since people's focus is on getting a reward instead of doing a good job. When you reward employees based on outcome, they will take the shortest path to that outcome.[7] Bad behaviors with dysfunctional side effects undermine the organization's performance, while the employees walk away with a bonus or with their colleagues' pension fund.

Extrinsic motivation, with big incentives based on outcomes, is like a hot air balloon with a basket of gold. It's expensive, and it's hard to make it fly.

Intrinsic Motivation

Fortunately, there is some good news as well. Rewards that trigger *intrinsic motivation* are more effective, more sustainable, and usually cost less money. Intrinsic motivation is defined as behavior that is triggered from within a person. In other words, the people are rewarding themselves.

> Influence masters first ensure that vital behaviors connect to intrinsic satisfaction. Next, they line up social support. They double check both of these areas before they finally choose extrinsic rewards to motivate behavior.

Kerry Patterson[8]

Rewards can work *for* your organization, and not *against* it, when you take the following six rules into account:

Don't promise rewards in advance.

Give rewards at unexpected times so that people don't change their intentions and focus on the reward. Research shows that, when acknowledgment of good work comes as a surprise, intrinsic motivation will not be undermined.[9]

Keep anticipated rewards small.

Sometimes, you cannot prevent people from anticipating a potential reward. In such cases, according to research, big rewards are likely to *decrease* performance. But with small rewards, the risk of hurting performance is negligible.[10]

Reward continuously, not once.

Do not look for something to celebrate just once per month or once per year. Every day can be a day to celebrate something. Every day is an opportunity for a reward.[11]

These six rules for rewards give you the best chance at increasing people's performance and their enjoyment of work, while *encouraging* intrinsic motivation instead of *destroying* it. Notice that an incidental compliment addressed to a colleague in a meeting for a job well done satisfies almost all six criteria. A well-aimed kiss, blown carefully across a conference table, can also do wonders, I've noticed. (Just kidding!) It's not that difficult to implement rewards well.

Reward publicly, not privately.

Everyone should understand what is being rewarded and why. The goal of giving rewards is to acknowledge good practices and have people enjoy the work, too. To achieve this, a regular public reminder works better than a private one.[12]

Reward behavior, not outcome.

Outcomes can often be achieved through shortcuts, while behavior is about hard work and effort. When you focus on good behavior, people learn how to behave. When you focus on desired outcomes, people may learn how to cheat.[13]

Reward peers, not subordinates.

Rewards should not come just from the manager. Create an environment in which people reward each other because peers often know better than managers which of their colleagues deserve a compliment.

Kudos

Money is only advised as a reward when you need to motivate people to do an uninteresting or repetitive job.[14] And even in the case of creative work, it's OK for rewards to cost a little bit of money, as long as you don't overdo it.

In one of my workshops, Paul Klipp, former president at Lunar Logic Polska in Poland, told me how he created a reward system.[15] He explained that his employees could give anyone a gift worth 20 euro. They called it **kudos** and it could be implemented as an e-mail to a central mailbox, or by slipping a note into a cardboard box.  The management team never questioned why someone was rewarded. When anybody in the company felt someone deserved a reward, the person received it. Paul would personally bring a handwritten kudo note and a tray of gifts from which the receiver could pick one item. And everyone would hear about it on Facebook and on the internal chat system. Paul told me these gifts worked extremely well, and he loved the fact that all employees were involved in recognizing people doing good things. It was a low-cost reward system, and trust was never abused.

© 2014 Kamil Sowa

but, kudo
is not a word!

Some readers have suggested that *kudos* is a singular word and therefore using the word *kudo* is wrong. But kudo is simply a back-formation from the Greek *kydos*, meaning "glory" or "fame," which is misunderstood as being plural. The words *kudo* and *kudos* were introduced into the English language in the previous century. Sure, the singular and plural forms began as a misunderstanding, but the same applies to many other words we now take for granted.

A similar system was implemented by Philip Rosedale, former CEO of Linden Lab, which created the virtual reality platform Second Life. Rosedale called it the *LoveMachine*.[16] It was a tool that enabled employees to send notes of appreciation to their colleagues. According to Rosedale, recognizing each other's hard work makes everyone feel great. And because everything is transparent, managers gained useful insight into which people were appreciated often and which people never received a compliment.

There are many other names in use for the same system. For example, at Zappos they call them HERO *awards*.[17] But no matter what you call it, a public system that enables people to give each other small, unexpected tokens of appreciation for doing a good job meets all six basic principles of good rewards. A gift attached to the compliment is of course optional. It is the intention that counts. However, experience suggests that a tangible gift helps a compliment to have a bigger impact on the receiver. The gift enables the person to touch, hold, and cherish the compliment. And that has value, too.

should the kudos be anonymous?

Should they be private?

I remember one occasion when I received a nice message from someone anonymously. Even now, after 20 years, it still bothers me not knowing who gave me that compliment.

Maybe you are different. Maybe you love the mystery of giving or receiving an anonymous reward. My advice here is simply to leave this decision to the givers and receivers in the company. They can decide best, given the context of the compliment and the culture of the organization, whether they want the identity of the giver to be known or not.

Whether kudos should be given publicly or privately is also a matter for discussion. The generic rule says that public rewards usually work better to improve an organization's culture. Some people, however, shy away from public praise. Again, it is best to investigate your organization's culture and people's preferences to see what works best for you and them.

THANK YOU!

Thanks for stepping forward at the end of the open space session at #ale 2012

Jurgen

29 August 2012

But What If...?

I noticed there is always somebody who asks, "What if?"

"What if our workers don't play fair?"

"What if two people abuse the kudo box system to get free movie tickets?"

"What if someone just wants to gain the boss's favor with a kudo card?"

To these questions I have just one reply: "What if you see such risks because you have a low level of trust in others? What if this low level of trust is a result of your company's culture? What if the kudo box is exactly the kind of practice that is needed to *change* this culture of distrust in a relatively harmless way?" Yes, there is always a risk that unexpected behaviors will occur. When I give away free books at a conference, some people might use them as paperweights or doorstops. Should this hold me back from doing a good thing?

When cheating *does* occur, it is probably best to let this behavior emerge and evolve naturally, in a transparent way, so others can respond. Let the community decide what to do about cheating. Try not to delegate such matters to upper management, because management is like government. When you expect team members to reward *good* behaviors and you prefer that management deal with *bad* behaviors, you increase the gap between managers and nonmanagers. This gap makes the organization's culture worse, not better! In the end, everyone will be gaming the system, and management will have a full-time job making rules for "proper" rewards, creating elaborate forms for rewards, and depleting the rewards budget for their own benefit. We all know how governments work. :-)

> Let the community decide
> what to do about cheating.

Another question I sometimes get is, "What if people *expect* to be rewarded? When one person gets a compliment for doing X, his colleagues might then also expect to get a reward for doing X. Ultimately, everyone will feel entitled to a reward for doing the same thing."

I understand the problem. Most workers have a good sense of fairness. When they give a reward to one colleague, they might feel bad about not giving a reward to another who has done the same good thing. And before you know it, you have a situation where everyone automatically gets a reward for doing X. Obviously, this should be prevented.

The first rule for rewards says that they should come as a surprise. When people expect to be rewarded, the rewards system has gone off track. That's why I suggest that you frequently emphasize that praise doesn't work when it is required or demanded. You might also want to phrase your kudos in such a way that stresses the fact that this is the first time somebody did something or the unique nature of the contribution or the effort beyond expectation that went into the job. That would make it less likely that the next person will expect praise for the same thing. After all, it wouldn't be the first time, it wouldn't be unique, and it wouldn't be beyond expectation.

Finally, some readers have asked me, "Shouldn't we reward teams instead of individuals? Don't we want people to work collaboratively, instead of going at it alone?"

Well, yes, of course. But teamwork can only emerge as an outcome of people's individual contributions to that team. You could give a reward *because* of what an individual did for the whole team. Obviously, sometimes it could be worth praising a whole team, a whole department, or even a whole organization. Quite often, however, people's individual contributions to the whole have to be recognized first, *before* the whole unit performs in a way that deserves praise as well.

The kudo box not only adheres to the six rules for rewards; it also satisfies the three principles for Management 3.0 practices: The rewards are handed out for improving the work and delighting clients, and they engage people through intrinsic motivation. And as a bonus, the practice helps you get rid of bonuses!

> Teamwork can only emerge as an outcome of people's individual contributions to that team.

About our
"shout-out shoebox"

"Since the launch of our 'shout-out shoebox' at Brightside Group, we have had 19 cards put in the box, including a thank-you from one team to another. The whole team signed the card and it was proudly stuck up in the receiving team's area. Another great card was for a new starter who has been with us for just a few weeks but has impressed her team with her ability to 'hit the ground sprinting.' She was very touched with the gesture.

The manager, who was skeptical at first, has been surprised by the positive reaction to the scheme, and he now asked if the practice can be rolled out to his own teams. In fact someone has already left a card for one of his teams so it has already crossed over."

Gary Shepherd, *United Kingdom*

About our
Rippas

"Here at Virgin Mobile we have a thing called a Rippa (an Australian colloquialism for good work) which is given to people as a thank-you for a job well done, a token of appreciation, or just for the fun of it. Every person in the company gets a book of Rippas to give out, which are in carbon paper triplicate: One goes to the individual; one is for the manager; and the third goes in the Rippa Box.

Every three months there is a draw and about 10 people win shopping vouchers. Similar to kudos, our system is about giving instant feedback to someone who has helped you out in some way."

Paul Bowler, *Australia*

How to Get Started

Now it is time for you to start implementing your own kudo box.

1. Secure commitment from upper management to spend a small sum each month on a new rewards system. If management is fearful of the costs, you can agree temporarily on a maximum amount that will be spent per month. (And make it available through a draw of winners.) If management doesn't cooperate (yet), simply introduce the system without the gifts.

2. Implement the practice at a high level, throughout either the whole company or the whole department. If this is not possible, experiment with one team, but aim to expand it as soon as the practice shows good results.

3. Create a central mailbox, or place a colorful cardboard box in a central location, and name it the "kudo box" or choose your own local terminology. Print kudo cards and posters to support the new initiative, and give someone responsibility for the kudo box. (If you want, you can download our free kudo card designs from m30.me/kudo-cards.)

4. Let everyone know that any employee is allowed to reward any other person with a small reward, by slipping a note or kudo card in the box. Tell them explicitly that you trust everyone not to abuse the system, or else . . . the employees should self-organize and take action.

5. Define the upper limit of the value of the gifts, and give some useful examples (movie tickets, flowers, lunches, gift certificates, cash, copies of this book, etc.). But allow people to be creative.

6. Check the box every day, and announce publicly who received a compliment and why. You might have to bootstrap the practice by handing out plenty of kudo cards yourself.

Tips and Variations

I use kudobox.co to send nice-looking kudos to remote workers. We printed our corporate values on the kudo cards to connect rewards to our organization's culture.

New kudo cards should be easily accessible. Place them near the coffee machine or the water cooler.

Remove all barriers to finding the cards. Even bending over and opening a drawer can be too much work for some!

We safely tried the practice in one team and, after it was successful, we broadened the scope.

I started with a team that had the worst communication patterns, just to show the practice works for everyone.

Print the company's purpose on the cards. It reminds people why they are giving each other compliments.

We give the cards personally. It makes a lot of difference when you look a person in the eye and say, "Thank you."

Have people pin the cards to a dedicated Kudo Wall, preferably in an area with heavy traffic.

We organize a weekly roundup of new kudo cards; we read them out loud and we celebrate.

The design of the kudos can make a lot of difference. Make sure the cards themselves look happy!

Download the free kudo card designs from m30.me/kudo-cards. Find more ideas at m30.me/kudo-box.

2

personal maps

Improve Communication and Understanding

People should get closer to the work of others in order to better understand what is going on. They can do this by moving their feet, moving their desk, or moving their mike. Decreasing the distance between yourself and others helps to increase communication and creativity. A great exercise for a better understanding of people is to capture what you know about them in personal maps.

> Our main business is not to see what lies dimly at a distance but to do what lies clearly at hand.
>
> Thomas Carlyle,
> Scottish writer
> (1795–1881)

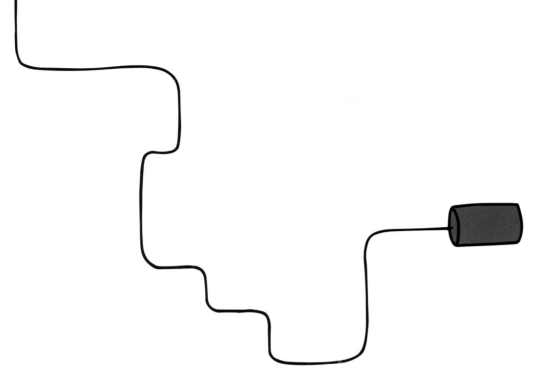

When I just started as a manager 16 years ago, I had my own big office with a shiny desk, a fast, new computer, and a desk phone with more buttons than the ceremonial suit of your average dictator. There was also a small workforce, consisting of a dozen or more software developers, to boss around as I pleased. There was just one thing I lacked: I had no clue what was going on in their minds.

Raised as a software engineer, I saw developers as unreliable computers with legs, and too much hair. My desperate attempts at programming them failed because they rarely followed my instructions. And my attempts at debugging produced some nasty side effects. After a while, I started to see the discrepancy between computer programming and people management. I started learning. Now it is my estimate that management is 5 percent instruction (what I want done) and 95 percent communication (what they need).

Management is 5 percent instruction and 95 percent communication.

Improving Collaboration

When I investigated my communication issue, I realized the solution follows naturally from scientific research, as well as common sense. It is crucial to understand the way in which communication flows in an organization.

Whether they intend it or not, people continually disperse information about their mood, their work, their feelings, their preferences, and many other personal attributes and activities. Other people are able to pick up on some of that information. For example, when you feel stressed, you inevitably give off signals indicating this, and someone around you is bound to pick up on these signals and may ask what's amiss. Or when a colleague is working on a tough challenge, you might unknowingly radiate some information that helps solve the problem. The picture on your desk communicates that you have two kids. The background on your computer screen clearly says you like cats. And the shopping bag next to your chair radiates that you're probably having friends over for dinner.

Software development expert Alistair Cockburn explains that the information flow across a team or an organization can be compared to the dispersion of heat or gas.[1] Not surprisingly, for the dissemination of information, sitting side by side in the same room is more effective than having two people sit in private offices next to each other. This, in turn, is more effective than having two people half a building and several coffee machines apart. For an optimal flow of communication, sharing the same room with other people works best because this allows a person to pick up other people's emitted information (either intentionally or unintentionally) which would otherwise never be appreciated. It's the same with heat and gas.

The obvious conclusion is that the effectiveness of collaboration between people heavily correlates positively to their proximity.

> In a study conducted at Bell Labs, researchers tested for factors that determine whether two scientists might collaborate. The best predictor was, you guessed it, the distance between their offices.... The probability of collaboration sharply decreases in a matter of a few feet.

Kerry Patterson, *Influencer* [2]

Sadly, miscommunication is the norm in all organizations.[3] When you understand that distance reduces communication, you can try to improve communication by optimizing your proximity to others. The "how" part of reducing the distance between managers and other people has been described in many books and articles. The suggestions differ in detail, but most of them boil down to the same thing: People should get closer to the work that is important to them. Of course, this does not only apply to managers. It applies to any creative worker who is working with other people and is trying to do a good job.

People should get closer to the work that is important to them.

Management by Walking Around

The advice to walk around in the organization  is often presented under the Japanese name *gemba* (meaning: "the real place"). The practice of gemba states that a person ought to be where people are working in order to understand how well they can do their jobs and what they need from you.[4] But seeing things with your own eyes also helps to solve any problems people might have. Improvement works better when you use facts and not assumptions.[5] Other terms you may find in literature are *genchi genbutsu*, "go and see," [6] face-time,[7] and management by walking around (MBWA). And, in the case of distributed teams, this could easily become management by flying around (MBFA).[8] The practice has more names than His Majesty King Willem-Alexander Claus George Ferdinand, King of the Netherlands, Prince of Orange-Nassau, et cetera, et cetera. Therefore, you might assume it is pretty important.

Some experts suggest that when walking around the people who are important to you, you should not follow a strict schedule, but rather try to do this randomly. You listen to them, talk to them, consult with them, and advise them. At random, you may decide to attend a team's planning meeting, a stand-up meeting, a demo meeting, or you may catch them near the water cooler. (This is far more challenging with remote teams, but we'll address that topic in a moment.) It is important that you do not give your team the impression that you are *checking up* on them because your aim is better *communication* and *understanding*, and not better *instruction*. It's about managing, not programming. And face-time doesn't have to focus on just work. Social time (during lunch breaks, near the coffee machine, and after work hours) counts as well.

> Social time turns out to be deeply critical to team performance, often accounting for more than 50 percent of positive changes in communication patterns.

Alex Pentland, "The New Science of Building Great Teams"[9]

Despite the fact that walking around is a great practice, I have a small problem with this approach. The problem is that you still have to get up and start walking around. This is great when, like me, you need daily exercise. (And after all, this book *is* about great exercises!) But collaboration with other people, no matter how sincere, may still come off as artificial or stilted if you have to get up from your desk and head out of your office in order to talk to your team.

Management by Sitting Around

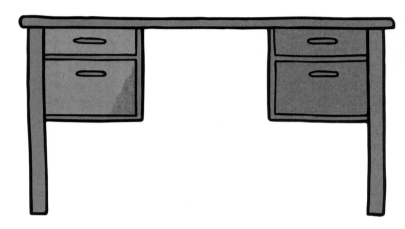

The best computer systems in the world cannot substitute for being there, talking about what's going on and responding at once to subtle situational clues.

Tim Harford, *Adapt* [10]

The more I thought about the idea of walking around, the more I got the feeling that the practice is suboptimal. Years ago, I realized that the concept of "being where the work happens" can be taken a step further. I solved it by picking up my stuff and moving to an ordinary desk alongside with my team. ▉▉ It might have been the best management decision I ever made. It vastly increased the amount of social time I could enjoy with my team members.

After I had moved my desk, no matter what happened, I was always around. This allowed me to pick up more information about what was going on and understand much better what other people cared about. Team members regularly asked for my opinion, something that used to occur only when I happened to be walking around. And I picked up signs of joy and frustration, which I wouldn't have noticed if I had not been there. This convinced me that MBSA (management by sitting around) could sometimes beat both MBWA and MBFA.

Interestingly enough, not everyone is of the same opinion. Richard Branson, the famous founder and chairman of the Virgin Group, has always practiced the opposite approach. He prefers *not* to sit with any of his management teams because, in his view, this could inhibit their creativity and self-reliance.[11] Instead, he prefers to leave them all to their own devices most of the time, but he guarantees regular face-time with everyone by flying around all the time. (This is of course easy to do when you have your own airline.)

MBSA

"I once worked in a project management role, and it seemed plausible to have a small office with another senior so I could discuss important matters and make confidential calls.

At one point, I started to collocate the people who were working on my project because communication between them was bad. I don't remember the exact reason, but I also moved from my own cozy office to where the project was happening. I guess it was to show that I was not only moving others around, but I was moving myself as well.

The effect for me was dramatic. Suddenly, I felt the pulse of the project and learned of people's problems directly. I was able to moderate discussions between workers, and they now found it much easier to ask me questions. Another effect was that sitting together showed that we were all in the same chain gang on this death-march project. For me as a new manager it was tremendously helpful to build trust. Later changes, such as the introduction of agile approaches, have been much easier because I had a better understanding of how the team felt."

Peter Rubarth, *Germany*

Management
by Skyping Around

In February 2013, Marissa Mayer, the CEO of Yahoo!, sent a memo to her employees, saying that working from home was not acceptable anymore, and that all Yahoo!'s remote workers would soon be expected to either relocate to the office or else quit their jobs.[12] She said the main reason for this decision was that collaboration and communication are improved when people work together in the office and when they can see each other face to face. Marissa Mayer was right.

She was also wrong. Plenty of research and case studies confirm that *creative* people who work remotely are, on average, *more* productive than their colleagues who work at the office.[13] Marissa Mayer's claim that "speed and quality are often sacrificed when we work from home" might have been true for herself or for some of Yahoo!'s employees, but, in general, this claim doesn't stand up to scientific scrutiny. Richard Branson's reaction to Marissa Mayer's decision was, "Yours truly has never worked out of an office, and never will."[14]

The answer to the question, "Should people work from home or in the office?" is, as always, "It depends." People *can* be more creative on their own when they work remotely, but creativity is fruitless without a frequent gathering of the minds and mixing of ideas. On the other hand, communication *can* be improved when people are collocated most of the time, but communication is useless without good productivity, which many people often best achieve *alone*. Somehow, you must optimize both. Anyone who optimizes one over the other is missing the point.

The best approach for your organization is to find your own optimum. This means asking people to optimize both creativity *and* communication in ways they believe are best. It also means giving them the means for high-bandwidth communication across distances, in the form of Skype calls, Google hangouts, and any other tools you can think of that include both audio and video.

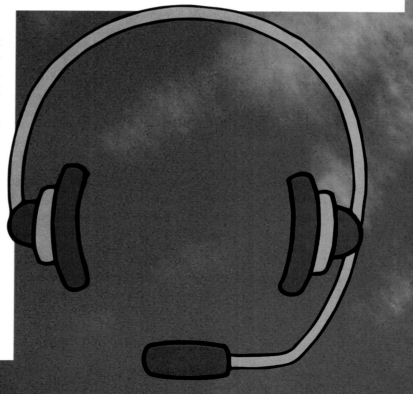

Is the trend toward working remotely good or bad?

In many industries, companies prefer to keep people together in one building and then they try to compensate by giving workers individual offices or cubicles. (Banking, software, and government come to mind. Maybe Yahoo! as well?) In other industries, many businesses prefer to let people work in a distributed way but then they compensate by frequently getting creative workers together for collaborative and productive meetings. (One can think of entertainment, media, and fashion. And Virgin.) There is indeed a trend among office-oriented companies to allow more people to work remotely.

At the same time, there is an opposite trend among creative businesses to relocate to shared spaces and city areas where different organizations can work more closely together. Neither direction is good or bad. What's good is that people try to find an optimum between two extremes.

The Observer Effect

Communication with coworkers is a crucial habit for everyone in a business. It doesn't matter if you're a manager, a team member, or an independent worker. You should move yourself around, and you should help others do the same.

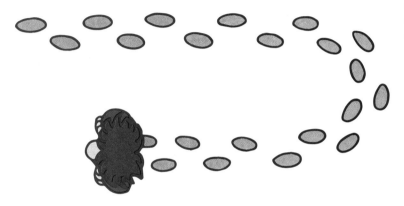

But no matter whether you move your feet, your desk, or your mike, you must keep in mind that objective observers don't exist. When you get closer to other people who are doing work, you are influencing them. This is called the **observer effect** or **observer's paradox.** This doesn't have to be a problem, as long as you are aware of the fact. You can even use it to your advantage!

> When you observe other people doing work,
> you are influencing them.

Your proximity to other people can help you create trust. It also can help create awareness among your team members that you care about what they are doing. Your proximity itself is an information radiator and has an impact on people's work. The consequence of moving around and paying attention to what others are doing is not only improved communication; it can also mean improved behavior and better performance.

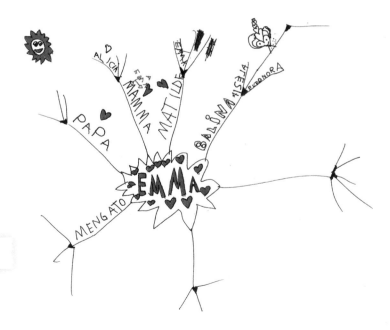

Close Proximity

I know what you're thinking. Moving around sounds like a great idea, but what can you do if you are involved in many teams? What if the teams work in different buildings or in different countries? What if you are the founder of 400 companies? My answer is: First, make sure at least one of them is an airline; second, figure out a good way to combine the three approaches mentioned earlier by applying these proximity principles:

Running a productive organization means finding the optimum between creativity and communication. Creative people need time to themselves. If you let them be, don't disturb them with trivial phone calls, and allow them to work wherever they want, most will be *more* productive, not less. On the other hand, some have a tendency to focus a bit too much on their creative work, not realizing the organization needs collaboration as much as it needs creativity. It is up to you to see to it that both are balanced.

The **First Proximity Principle:**

- Match your proximity to people with the importance of their work.

Is there an important project or deadline? Go sit with that team for a while. Is one team lagging behind the others significantly? Move your desk to their working area. Are you working with two teams that need special attention? Sit with both of them by alternating your workplace from day to day, or week to week. Show people that you care about them and what they're doing and that you understand what's going on by *being there*.

The **Second Proximity Principle:**

- Keep your proximity diverse, flexible, and unpredictable.

You should not allow an important team to claim your full attention while leaving other people unattended. Optimize your communication with others using walks, trips, flights, and video calls. There should be diversity in your distance to people, which will depend on the diversity of their locations and their work. But whatever you do, don't wait for problems to find you.[15] The so-called open-door policy rarely works. You shouldn't wait for people to come to you. You should go to *them*.[16]

Great Conversation Topics

I find it hard to stay interested when people discuss the weather, sports, business, or celebrity gossip. One of the deepest discussions I enjoyed was when I shared a sauna in Finland with fellow speakers after a conference. We debated politics, philosophy, and the meaning of life in 20 minutes.

When I met with my fellow management team members of Happy Melly for the first time, I suggested that we not only discuss ideas, projects, and tasks, but also some personal stuff. I came up with the suggestion that each of us should ask the others one interesting personal question, and we should answer the question ourselves at the end of each round. The first question, offered by yours truly, was, "What part of your culture do you recognize in yourself?" The other team members followed suit with, "What is your favorite movie and what does this say about you?" "How do you exercise physically?" "What is it you don't understand about other people?" "Which book changed your view on the world?" and "What happened in your past that made you join this team?"

With a little effort, you should be able to come up with dozens of similarly interesting and challenging questions. It could be useful to memorize a few of them so you can ask them of anyone at any time. You could really impress your colleagues the next time you share a sauna.

Besides asking deep questions, there are plenty of other things you can do to engage in interesting conversations with fellow team members. You can organize one-on-ones, discuss Gallup's famous 12 questions,[17] or you can play delegation poker (see Chapter 3) or moving motivators (see Chapter 10). You can investigate people on social networks, such as Facebook, LinkedIn, and Twitter, or at social events, such as dinner parties or community gatherings. On the less serious side of the communication spectrum, we find personality tests, such as MBTI or 16PF,[18] and even horoscopes and numerology, which can all be useful for discussing "typical" personality traits. (You may find it hard to believe, but I recently found out that according to numerology, I am a "typical 5," which has been my favorite number ever since I was 10 years old.)

Whatever you do to improve communication, keep in mind that the best approach to understanding a person depends a lot on that person's preferences. What works with one may not work with the other. For example, half the world knows that I don't drink beer and that I need private time each day because I'm an introvert. By offering me a beer after a busy day full of social activities, you communicate to me that we're not socially close. My friends would never suggest that. This may actually *reduce* my willingness to open up and share my thoughts.

You can make amends by buying me a caffè latte the next morning.

Chit chat

"One point you didn't explore and expand on is to make room for a little chat during the day-by-day activities. It is one of those things so obvious, we keep forgetting about it. Whenever I am in a conversation at work, I have the habit of starting or closing the conversation with trivial stuff, just to confirm the informal relationships we have together. By doing this I not only make room for a personal connection; I also avoid giving people the feeling that I'm only interested in checking on their work."

Riccardo Bua, *Belgium*

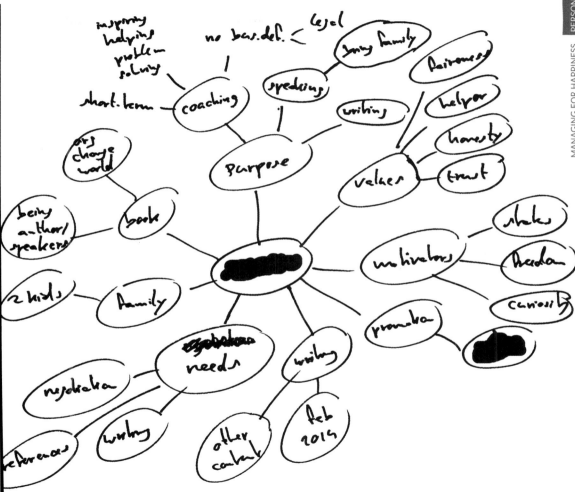

You Are Always on My Mind Map

In an earlier version of this chapter, I suggested that you could draw a proximity map indicating where you are, where your most important people are, and how you plan to see them regularly. But I was never satisfied with my own suggestion. I didn't see the point of praising the merits of flight plans and Google maps, and I realized I was on the wrong track.

> It's not about geographical distance, it's about mental distance.
>
> Jim McCarthy,
> keynote at Agile Lean Europe 2012
> in Barcelona

I noticed many times that the relevance of *geographical* distance has been shrinking steadily for years, thanks to globalization and technological progress. Unlike a decade ago, the connections to the people closest to me are almost literally under my fingertips. At the same time, it seems that the *mental* distance between people has been increasing steadily. Those same technologies have allowed me to be "friends" with thousands of people I hardly know while quality time with my closest friends and relatives suffers from the noise of status updates, photos, videos, likes, retweets, +1s, and personal messages through a dozen social channels.

An idea came to me during a car trip from Amsterdam to Brussels. I was staring off in the distance while driving, attempting to solve an issue that had been bugging me for months. I was disconnected from the whole world except for Raoul, who was sitting next to me, but he was graciously keeping his mouth shut for a while. Needless to say, it was the perfect time for me to have a creative thought. And I had one. I suddenly realized that we don't need more *geographical* maps. We need better *mental* maps.

Mind mapping is a simple but powerful technique that allows anyone who can hold a pen to visualize the relationships between concepts. By creating a **personal map** of a colleague, you make an effort to better understand that person. You start by taking a sheet of paper, an empty page in a notebook, or a blank screen on your tablet computer, and you write the person's name in the middle. You then write categories of interest around your colleague's name, such as *home, education, work, hobbies, family, friends, goals,* and *values*, and you expand the mind map by adding the relevant things you know about this person. Is this person's biggest passion his or her dog? Write it down. Did you attend the same university as your colleague? Write it down. Does your colleague hope to emigrate to another country? Write it down.

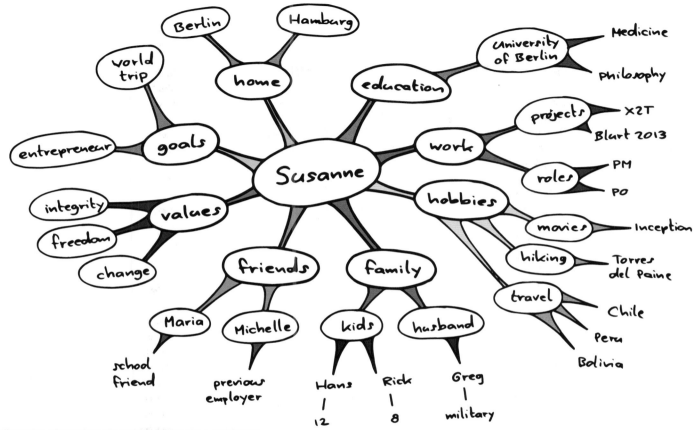

By creating a personal map of a colleague, you make an effort to better understand that person.

When you start creating personal maps for your team members, you might be surprised at how little you know about them. The empty pages stare at you like a glacier at a Patagonian hiker. If this happens, then it's probably a pretty good hint that you need to organize some face-time and ask a few interesting questions. You might be surprised how much people appreciate a genuine interest in their backgrounds, needs, and desires.

this is creepy!

In a world where people still remember the immoral scrutiny of former secret service agencies such as the KGB or the Stasi, and where many, nowadays, loathe the activities of the American NSA and its counterparts worldwide, it is no wonder that I sometimes get the question, "Isn't it wrong to collect information about people?"

Well, it depends on how secretive you are and what you do with the results.

Is it wrong for my mother to have a calendar where she writes down other people's birthdates so she can send them a birthday card? Is it wrong for me to copy e-mail addresses from business cards so I can invite my contacts to my book launch? Is it wrong for you to write down a few personal notes about coworkers so that you can help them to feel engaged, improve their work, and delight your clients?

How to Get Started

1. Grab a sheet of paper and write the name of one of your team members. (If you don't have any, try writing my name.)

2. Write the words *home, education, work, hobbies, family, friends, goals,* and *values* around the name, and connect those words with the name in the middle.

3. Now, work toward the outer edge of the paper, writing words, names, and concepts that you are able to recall about this person, and connect them to the words you had already written. (If you wrote my name, try to find the hints I gave throughout this text.)

4. Evaluate the mind map you have just created and recognize where you have empty areas. Decide what would be the best approach to improving communication with this person and filling in the blank spots on your map. (Adhere to the first proximity principle.)

5. Do the same with other people. Think about how you can use different approaches with different people in order to enjoy optimal face-time with all of them. (Adhere to the second proximity principle.)

6. Get an office chair on wheels, and connect it to Google Navigator. (Just kidding.)

Tips and Variations

The personal maps exercise is a great icebreaker in workshops. While people arrive, get them started on drawing their own.

We make papers available with a few empty bubbles on them. This makes it easier for people to get started.

I keep helpful notes about my colleagues: their birth dates, names of their kids and partners, and how they like their tea or coffee.

Have colorful pens, markers, or pencils available. Some people can better express themselves with colors.

Put all personal maps of people on a wall and try to find similarities and differences.

I organized a personal maps exercise as part of a team retrospective.

Instead of my name, I prefer to start with something else in the middle. For example, my purpose in life.

Ask people to present each other's personal maps and ask questions about them.

Take photos of the mind maps (with permission) and share them on the company's social Web.

We found that it helps to have examples available. People get more creative when they can see what others are doing.

Do NOT let people present their own personal maps. Some people go on and on talking about themselves!

Hang them near a watercooler or coffee machine, so that people have something to talk about.

Find more ideas at m30.me/personal-maps.

3

delegation boards and delegation poker

Empower Workers with Clear Boundaries

It is said that power corrupts, but actually it's more true that power attracts the corruptible. The sane are usually attracted by other things than power.

David Brin,
American scientist
(1950–)

Delegation is not easy. Managers often fear a loss of control when considering allowing teams to self-organize, and creative workers sometimes don't know how to self-organize. A delegation board enables management to clarify delegation and to foster empowerment for both management and workers.

I once went horseback riding on a mountain in Chile. The trip lasted four hours and a guide led four tourists, including me, through an Andean forest. During our ascent of the tree-covered mountain, I wondered why my horse would stop occasionally and glance backwards until the guide offered an explanation. She suggested that I should keep my horse away from the other horses and preferably let it drop back to last in line because my horse was known to have a bad temper. Mine was the only white horse among four black horses, and our guide explained that horses can be as xenophobic as humans. My poor white horse had been traumatized as a result of being mistreated by the black ones, and my horse wouldn't hesitate at a chance to kick the others in the head.  Sure enough, at an unexpected moment, when we were relaxing and enjoying the scenery, my fierce white horse bolted toward my partner's discriminating black horse. The black one had probably given mine a funny look or nickered something insulting, and I could barely prevent my animal from biting the black one's eye out. If I had not masterfully and heroically handled the reins, we might have never married. I mean a marriage with my partner, of course, not with the horse.

Managing an organization is like leading a horse. Some organizations are like the powerful, lean horses we see on the racetracks. Others are like the sturdy horses that pull carts full of groceries. Some organizations are like horses in Chile carrying bored tourists and heroic writers. Other organizations may best be compared to pink, fluffy unicorns. Whatever kind of horse your organization is, I'm sure it needs care, food, love, grooming, currying, brushing, and an occasional firm tug on the reins.

Managing an organization is like leading a horse.

Distributed Control

Let's dismount from the horses and climb onto organizations. Some-one close to me has a very inquisitive boss. She's always busy check-ing everyone's work and has remarks, criticism, and corrections for everything. It's not surprising that the workers are a bit scared of her, especially because she can respond like a rabid dog whenever she finds something objectionable. Meek horses and vicious dogs don't go well together.

In her defense, as the manager of a government agency, she has a lot of responsibility. She is held accountable for everything that is produced in her office. Therefore, it's crucial that she keep an eye on things; isn't it? That sounds reasonable. But people behave according to how they are treated. When the boss always corrects everything you deliver, why bother producing a polished result? It'll all get changed anyway! Thus, the quality of the work goes down, and the boss has to tighten control even more. An intrusive management style generates contin-uous confirmation that the boss's worldview is correct. The workers *are* sloppy, and they *do* deserve some growling and snapping! If the horse is used to being bitten, it will only move forward when being bitten. Here we have a perfect example of a self-fulfilling prophecy.[1]

We can only escape this typical management trap and increase the quality of work when we distribute control in our organizations. All around us (and inside us) complex systems self-organize success-fully *because* control is rarely centralized. 🐌 There is no master T-cell that controls your immune system, no primary pacemaker cell that regulates your heartbeat, and no central neuron in your brain to create consciousness. In complex systems, control is typically dis-tributed among the parts. And that's a good thing! If your immune system had a control center, it would be very easy for viruses to take

it down. And if your heartbeat were managed by just a few cells, you wouldn't survive long enough to read the remainder of this book.

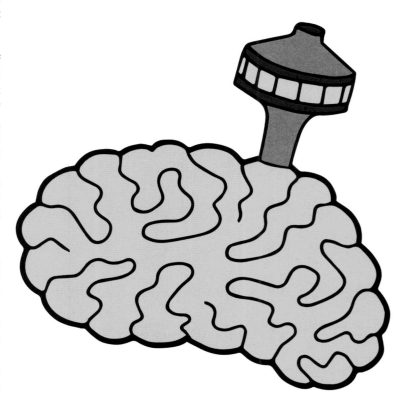

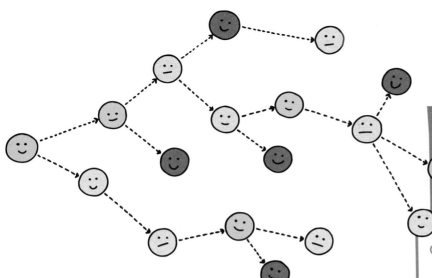

So, why not get rid of the hierarchy **completely?**

Another reason for distributed control can be found in the **darkness principle**. This principle says that each part in a system is not aware of all the behaviors that occur elsewhere in the system. If one part "knew" the entire system, the complexity of the whole system would have to reside in that single part. The darkness principle explains that each worker has only an incomplete mental model of all the work. And the same goes for the manager too! Only the whole organization understands all the work. That is why it's best to distribute control among everyone.[2]

Complex systems survive and thrive *because* control is distributed. It is why the Internet cannot be destroyed. It is why terrorist groups form independent, self-organizing units. And it is why organizations require workers to have a high level of control over their own work. A top-down style of management is undesirable because it stifles an organization's ability to deal with complexity.[3]

Companies differ from natural systems because of *legal authority*. The people in an organization are not allowed to break any laws. Managers are *authorized* by the business owners to hire and fire people, to commit the whole business to services and payments by signing contracts with customers and suppliers, to take care of the money that goes in and out of the organization, and to delegate work to other people. This all passes through the organization in a hierarchical fashion to enable *traceability of authorization.* As far as I'm concerned, that's one of the very few things for which a hierarchy can be useful.

Employee Empowerment

What scientists call distributed control is usually called **empowerment** by management consultants. However, some experts don't like the term.[4,5] The word seems to suggest that people are "disempowered" by default and need to be "empowered" by their managers.[6] Perhaps that was indeed its original meaning, and I agree that this could be seen as disrespectful.

On the other hand, I believe networked systems are more powerful than hierarchical systems because it's so much harder to destroy them. By distributing control in an organization, we not only empower workers, we also empower the managers. Maybe we should see it as empowerment of the *system*, not of the *people*. Remember the last time you were sick? I bet you felt quite powerless as an individual person against that tiny distributed virus. I'm just glad your distributed immune system was even more powerful, or else I would have one less reader!

> We should see it as empowerment of the system, not of the people.

Management literature cites plenty of arguments in favor of empowerment, such as improving worker satisfaction, increasing profitability, and strengthening competitiveness.[7] All of these are true. But never forget that the real reason for empowerment is to improve system effectiveness and survival. We enable the organization to have more resilience and agility by delegating decision making and distributing control.

Unfortunately, empowerment sounds easier than it is. For some organizations, it requires a total culture change, which doesn't happen overnight. This is one of the reasons why many empowerment programs, despite the best intentions of those involved, often don't provide immediate results.[8] But there is no alternative. The organization *must* be empowered so that people can make their own decisions. All over the world, creative networkers are becoming better educated and better able to take matters into their own hands. And the more educated people are, the less effective authoritarian power is.[9] In many organizations, teams understand their work better than their managers do. Most horses know quite well how to eat, run, and not fall off a cliff without detailed instructions from their riders. Therefore, the primary concern of management should be empowerment, not supervision.[10] We aim for a more powerful system, not better-controlled people. We just need to learn how to implement this system better. It's time for managers to dismount from their rocking horse and learn how to handle a live one.

Defining Boundaries

All I know about horses is what I picked up from fantasy literature. I know they often have saddles, bridles, spurs, bits, shoes (not Italian), and long, beautiful manes that always blow the right way when warriors need to stab an enemy to death. The ones who just sit on a wild horse and yell "yee-haw!" are usually dead before page 50.

I compare teams and organizations—not people!—with horses, and I believe in mutually respectful relationships between horses and their caretakers. The caretaking of horses includes giving direction and setting boundaries. Quite often, when managers delegate work to teams, they don't give them clear boundaries of authority.[11] By trial and error, teams need to find out what they can and cannot do, usually incurring some emotional damage along the way. This was described by Donald Reinertsen as the "discovery of invisible electric fences."[12] Repeatedly running into an electric fence is not only a waste of time and resources, but it also kills motivation, and it ruins the coat of the horse. With no idea of what the invisible boundaries are around it, the horse will prefer to stand still or kick another in the head.

Reinertsen suggests creating a list of **key decision areas** to address the problem of not setting boundaries. The list can include things like working hours, key technologies, product design, and team membership. A manager should make it perfectly clear what the team's authority level is for each key decision area in this list. When the horse can actually *see* the fence, there will be less fear and pain. And the farther away the fence, the more the horse will enjoy its territory.

It also works the other way around. A team usually delegates work to management, such as rewards and remuneration, business partnerships, market strategy, and parking space. The horse is not required to simply accept any kind of boundaries, constraints, and abuse. Nature gave the horse strong teeth and hind legs for this very reason. My fierce white horse in Chile used them well.

The 7 Levels of Delegation

Distributed control in a complex system is achieved when authority is pushed into all corners of the network. However, people prefer not to "lose control." Therefore, in order to make them feel safe, we must play along with the assumption that they have at least *some* control over their situation. That's why a person wanting to delegate can benefit from the use of the *seven levels of delegation*.[13]

© 2014 Koen van Wijk

1. **tell**
   You make a decision for others and you may explain your motivation. A discussion about it is neither desired nor assumed.

2. **sell**
   You make a decision for others but try to convince them that you made the right choice, and you help them feel involved.

3. **consult**
   You ask for input first, which you take into consideration before making a decision that respects people's opinions.

4. **agree**
   You enter into a discussion with everyone involved, and as a group you reach consensus about the decision.

5. **advise**
   You will offer others your opinion and hope they listen to your wise words, but it will be their decision, not yours.

6. **inquire**
   You first leave it to the others to decide, and afterwards, you ask them to convince you of the wisdom of their decision.

7. **delegate**
   You leave the decision to them and you don't even want to know about details that would just clutter your brain.

The seven levels of delegation are a symmetrical model. It works in both directions. Level 2 is similar to level 6, when viewed from the opposite perspective. And level 3, asking for input, is the reverse of level 5, which is about offering input.

The seven levels of delegation should *not* be applied to individual tasks and deliverables. Instead, they should be applied to key decision areas. Defining key decision areas is analogous to erecting a fence around the horse. Increasing and decreasing the delegation level (per key decision area) is similar to tightening or loosening the reins while riding the horse.

The seven levels of delegation can be used to define how decision making is delegated from a manager to an individual or a team, from a team or individual to a manager, and between individuals or teams in a peer-to-peer manner.

Some examples:

- A CEO has set mergers and acquisitions at delegation level 1 and therefore simply **tells** all employees in an e-mail about the takeover of another company.

- A project manager has set project management method at delegation level 2, and therefore he **sells** the idea of introducing an agile project management framework in the project team.

- Team members have set vacation days at level 3, and therefore they **consult** their fellow team members first whenever one of them wants to go on a vacation.

- The facilitator of a workshop has set topics and exercises at level 4 and therefore discusses the available options with her class; together, they **agree** on the details of the program.

- A consultant knows that key technologies for his customer are set at level 5 and therefore **advises** his customer about which technologies to use, but he lets the customer make the final call.

- A mother knows that boyfriends cannot be anything else than level 6, and, therefore, she gently **inquires** about the name and background of her daughter's latest object of desire.

- A writer **delegates** printing and binding at level 7 to his professional printer because, as a writer, he has absolutely no clue how to get his words stuck onto the thin slivers of a deceased tree.

The right level of delegation is a balancing act. It depends on a team's maturity level and the impact of its decisions. Distributed control in an organization is achieved when delegation of authority is pushed as far as possible into the system. However, circumstances may require that you start by telling or selling, gradually increasing the delegation level of team members and widening their territories.

The Delegation Board

Empowerment boards

There is an easy tool people can use to communicate the type of delegation between a manager and a team, or between any two parties. This tool can also help both parties be open and transparent about what they expect from each other. I call it the **delegation board**.

	1	2	3	4	5	6	7
WORKING HOURS					☺		
PROJECT SELECTION						☺	
TEAM MEMBERSHIP			☺				
SALARIES		☺					
OFFICE DECORATION						☺	

Originally, I referred to these boards as authority boards, but I think delegation boards sounds better. Now, I have people suggesting that maybe they should be called empowerment boards because empowerment is what we aim for and is what the tool achieves! I've gotten used to the term delegation board myself, but please feel free to call them empowerment boards if you prefer.

It is a physical board (or a spreadsheet, or the window that looks out onto your neighbor's kitchen) that vertically lists a number of key decision areas that someone delegates to others. In the horizontal dimension, the board shows the seven levels of delegation. For each key decision area, the board has a note in one of the seven columns, clearly communicating to everyone how far authority is delegated in that area. Are people somehow involved in the decision process (level 3: consult)? Is their agreement on certain topics required (level 4: agree)? Are they expected to inform the manager about their decisions (level 6: inquire)? The delegation board can tell everyone.

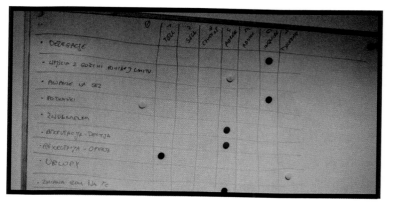

© 2015 Mateusz Gajdzik

Stand-up meetings, retrospectives, and one-on-ones can reveal confusion about authority (who gets to decide what), which can be resolved with the delegation board (or empowerment board). For example, new key decision areas with unclear authorization can be listed, or specific people/teams can be identified and listed by name (or a crude approximation of their physical appearance) using the notes on the board. Furthermore, as in the case of regular task boards, the notes can move from left to right, indicating that more and more control is being delegated from one party to the other. In fact, by visualizing delegation like this, there might be an *urge* to have things flow steadily from left to right!

Teams don't have to wait for managers to create a delegation board. When a team needs more clarity about the control of its territory, the team members could simply visualize their assumptions with a board and ask their manager to come and have a look. Of course, the one who delegates control is the one who decides where to put the notes, but the ones who do the delegated work are responsible for agreeing to their accountability! And remember, teams also delegate work. There is nothing to prevent them from defining *another* board with other key decision areas.

Teams don't have to wait for managers to create a delegation board.

The delegation board is useful in various ways. It models the creation of boundaries and the balancing act of authorization, both of which are needed to get the best out of self-organization. Second, by visualizing key decision areas and delegation levels, the board can act as an information radiator, influencing and directing anyone who takes a closer look at delegation. Last but not least, a delegation board gives managers something to control. When they feel they are losing control, I prefer to see them pushing around some notes on a board rather than the people in their organization. I have no problems telling managers that they can "control self-organization" with a delegation board when this gives people clarity of boundaries and an opportunity for expanding their territory.

Self-organization
gone too far

Even with my own workshops, I struggle with delegation regularly. I recently saw on Twitter the announcement that I would be running an event in Germany. That was a surprise to me. I didn't know! Apparently, local organizers had applied delegation level 7 and forgot to involve me in their decision. Who was at fault here? *I* was, of course! I had not properly communicated the key decision areas and delegation levels for my workshops. I added the delegation board to my website in a matter of days. It was a great reminder for me to apply the exercise to my own work!

Delegation Poker

The delegation poker game was first played at a scrum gathering event in Amsterdam in 2010. Since then, I have played it with people at hundreds of events worldwide, and always with great success.

The purpose of the game is to teach people that delegation is not a binary thing. There are plenty of shades of gray—or colors—between being a dictator and being an anarchist. Delegation is also a step-by-step process. You hand over responsibilities to other people in a controlled and gradual way. And delegation is context dependent. You want to delegate as much as possible, but if you go too far, chaos might unfold.

The game is played with a small group of people (usually three to seven). Each participant gets a set of cards numbered 1 to 7, which correspond to the seven levels of delegation. They can use the "official" Management 3.0 cards (see m30.me/delegation-poker), but it's also easy to let people self-organize and create playing cards out of sticky notes, laser printer paper, or the CEO's business cards.

At the start of the game, you ask the group what kind of key decision areas they would like to discuss. I often give the simple example of vacation days. Does the manager tell everyone on which days they should have their vacations (delegation level 1)? Probably not. Does the manager accept it as a daily surprise who is working and who is not (delegation level 7)? Again, probably not. Most likely, the key decision area of "taking vacation days" is delegated to a level somewhere in between 1 and 7. Let the group decide which other areas they want to explore. Tool selection? Office layout? Project deadlines? Remote working? Financial compensation? For some groups, it is useful to have a set of pre-defined cases for people to discuss. For example, in my workshops, I often offered people 10 management stories, such as this one:

You wish to involve existing team members in the recruitment of new employees. What delegation level will you give them for hiring decisions concerning various job candidates?

Last of all, it is important that participants can refer to the seven levels of delegation while they're playing the game. I usually show the seven levels projected or taped on the wall. A handout is also quite useful.

Rules of the Game

The participants will (repeatedly) perform the following steps:

1. The group picks a key decision area and makes sure everyone understands what it means.

2. Every player *privately* chooses one of the seven cards, which reflects how far they would delegate decision making if they were the manager.

3. When all players have decided, at a count of three, they reveal their selected cards simultaneously.

4. The choices people made will probably be different. Let the people with the highest and the lowest cards explain their choices.

5. Ask the group to achieve consensus about one delegation level (or perhaps a small range).

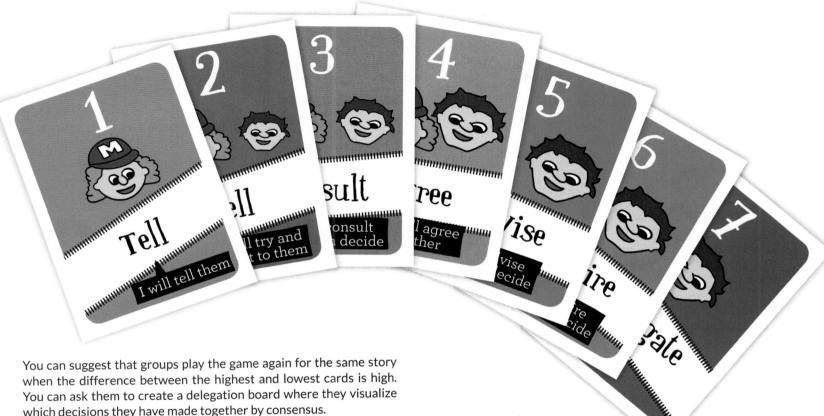

You can suggest that groups play the game again for the same story when the difference between the highest and lowest cards is high. You can ask them to create a delegation board where they visualize which decisions they have made together by consensus.

It is obvious, but perhaps still necessary, to note that self-organizing teams do not decide for themselves what the "correct" delegation levels are for key decision areas delegated to them. After all, the horse does not make its own fence. But the game can be very useful to reveal misconceptions and hidden assumptions. The purpose of the game is not to draw the lines but to get a common understanding of where the lines already are.

Delegation often comes down to either "I do it" or "you do it." But that's too simple. Use delegation poker to make clear who's responsible for what and to what extent. The game encourages employee engagement through controlled self-organization and clarified decision making.

About learning to
self-organize

"I coached a team that was formed with the 'instruction' to be self-organized. But the team was new to this and had only experience with a more command-and-control mindset. They were left to their own devices with no advice on how to 'self-organize.' The result was team conflict, low effectiveness, and decision paralysis, and the manager got more and more irritated about being asked to help them out all the time. Traditional micromanagement was the inevitable result.

I helped the team to list their key decision areas, and we used the delegation poker game to facilitate discussions and agree upon delegation levels. The result was their first delegation board. This helped the team to make much better progress, and the manager was happier as well, because he could finally take a few steps back."

Inga-Lill Holmqvist, *Sweden*

About combining with
competence levels

"At VI Company, we use delegation in combination with competence development. We define different roles and competence levels and communicate clearly what authority level people have, which depends on their agreed-upon job levels.

For example, a junior developer is at level 3 in the area of technical documentation, which means his manager makes a commitment to ask for his input. A mid-level developer is at level 4, which means he and his manager are jointly responsible for documentation.

For senior developers we've set this at level 7, meaning they have earned our complete trust to do whatever they think is necessary in this key decision area."

Ivo van Halen, *The Netherlands*

How to Get Started

Now it is time to define the territory of the horse and to handle it with trust and care.

1. Determine where in the organization people seem to have some issues with delegation and authorization.

2. Decide together what the key decision areas are for these workers. Try not to define the areas as too low-level ("picking up the phone") but also as not too high-level ("doing work").

3. Decide what the assumed delegation levels are per key decision area. You may want to play delegation poker to find out.[14]

4. Create a delegation board (or empowerment board) to visualize delegation to everyone involved.

5. Ask the manager to check if you've made the correct assumptions for all key decision areas and delegation levels. This may lead to an extra discussion or two to narrow down all the opinions.

Tips and Variations

Make it clear which boundary the delegation board is supposed to clarify. Between a manager and an entire team? Between a team lead and specific team members?

We added two levels (0 – Don't Tell and 8 – Ignore), which made sense to our team. Feel free to experiment with your own adaptations.

I used the delegation levels to define or clarify job descriptions.

You can also discuss a delegation board and play delegation poker with other stakeholders, such as product owners and project managers.

I use delegation levels to decide what is the difference between a junior and a senior employee.

My team members were surprised at the level of trust I communicated with the delegation board. They had never been aware of that.

It's good to hang the delegation board on the wall, so you can refer to it whenever needed.

Regularly review the key decision areas and delegation levels and move the levels further when you see growth and maturity in decision making.

We prefer to call it a delegation matrix. Somehow, our people find that easier to understand.

Visually, it can be more interesting to write delegation levels vertically (and key decision areas horizontally) and then have checkmarks or sticky notes move up or down.

We had two sessions: one delegation board by management and another created by the teams. Afterward, we all got together, compared the results, and had great discussions and good progress.

Play delegation poker at the start of a workshop to get people talking about lunch hours, topics to discuss, use of phones and computers, and so on.

Find more ideas at m30.me/delegation-boards and m30.me/delegation-poker.

value stories and culture books

Define the Culture by Sharing Stories

```
C R E A T I V I T Y
    N
  M       T O L E R A N C E
B A L A N C E
  S       G           B
  T   R   R   T R E S P E C T
  E   I   I   U         A
  P R A G M A T I S M    U
  Y   O   Y   T         T
      R               Y
```

> Lasting change is a series of compromises. And compromise is all right, as long as your values don't change.
>
> Jane Goodall,
> British primatologist
> (1934–)

There are all kinds of values that both groups and individuals can recognize. Some of those values come naturally to you. Without them, you wouldn't be yourself. Other values are the ones you aspire to have. It will take effort for you to embrace them. For best effect, you should spin your values into a personal story.

> Self-interest works only as long as there's a containment vessel—a set of ethical principles that ensures enlightened self-interest doesn't melt down into unbridled selfishness.

Gary Hamel, *What Matters Now*[1]

When I signed the contract for my first book, *Management 3.0*, my publisher and I agreed on the deadline of August 1, 2010, for the delivery of my completed manuscript. The editor added that this deadline was just a formality. "We know you authors," he said. "You almost never meet your deadlines, and that's okay. Just deliver whenever you're ready." But I replied, "No, I'm not one of those authors. I intend to deliver my book on schedule." And I did. I e-mailed the completed manuscript to the editor on August 1, 2010, four minutes before midnight. I even had time to pour myself a drink.

Apparently, meeting the deadline was important to me. It was a matter of *discipline* and a matter of *honor*. I wanted to prove something to myself. As a beginning author, I thought it was in my own self-interest to be able to keep a promise.

Honor and *self-discipline* are two examples of **values**, or virtues, of human beings. They are important. Without respect for existing value, the creation of new value easily melts down into selfishness.

I can tell you similar stories of how I pay all my suppliers within two weeks of receiving their invoices (*fairness*), how I never require contracts for my speaking engagements (*integrity*), how I use a daily reminder for myself to say "thank you" to someone (*gratitude*), and how I spent weeks trying to figure out which charity organization to contribute to (*generosity*). I do these things because I find them important. They are important to *me*. Not only do they help me be happier with myself, but having an inspiring purpose and clear values also helps me to keep focus in my work and make decisions more easily. Purpose and values allow people to say either "yes" or "no" to requests and opportunities with more conviction. Research confirms that clarity of values and direction makes a significant difference in behavior at work and is a force behind motivation, commitment, and productivity.[2] Many employees in the world are in need of these clearer boundaries, because most of them suffer from cognitive overload: too many choices and too little direction.[3]

Creating Value

When you see an organization as a network of people creating value (as I do), then you inevitably come to the conclusion that all clients and stakeholders participate in this network in order to derive value from it. Customers, shareholders, employees, suppliers, banks, communities, business partners, governments—in short, everyone who is economically involved with the organization—try to get some value out of it. Otherwise they would not contribute to that collaborative project that we call a business.

You can only create new value when you protect what is already valuable. When you delight customers while screwing suppliers, you're not *creating* value; you're just *moving* it from one stakeholder to the other. When you increase short-term productivity while cutting corners in quality, you're not creating value; you're just *stealing* it from the future. And when you think you create shareholder value by depleting natural resources, you're not creating value; you're just *transforming* part of an ecosystem into an economy.

You can only create new value when you protect what is already valuable.

True value creation happens when you respect the things that are already valuable to some clients. This means taking into account the values of people at all levels of the organization and in all corners of the network.

> Rather than viewing organizational processes as ways of extracting more economic value, great companies create frameworks that use societal value and human values as decision-making criteria.
>
> Moss Kanter,
> "How Great Companies Think Differently"[4]

"But," I hear you think, "what is valuable to clients and stakeholders? Which values should we respect and uphold? I want to be a true value creator, but how do I do it?" Well, it seems you're showing signs of *curiosity*, *enthusiasm*, and *determination*. Great! That means you're already on your way to knowing the answer.

Value List

As the result of a bit of searching and some spare time on a flight from Shanghai to Dubai, I created the following list of 250 values, from a collection of multiple sources. I ignored words such as *religiousness* and *sexiness*, or any other words that did not seem very businesslike (unless your business is a church or a brothel, or both). You can use this list to find and select your favorite values. (A smaller version of this list was offered in my first book.[5]) You can randomize the words and pick your favorites from a pile, or you can apply dot voting where several people make a mark on their preferred values in order to narrow the list down to three or five words. Whatever approach you use, discussing core and wish values is a great management exercise.

Acceptance	Balance	Commitment	Dependability	Expressiveness	Hospitality
Accessibility	Beauty	Compassion	Determination	Extroversion	Humility
Accomplishment	Benevolence	Competence	Devotion	Exuberance	Humor
Accountability	Boldness	Concentration	Dignity	Fairness	Imagination
Accuracy	Bravery	Confidence	Diligence	Faith	Impartiality
Achievement	Brilliance	Conformity	Directness	Faithfulness	Independence
Activeness	Calmness	Consistency	Discipline	Family	Ingenuity
Adaptability	Camaraderie	Contentment	Discovery	Fearlessness	Initiative
Adventure	Candor	Cooperation	Discretion	Ferocity	Innovation
Aesthetics	Capability	Courage	Diversity	Fidelity	Inquisitiveness
Agility	Carefulness	Courtesy	Drive	Fierceness	Insightfulness
Alertness	Caution	Craftiness	Duty	Fitness	Inspiration
Ambition	Change	Creativity	Dynamism	Flexibility	Integrity
Appreciation	Charity	Credibility	Eagerness	Fluency	Intelligence
Approachability	Cheerfulness	Cunning	Education	Focus	Introversion
Assertiveness	Clarity	Curiosity	Effectiveness	Frankness	Intuitiveness
Attentiveness	Cleanliness	Daring	Efficiency	Freedom	Inventiveness
Availability	Cleverness	Decisiveness	Elegance	Friendliness	Joy
Awareness	Collaboration	Dedication	Empathy	Friendship	Justice
			Encouragement	Fun	Kindness
			Endurance	Generosity	Knowledge
			Energy	Gratitude	Leadership
			Enjoyment	Growth	Learning
			Entertainment	Happiness	Liberty
			Enthusiasm	Harmony	Logic
			Equality	Health	Love
			Excellence	Helpfulness	Loyalty
			Excitement	Heroism	Mastery
			Experience	Honesty	Maturity
			Expertise	Honor	Meticulousness
			Exploration	Hopefulness	Mindfulness

Cultural backgrounds have an impact on the choices people make when picking their values.

Modesty	Preparedness	Self-reliance	Thrift
Motivation	Privacy	Sensitivity	Timeliness
Neatness	Proactivity	Serenity	Tolerance
Open-mindedness	Professionalism	Service	Tranquility
Openness	Prudence	Sharing	Transcendence
Optimism	Punctuality	Silliness	Trust
Order	Purposefulness	Simplicity	Trustworthiness
Orderliness	Rationality	Sincerity	Truth
Organization	Realism	Skill	Understanding
Originality	Reason	Solidarity	Uniqueness
Outlandishness	Reflection	Speed	Unity
Outrageousness	Regularity	Spirituality	Valor
Passion	Reliability	Spontaneity	Variety
Patience	Resilience	Stability	Vigor
Peace	Resolution	Status	Vision
Perceptiveness	Resolve	Stealth	Vitality
Perfection	Resourcefulness	Stewardship	Warmth
Perseverance	Respect	Strength	Willfulness
Persistence	Responsibility	Success	Wisdom
Persuasiveness	Responsiveness	Support	Wittiness
Philanthropy	Restraint	Sympathy	Wonder
Playfulness	Rigor	Synergy	Zeal
Pleasure	Sacrifice	Teamwork	
Power	Security	Thankfulness	
Pragmatism	Self-control	Thoroughness	
Precision	Self-discipline	Thoughtfulness	

Human values and virtues are interesting topics, not in the least because they are so heavily influenced by culture. This is wonderfully illustrated by social psychologist Geert Hofstede and his cultural dimensions theory.[6] For example, Hofstede's *power distance index* shows that in Latin, Asian, and African countries, there is a tendency to defer to authority figures, while in Anglo and Germanic countries this power distance is much lower. His *individualism index* shows a clear gap between the improve-yourself attitude in western countries and the stay-with-the-group mentality in eastern countries. Equally interesting are the *uncertainty avoidance* scores, which are high in southern and eastern Europe, and low for the northwest of the continent.

People also reported to me that significant cultural differences can exist between generations within the same region. For example, in Eastern European countries, the older generations, who have experience with socialism and communism, are more inclined to expect that the state and government be there to help everyone, while the younger generations learn that, basically, their future is their own responsibility. Obviously, such cultural backgrounds have an impact on the choices people make when picking their values.

Team Values

So far, I have discussed values from both personal and organizational perspectives. But, like the formation of identity and purpose, the selection of values could also be considered and performed at every organizational level. What about the values of a team? What about the values of the department or the business unit? Clarifying your own values is important, but equally important is understanding the values of others.[7]

The behavior of a team depends on the personalities of the team members, their relationships, and their environment. An important change in their relationships or the environment can lead to a different set of desired behaviors for the team and can, therefore, be a reason to reconsider the team's values.

Using the value list, a team may discuss their most important values. A useful exercise, offered in my first book, is to have management do the same thing and then compare and discuss the results.[8] The same approach was applied at Atlassian, a tool vendor company, which resulted in such fascinating company values as "open company, no bullsh.t" and "don't f..k the customer."[9]

Once the values are selected, people can print them on walls, task boards, T-shirts, screensavers, coffee mugs, and anything else you can think of.

What about
values at other levels?

The selection of values can happen at any organizational level. If that happens (and I certainly suggest that you give it a try), you could end up with a lot of value lists. Isn't that confusing?

Maybe.

But it's not any more confusing than knowing that different organizational levels have different bosses, conflicting policies, multiple identities, and numerous faces. Human beings are masters at reconciling such differences. And if some multilayered value lists are indeed too confusing, I see no reason why people cannot simply sit together and simplify the results. In most organizations, the problem is too little guidance in regard to values, never too much. Remember that the goal is for people to create and respect value and achieve happiness. The goal is not to fight over 250 simple words.

Employee Handbooks

In a land far, far away, and in a time long, long past, I was a senior student at the Technical University in Delft, the Netherlands, employed by the Faculty of Computer Science as a student assistant. I was one of the people paid to evaluate the programming assignments of first-year students, which meant I could tell them that the word *end* had to be properly aligned under *begin* and that the purpose of indentation was to make code readable, not to balance the white space equally in both margins.

One of the things I did, from the bottom of my big compassionate heart, was to create a Freshmen's Guide. It was a simple little book, explaining where to find exams and grades, where to find the student's society, where to go with study problems, and where to find the better parties. I added plenty of handmade illustrations and silly jokes because I wanted the students to find it an interesting read. I am happy to say that my booklet was not only supported by the student's society and paid for by the faculty, but the idea was also copied by some of the most famous companies in the world many years later. (Just kidding!)

IDEO is arguably the most famous design company in the United States, and for good reason. Its *Little Book of IDEO* spells out the important values of the organization, such as "be optimistic," "embrace ambiguity," and "learn from failure." One statement I like in particular is "make others successful," which means that employees should always strive to help each other out. Unlike my own Freshmen's Guide, IDEO's little book can be downloaded from the Web.[10,11]

Valve, a highly successful gaming company, has a Handbook for New Employees that was created by a small team of developers and designers. The handbook, which contains great illustrations—yes, better than mine—and nice jokes and stories, was published first as a print edition and later made available as a downloadable PDF. The document not only inspired many companies in the world as a shining example of a flat organizational structure, but it also showed that employee handbooks don't have to be boring and can be created by employees.[12]

Another example is offered by online retailer Zappos, a company with an official Culture Book, which is also written by its employees and updated every year. The book tells stories of how people feel about the company, and the employees take care that the company's culture is developed and reinforced all the time. Like the Valve Handbook, Zappos's Culture Book is freely available for download.[13,14]

Obviously, such handbooks and culture books only work when employees actually use them and know what they say. All too often, employee handbooks are created by human resources departments, not by employees themselves, and are devoid of any emotion. Values are offered as bullet points and accompanied by rules, policies, and legal disclaimers. It's no wonder that, with such handbooks buried deep down in file systems, employees usually have no affinity with any core or wish values of the company. The real culture communicated in cases like these is "culture is defined by managers" and "we're not supposed to have fun."

In one organization, we asked three managers what the mission was and what was the most important organizational goal. . . . We were told that the values were "in the employee handbook," but those values were disconnected from how people acted or how people were incentivized.

Robin and Burchell, *No Excuses*[15]

Perhaps the most famous example of a great culture book that actually worked is the Netflix Culture document, which says that it all starts with *freedom* and *responsibility* at this company. At Netflix, they actually practice what they preach because the company offers total freedom with regard to vacations, flex-time, and travel expenses (see Chapter 6).[16,17] Some say, as an example of how a company can create and reinforce a culture with values, it is the most important document ever to have come out of Silicon Valley.[18]

Our value wall

"Creating team values was harder than it sounds, as we needed to get the team and company behind it and demonstrate that this offered value (spot the irony). After creating a compelling business case, complete with Gandhi quote, we were able to decide on a set of team values. Once this was in place, we were able to create a Value Wall. A shiny movie picture showcasing each value along with a brief description printed on A3 adorned our Value Wall. Having read about intrinsic motivators, I was keen to make this a thing accessible to all without any agenda other than giving people a 'shout out.' We took a simple approach by putting bright Post-Its with stories on top of the values with the name of the person and a stated observation. However, because it was a room full of blokes, we didn't ring a bell to announce any new additions. In fact, we didn't do any roll calls at all. What happened was more subtle. People casually walked past the Value Wall and took a genuine interest. After a month of doing this, it was clear to see by people's engagement and satisfaction with these stories that it was a hit. You could say this was a lo-fi approach to value stories."

Paul Holden, *United Kingdom*

Living Your Values

Enron, which went bankrupt because of fraud by its top management, had the values *integrity, communication, respect,* and *excellence* displayed in its corporate lobby. Apparently, only showing words to everyone is not enough. After you have determined what your values are as a team or as an organization, it's time to put your money where your mouth is. Turn your values into action! Create your own story!

Are you aiming for *honesty, excellence,* and *service*? Get the team in a car, drive to a client where something went wrong with your product, and sing a song about how sorry you are while handing over a big bouquet of flowers. Should your work be focused on *creativity, discipline,* and *orderliness*? Get your team to make a perfectly executed work of art out of sticky notes, carefully measured out and modeled on the computer. The key is not only to *promise* to keep these values in mind but to actually *do something* to prove that these values matter and guide people's behaviors and decisions.

> At the end of the day, you just ask yourself, "How did our vision and values influence decisions I made today?" If they did not, then they are pretty much BS.
>
> Senge, *The Fifth Discipline*[19]

The culture should drive the business at your organization, not the other way around.[20] Proper values, visualized and communicated with stories, help you define and reinforce that culture.

Videos and books

"After formulating our vision for Future Processing, we decided to present it to our teams in a three-minute animated video. The video presented our goals in the form of a story. We even hired one of the most popular Polish TV presenters to do the voice-over. The effect was that people watched and shared the video much more willingly than they would with the best written corporate document in the world.

What we also did was to make a Christmas present from the teams for our CEO. We gathered some of the best stories in the company and published them as a book. Not only did our efforts result in a nice gift; now we also have an amazing source of funny and inspiring stories about our company that explains our culture and spirit. We share these with new employees, and we also plan to print them for display in our new office building."

Agnieszka Zimończyk, *Poland*

How to Get Started

Does your team have its own values? Do you have a culture book? If not, maybe you can do this:

1. Collect stories of past behaviors that you feel exemplify and illustrate the culture of your team or organization.

2. Print the big list of team values, one copy per person, and let each team member pick core values and wish values, based on the stories you've collected. (You can download the Big Value List from m30.me/value-stories.)

3. Ask management to do the same, and compare the results. Choose a final set that everyone can agree on, both employees and management.

4. Make the values easy to refer to, by keeping them visible around the office. But also find a way to retell the stories around them.

5. Consider turning your values and stories into a culture book that is (preferably) maintained by employees, not by the HR department.

Tips and Variations

Try not to have too many values. The ultimate test is: Can you remember them?

We used a channel in our organization's communication tool (Slack) to post and discuss value stories.

Add values to your kudo cards or merit money practices (see Chapters 1 and 8) to connect people's behaviors to team values.

Use photos or videos to capture great moments and share these in a book or movie.

If you don't know which values to pick, start with stories of things that made people happy. Then you'll find the values.

Organize a company-wide Values Day where everyone is invited to reflect on the organization's values and how people lived up to them.[21]

Make sure you communicate your values in a fun, colorful, and inspiring way.

Every now and then, test if people know the values. Ask them. If they don't know, the values are not working.

We make it a habit to start our weekly meetings by sharing one or two value stories. It gets everyone aligned and in the right mood.

Don't forget that bad things that happened are also worth talking about.

Write a constitution that lays down the way the company operates, the value it generates for everyone, and what it serves to protect.

Always reward people and blame the system, not the other way around.

Find more ideas at m30.me/value-stories and m30.me/culture-books.

5

exploration days and internal crowdfunding

Make Time for Exploration and Self-Education

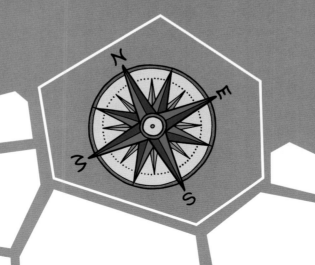

> I am always doing that which I cannot do, in order that I may learn how to do it.
>
> **Pablo Picasso,
> Spanish painter
> (1881–1973)**

Many organizations struggle with self-education of employees. A very effective way to make learning enjoyable is for people to organize exploration days. Sometimes called hackathons or ShipIt days, these days are meant to invite employees to learn and develop themselves by running experiments and exploring new ideas.

My favorite vacations have always been the ones where we fly to some faraway country, rent a car, buy a map, and start exploring. 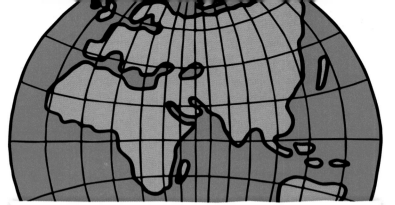 I like to believe this is similar to what they did centuries ago: sailing off across the ocean and discovering new continents, new cultures, and new diseases.

Exploration is also the most effective approach to learning—a topic that appears to be a challenge in many organizations. An emphasis on learning is crucial for all businesses, no matter how successful they already are. After all, you won't have a *first mover advantage* for long if somebody else has the *fast learner advantage*.

You won't have a first mover advantage for long if somebody else has the fast learner advantage.

In modern organizations, more and more people are expected to be self-organizing. Sadly, I have noticed that self-*organizing* teams are not always self-*developing* and self-*educating* teams. I worked with software teams in which developers were very competent at playing Halo or Quake. But important software development practices, such as test-driven development and continuous deployment, were regrettably not among their core competencies.

The problem of team members needing more education can be a significant challenge because, in the words of science fiction writer Isaac Asimov, the only real form of education is *self-education*. Similar opinions have been offered by many management experts. We cannot educate employees. They can only educate themselves.

People don't explore if they just follow the leader or the crowd.

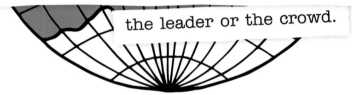

Development is always self-development. For the enterprise to assume responsibility for the development of a person is idle boast. The responsibility rests with the individual, her abilities, her efforts.

Peter F. Drucker, *Management* [1]

I agree with the experts; education of employees is not the prime responsibility of the organization. On the other hand, waiting for people to start developing themselves is not always a successful approach, either. People don't explore if they just follow the leader or the crowd. So what can we do? How can we create an environment that fosters learning and nudges employees to start their own exploration?

Education Days

I once introduced the concept of **education days** in the company where I worked. Every employee was entitled to a number of days per year (we started with 12) that they were encouraged to use for self-education. It didn't matter whether they spent it reading a book, attending a conference, experimenting with new technology, or building a prototype of some crazy idea. Anything was fine, as long as they *learned* something. It was almost the same as vacation days, but instead of spending those days exploring bars and beaches, we expected people to explore techniques and technologies. It touched upon intrinsic motivators such as *mastery, curiosity,* and *freedom.* I thought it was a good idea.

Well, it was. But it didn't work.

The idea was worth trying because apparently it *does* work in some other organizations. Google has its famous 20 percent time, a policy that says employees are allowed to spend 20 percent of their time working on any idea that interests them.[2] It has not only worked as a good motivator; the practice has also generated many great ideas for the company. Products such as Gmail and AdSense were conceived in 20 percent time. Interestingly, it was reported recently that Google has downplayed the importance of its 20 percent time policy[3] in favor of a more top-down approach to innovation and more reliance on employees to develop themselves in their own free time.[4] Apparently, Google has realized that having a fixed number of hours for exploration and learning is neither the best way to get people to develop themselves nor an adequate approach to building innovative products.

At Cisco Labs in Norway, they don't budget the time for people's self-development. Employees are allowed to spend any amount of time they want on their pet projects, and for some that means upgrading the foosball table in their lunch area. During my visit to Cisco Systems, I was shown their foosball table, which had a card reader installed that was used to sign in players using their security badges. Goals were registered with a built-in laser and shown on an LED-display on the table. Even the speed of the ball was measured.[5] Cisco's employees had made all these modifications themselves because, for them, the foosball table is their technical research lab. Olve Maudal, who showed me around the company, told me that other organizations often try to encourage creative ideas by providing lounge areas with fluffy cushions and colorful wallpaper. Olve stated it was more effective to just allow people time to play and experiment. I agree. It wouldn't surprise me if, by now, the foosball table in Norway supports Google Glass and has drones flying over it, capturing live video that is streamed to YouTube.

Unfortunately, my organizational reality several years ago proved a bit more stubborn and less playful than the examples I gave from Google and Cisco. Our employees argued that they had no time to learn and always had more urgent things to do. They had project deadlines to consider, customer demos to prepare, and meetings to attend. Therefore, they told me they saw no opportunity to make use of their education days. I thought this was strange because the same people had no problems making use of their *vacation* days. A more logical explanation seemed to be that they didn't consider their *education* to be as desirable as their *vacation*. Education, in their eyes, was just another task to be prioritized by management. Important, maybe, but not urgent.

Experienced creative workers know that important things and urgent things rarely overlap. Doing what's good for you and developing useful habits—such as flossing your teeth, eating vegetables, and going to the gym—take motivation and discipline. People need to grow into it. (I've managed the first one, but I'm still working on the other two.) Because organizations cannot really change people and educate them, a good alternative is to tweak the environment so that people change themselves, educate themselves, and start developing the desired habits.[6]

ShipIt Days

One company that understands this well is the Australian software company Atlassian.[7] Once every three months, they select a day on which everyone in the company works for the entire day on an idea of their own choosing.  The requirement is that they deliver a result in just 24 hours, hence the name **ShipIt day**. (The original name was actually *FedEx day*, but the FedEx Corp. started to voice concerns about this.) Several other organizations, including Facebook and Spotify, organize similar internal events called **hackathons**[8] or **hack days**. It pretty much boils down to the same thing. Business stands still for one day—some people even stay at the office for a whole night—and everyone learns.

On a ShipIt day or hack day, you can work on whatever you want, as long as it isn't part of your regular work.[9] You can choose to do it alone, but it's probably more fun to team up with some of your colleagues. Such days can be wild and spontaneous, but they work better when they are planned.[10] At Atlassian, they usually have a "ShipIt organizer" who prepares meetings to come up with ideas that can be turned into projects.[11] At Facebook, they have a group called Hackathon Ideas where people post ideas during the week leading up to a hackathon, so that teams can form organically around them.

How often
should we do this?

At Atlassian, they organize a ShipIt day every three months. At Facebook they organize their hackathons roughly every six weeks. Doing it more often has too much of an impact on people's regular projects and work lives, and less often means people get impatient, waiting for the next one. My guess is that the optimum for most organizations is somewhere between one and three months.

According to the people at Atlassian, ShipIt days work well because they stimulate creativity, help solve actual problems, increase knowledge and experience, and are a lot of fun.[12] The people at Facebook and Spotify seem to agree that hack days lead to more focused and open working environments. And they not only involve developers, but designers, marketers, and other experts as well. Last but not least, these "synchronized education days" seem to help increase social connections between people, help them to self-organize, and increase commitment among employees.

What ShipIt days and hackathons add to education days is that peer pressure makes it harder for employees to claim that they are "too busy," an argument that is also heard among Google's employees.[13] Second, the commitment to present the results in 24 hours gets rid of the free format of the education days. Third, handing out an award for the best idea, as a token of recognition among peers, seems to target people's sense of *honor* and *mastery*. Fourth and finally, when some people's ideas evolve into actual new products, this will clearly satisfy their desire for *status*. (And I think employees will rarely spend such days playing Quake or Halo.)

Should we be experimenting or delivering?

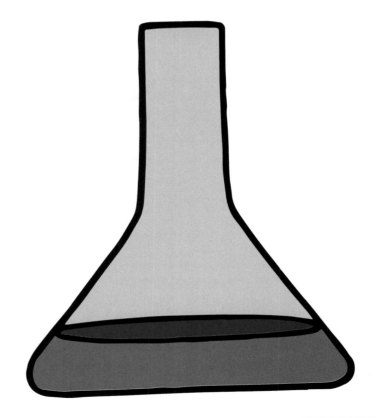

Everyone knows that the outcomes of research cannot be planned. (Otherwise, we could simply plan our way to vaccines for malaria and HIV. 🧪) Therefore, it's not required to deliver a successful idea at the end of a hack day. The goal is learning, not shipping. It is great when a team delivers a potentially shippable product, but it's also great when the explorers fail spectacularly by discovering the wrong continent, one they had never planned to find.

Internal Crowdfunding

When I was CIO, our management team felt responsible for gathering innovative ideas from employees. We appointed an innovation committee, with representatives from several departments, which had the task of choosing which ideas to invest in as a company.

That didn't work, either.

People submitted more ideas than we could handle, and many felt personally rejected when their idea was not selected by our innovation committee. The effect was the opposite of what we had intended: Instead of getting better ideas, the flow of new ideas dried up!

Some companies have discovered that it is better to leave the selection of innovative ideas to employees. They take the hackathon a step further and turn it into an **innovation stock market** by giving all employees a personal (virtual) budget that they can use for investing in ideas. 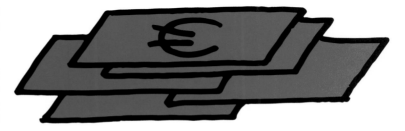 Any employee is allowed to float a new idea on the stock market, but will have to convince peers to invest in the idea. With this approach, there is no innovation committee needed because employees decide together, as a crowd, which of the ideas have the best chance of succeeding and generating a return on their investment. Basically, what you achieve with such a system is an internal version of **crowdfunding**.[14] This can work beautifully because the job of management is not to select the best ideas; it is to create a great system that allows for the best ideas to emerge.

A worker-driven idea stock market, however, is probably not enough to survive in an ever-changing global market. One cannot leave strategic product development to pure chance and self-organization among employees. This is one reason why Google replaced its free-format Google Labs experiments with its more focused and disruptive Google X program.[15] But a top-down pursuit of long-term strategic opportunities and bottom-up development of short-term ideas for improvement don't need to be in conflict with each other. Probably, you need both. You cannot bet the future of the company on whatever employees come up with as playful experiments.[16] But you do not have a future *at all* as a company without an incentive for employees to develop themselves, motivate themselves, and generate innovative ideas.[17]

> The job of management is not to select the best ideas; it is to create a great system that allows for the best ideas to emerge.

As with any other adventure, there are different paths to the same goal. When your regular education days and 20 percent time don't work, you might want to consider turning them into ShipIt days, hack days, or a more exclusive and secretive program like Google X. And it may or may not be interesting to add an idea market, powered by internal crowdfunding, as a complementary approach to any disruptive innovations that top management is working on. These are all useful contributions to people's self-education. They address intrinsic motivators such as *autonomy, mastery*, and *purpose*, but also *social connectedness* and *status*. People work on something they like to do for a cause they think is important. But people also see what their colleagues have worked on and why this matters to *them*. And there is nothing as rewarding as delivering something interesting in just 24 hours, except maybe seeing it being turned into a real product thanks to an internal crowdfunding system.

Some experts say you get the best out of employees when you treat them as entrepreneurs.[18] By making a bit of time available for them to work on their dream projects and allowing them to gain support from their peers to actually get those projects funded, you help people feel more connected to their coworkers, and you help the organization become more innovative. No committee in the world can achieve that.

> You get the best out of employees when you treat them as entrepreneurs.

Self-Education

Learning is different from training. Training is something organizations can do to teach employees how to handle a specific set of tasks. Learning is what employees must do *themselves* to cope with the complexity of their environment. And learning is optimal when people run experiments and explore unknown terrain.[19] That's why I prefer to use the term *exploration days*. 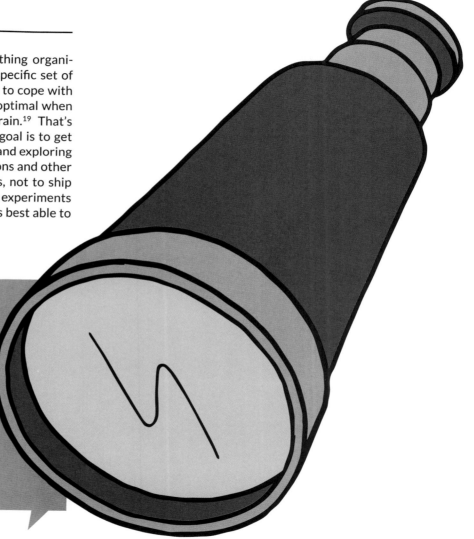 The goal is to get employees to learn as much as possible by generating and exploring new ideas. Experts agree that the purpose of hackathons and other forms of exploration days is to experiment with ideas, not to ship things.[20] And organizations must learn how to run such experiments regularly, because those that learn fastest are the ones best able to survive.

> The purpose of training is to reduce variety, to get a group of people tackling tasks in the same way; so training reduces variety. The purpose of learning is the exact opposite. Learning increases the individual's capacity to respond to different situations; it increases variety.

Patrick Hoverstadt, *The Fractal Organization*[21]

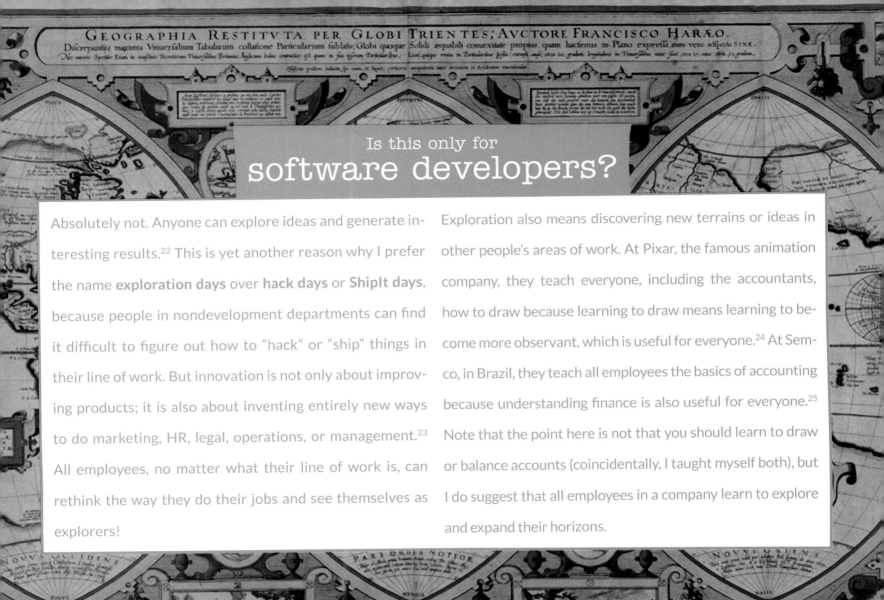

Is this only for software developers?

Absolutely not. Anyone can explore ideas and generate interesting results.[22] This is yet another reason why I prefer the name **exploration days** over **hack days** or **ShipIt days**, because people in nondevelopment departments can find it difficult to figure out how to "hack" or "ship" things in their line of work. But innovation is not only about improving products; it is also about inventing entirely new ways to do marketing, HR, legal, operations, or management.[23] All employees, no matter what their line of work is, can rethink the way they do their jobs and see themselves as explorers!

Exploration also means discovering new terrains or ideas in other people's areas of work. At Pixar, the famous animation company, they teach everyone, including the accountants, how to draw because learning to draw means learning to become more observant, which is useful for everyone.[24] At Semco, in Brazil, they teach all employees the basics of accounting because understanding finance is also useful for everyone.[25] Note that the point here is not that you should learn to draw or balance accounts (coincidentally, I taught myself both), but I do suggest that all employees in a company learn to explore and expand their horizons.

Our first ShipIt day

"We experimented with a ShipIt day in my company with eight colleagues. Our experience was that the requirement to do this in one day felt like a great incentive. People were enthusiastic and excited about participating, maybe because it was a new experience. There was great energy in the group. There's something special about concentrating on one topic during one day, and there was a great feeling of satisfaction of having achieved something in only one day.

The 24-hour format was a bit difficult for some people (understandably, some have to get their kids from school, etc.) and I felt a lot of preparation by the facilitator (including materials and ideas) was necessary to make things work well. But we enjoyed trying this for one day, and we will be sure to repeat this on a regular basis!"

Anthony Claverie, *France*

Rotation days

"I'd like to share a variation of exploration days called 'rotation days.' It's nothing fancy, but it does wonders. It was introduced recently in a section called 'Methodology, Interoperability and Architecture' at the European Commission. The section has five teams, with three to five members each, and all teams work in different areas. Once per month a member of one team works one full day in another team. The host team has to prepare an assignment, and at the end of the rotation day, both the guest and a member of the host team write a brief report about what happened, what they've learned, etc."

Ivo Velitchkov, *Belgium*

How to Get Started

Now it is time for you to start learning by doing.

1. Read more about exploration days (ShipIt days, hackathons, 20 percent time) in the referenced articles.

2. Organize an exploration day with just your own team, during the week or over a weekend.

3. Use the results of this experiment to convince other teams to organize another day together.

4. Consider setting up a stock market for ideas, where people can invest in each other's experiments and somehow reap the benefits of having supported a successful innovative project.

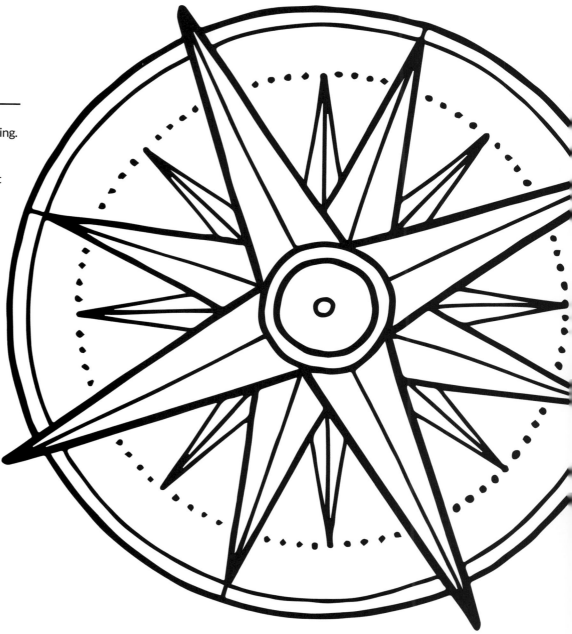

Tips and Variations

Don't make exploration days mandatory! Such days should be fun. It's no fun working with someone who'd rather be somewhere else.

It is easy for people to get carried away with a big idea, but they only have 24 hours. Make sure to keep everyone's expectations realistic.

Many hackathons are really 24 hours, meaning that people work on their ideas all through the night! Make the appropriate arrangements, if necessary.

We got people to submit ideas and experiments to a project board before the event so that they could find partners to collaborate with.

We got people to actually pitch their ideas a week before our exploration day.

Weeks before the event, communicate clearly to everyone in the organization that part of the workforce will not be available for 24 hours.

Remind people that hackathons are not only about developing products! Why not hack the office? Hack the culture? Hack your processes and procedures?

Some people may feel guilty for not doing any productive work on an exploration day. Remove this feeling of guilt by getting managers to participate as well.

Before the event, we defined some concrete success criteria, such as the level of participation, number of ideas generated, and average happiness level.

Don't invite burnouts during an exploration day! Convince people to take breaks, drink enough water, eat healthy snacks, and do some stretching exercises.

We promoted our exploration day with special posters that we put all around our offices several weeks before the event.

The best part of our event was when everyone briefly shared what they learned, which we did using a projector. Everyone who showed off their experiment got a big round of applause.

Find more ideas at m30.me/exploration-days and m30.me/internal-crowdfunding.

6

business guilds and corporate huddles

Share Knowledge, Tools, and Practices

An idea is a feat

of association.

Robert Frost,
American poet
(1874–1963)

Many organizations need to harmonize practices, procedures, and tools across teams and departments. They also need people to share knowledge and develop their craft by communicating across traditional organizational boundaries. This is the purpose and role of guilds and huddles.

The façades on the *Grand-Place* in Brussels, Belgium, look amazing. In the past, they were literally the images of the **guilds** of Brussels, representing some of the finest crafts in the country. Nowadays, the former guildhalls offer expensive Belgian chocolates to naïve tourists, who are unaware that the *really* good chocolatiers are situated on the *Grand Sablon* elsewhere in the city.

Medieval Guilds

In the Middle Ages, professional workers were called artisans, and they often organized themselves in guilds.  For several centuries, those guilds were formed around disciplines such as carpeting, carving, masonry, and many others. Sometimes, these associations of artisans were very strict. They dictated the rules of business for artisans throughout an entire country. Sometimes they were organized in a more relaxed way, with their guiding hands only reaching as far as the city boundaries. No matter how they were organized, the guilds enabled people to learn a craft in master–apprentice working relationships, and they defined proper procedures and behaviors for all who practiced the craft.

> Guilds [were] social networks that generated beneficial social capital by sustaining shared norms, punishing violators of these norms, effectively transmitting information, and successfully undertaking collective action.
>
> Ogilvie, "Guilds, Efficiency, and Social Capital"[1]

Unfortunately, when common sense devolved into politics, preserving power and making money became more important than sharing information and teaching students. With the help of the government, the guilds even became counterproductive in terms of innovation. It seems a classic example of management corrupting an idea that is intrinsically valuable but susceptible to abuse.

Communities of Practice

Fortunately, good ideas rarely die. Nowadays, the artisans within a company sometimes organize themselves in a modern version of a guild called a *community of practice* (COP).[2] A COP is a group of professionals who share a common interest or area of work, a common concern, or a passion about a topic. They can be organized around roles, technologies, interests, and anything else.[3] Since COPs are usually informal and self-organized, and membership is voluntary, the people who are involved are often passionate about their work.[4] This observation is closely related to one of Gary Hamel's "moon shots" for business, which says that companies should see themselves as "communities of passion."[5]

> Communities of practice are groups of people whose interdependent practice binds them into a collective of shared knowledge and common identity. . . . When people work this way, barriers and boundaries between people and what they do are often insubstantial or irrelevant, since a collective endeavor holds people together.
>
> Seely Brown, "Complexity and Innovation"[6]

The purpose of a COP is for participants to learn and share ideas, document lessons learned, standardize ways of working, initiate newcomers, provide advice, explore new technologies, and maybe even apply some forms of governance. A COP can cut across teams, products, business units, and other organizational boundaries. In doing so, it helps to strengthen the social network. Sometimes, a COP is in place for the duration of just one (big) project. Sometimes, COPs continue for as long as their members are passionate about an area of work that binds them.

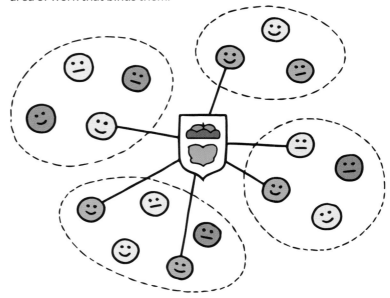

> A community of practice is a unique combination of three fundamental elements: a domain of knowledge, which defines a set of issues; a community of people who care about this domain; and the shared practice that they are developing to be effective in their domain.

Etienne Wenger, *Communities of Practice*[7]

In different contexts, people use different names for (roughly) the same idea, such as learning communities, tech clubs, centers of excellence, improvement communities, professional associations, or simply user groups. The COPs at Spotify, the popular online music company in Sweden, are actually called guilds.[8] It is the term I like best because it has an affinity with craftsmanship that is already centuries old. We could be more precise and call them **business guilds** to distinguish them from the bigger professional associations and user groups, which usually cover geographical areas instead of organizations. No matter what you call them, there are three things that business guilds all share. They cover a knowledge domain, a community of enthusiasts, and a set of tools and practices.

> Business guilds cover a knowledge domain, a community of enthusiasts, and a set of tools and practices.

Though the work of guilds is primarily about learning through collaboration, their usefulness can extend to other areas as well. For example, an interesting aspect of business guilds is that they may enable workers to have a bigger impact on the products, services, and business strategies of the organization, similar to the influence craftsmanship guilds had on the policies and laws of their city councils.

> Through guilds employees have an impact on the way they are working in the company and the way the company provides services to customers.

Piotr Anioła, "Guilds @ BLStream"[9]

When guilds become institutionalized (formally recognized by management), it is important to understand how conflicts of interest between people, guilds, and management will be resolved. For example, the Dutch gymnast Jeffrey Wammes (a professional) was originally not selected by the Dutch Gymnastics Federation (the guild) to represent the Netherlands at the London 2012 Olympics. Wammes didn't agree with that decision and took the case to court (the management), where the judge decided that Wammes had a good point, and that the federation had to reconsider its selection process.

In organizations, similar conflicts can arise. Perhaps some people desire that a product is delivered on a certain date, but a guild tries to block it because the product does not satisfy certain quality criteria. Management will then have to make it clear to everyone which people are authorized to make which decisions and play the judge in case there are different interpretations of the rules.

It's always up to the government (or management) to define the boundaries within which the guilds can make their rules but also to respect those boundaries. It is interesting to note that the judge did not simply overrule the decision of the Dutch Gymnastics Federation and give Jeffrey Wammes what he wanted. Instead, the judge said the decision had been made badly and ordered the two parties to start over. Likewise, in organizations, management can be a force that nudges people and guilds into a collaborative mode without making the decisions for them.

Business Huddles

For some purposes, starting a business guild might sound like too much effort with too little benefit. Sometimes, you just need to make a quick decision as a group, or you merely want a brief update on the latest news and gossip within your community of creative workers. That's where the *corporate huddle* comes in.

I remember lunch meetings at one of the companies where I worked that were among the most cringe-inducing practices our top management ever inflicted upon its employees. Once every three months it involved gathering everyone in the lunch area for one hour, paying for pizza or french fries, placing some department managers next to a computer and projector, and aiming PowerPoint slides decorated with bullet points at 200 glazed eyeballs. What I *don't* remember is anyone ever saying afterwards, "That was great! I wish we did this every week."

Corporate huddles are all-hands meetings that allow for quick, horizontal decision making among peers. They differ from traditional all-hands meetings in the sense that they are about peers informing each other and making decisions with each other, not managers informing nonmanagers about decisions that were already made without them.[10] Basically, you have a huddle when you get most members of a group in the same room and you invite everyone to contribute to a central discussion. That's the easy part. The difficult part is to make these huddles work and to have people say, "That was good! We should do this more often."

You can increase the chances of your huddles being successful by rotating the facilitator or leadership role of the huddle, by creating a regular schedule with an expected cadence, by injecting an element of surprise or fun (for example, with an outside speaker from the Netherlands, or with a small celebration), by keeping those who were not able to attend adequately informed, by keeping the PowerPoint projector locked away, and by *not* organizing it in a boring lunch or conference room.

If you organize your corporate huddles well, there is a good chance that you will never need a traditional all-hands lunch meeting again because everyone in the community is already informed about the decisions that they made together. People report that better cross-functional communication, less micromanagement, and breaking down barriers between teams and departments are the major benefits of regular huddles.[11] And when you focus some of your regular informal huddles on a specific topic or discipline, such as designing products, gathering user requirements, writing technical documentation, or giving presentations, you have the start of what could soon become a fullfledged business guild. Before you know it, you will be sharing insight and advice, helping each other to solve problems, discussing aspirations and needs, and developing shared tools, standards, and documents.[12]

> ## Corporate huddles are all-hands meetings that allow for quick, horizontal decision making among peers.

Tribes

Everyone can start a huddle or a guild. Is there something that interests you the most in your current job? Is there a topic, practice, or technology that you are passionate about? Could a group of peers in your organization benefit from a bit more coordination? Step forward and unite like-minded people across the organization by rallying them around a shared passion.

Your corporate huddle or business guild can start with a small group of enthusiasts gathered around a certain topic, but this can quickly evolve into an online discussion board, a wiki, brown bag lunches, off-site meetings, and anything else that helps you collaborate across multiple teams and departments.[13]

By initiating collaboration among peers, you will be forming your own **tribe**.[14] This is a good thing. Your tribe can define proper practices and rules of good conduct for professionals. It enables people across teams and projects to find appropriate levels of self-governance without getting management involved in the details.

However, management *does* play a role as an enabler of this practice. Many creative workers struggle with big task lists, full calendars, and strict deadlines. It can be hard for them to join a community that is focused on long-term learning rather than short-term results. Management should make it easy for workers by setting aside an appropriate amount of time and other resources for huddles and guilds.

One final word of advice for those who feel motivated to start a huddle or guild: Try not to allow politics and corruption to get in the way of your real purpose. Perhaps a code of conduct, or even a constitution, can help you prevent negative social behaviors by guild members from destroying the guild. You don't want your business guild to end up like the guilds of the old days, showing just a façade of their former glory.

Management should make it easy
for workers by setting aside
an appropriate amount of time
and other resources
for huddles and guilds.

Special interest groups

"I was a member of a management team working for an R&D organization where we frequently had discussions about how to encourage better collaboration across organizational boundaries. At the same time we had a senior project manager with an agile mindset who spontaneously started organizing brief meetings with other project managers in order to discuss common concerns, good practices, and communication in general. The management team discussed this idea with her, and it dawned on us that her informal huddles were a great way to tackle the collaboration problem that we had identified.

This thinking led to what we then called special interest groups (SIGs). Obviously, having people participate in SIGs led to discussions about the impact on our billing rate and utilization, not to mention the added travel costs for our distributed organization. But we were able to agree on the boundaries, and we gave the green light to the SIGs. Over time the SIGs proved their strengths. The feedback we received from the people in our organization clearly suggested that the SIGs were appreciated and that they generated genuine interest."

Juhani Lind, *Finland*

Guild KickOff day

"ComSysto is a fast growing consultancy company with teams distributed around Munich. To increase collaboration, knowledge sharing, and the feeling of being connected, we decided to implement business guilds in our own way.

We started with a guild kickoff day. Topics, goals, and members were not defined at the start of this day, but everyone was empowered to influence the formation of guilds. We did set a few constraints. For example, at the end of the kickoff day, each guild needed to have a contract, a minimum number of committed members, and a commitment to organizing one guild day per quarter. The kickoff day started with the opportunity for people to pitch one or more topics. Then, people self-organized around their favorite pitches, discussed them across various time slots, and the end result was that guilds were formed, common goals were defined, and contracts were signed among the new guild members to establish commitment.

We now support the guilds with Google+ and other communication platforms, so that communication does not only happen in regular guild meetings. Within months after the formation of the guilds, we are already able to feel an increase of collaboration, knowledge sharing, team growing, innovation, and happiness!"

Florian Hoffmann, *Germany*

How to Get Started

Now that you know what business guilds and corporate huddles are for, it is time to start applying the suggestions.

1. What topic (technology, discipline, or role) are you most passionate about? Or which kind of work do you believe is in need of some harmonization across the organization?

2. Which other people in your organization are interested in this topic and might be eager to join your cause?

3. Send those people this chapter. Organize a first huddle and start discussing tools, processes, procedures, people, and policies. Maybe you want to refrain from using the term *business guild* right from the start and just focus on discussing something valuable with each other. Once people start saying, "This meeting was great! Can we do this again soon?" you have a good reason to suggest the formation of a business guild.

4. Investigate how internal social networking tools, such as wikis and other collaborative platforms, can help your fledgling community build and sustain momentum.

5. Make sure that management knows about the huddles and that they stay away from the messy details of the guilds, as long as the guilds work in everyone's interests. (Obviously, this doesn't apply to corporate huddles that span an entire company or department, which are usually initiated by management.)

6. Ask management to set clear boundaries around self-governance so that the new guilds can prove their merits without cannibalizing other work and projects.

© 2010 Nordiska Museet, Creative Commons 2.0
https://www.flickr.com/photos/34380191@N08/4727639216

Tips and Variations

We have a weekly meeting with some people from several teams over lunch. It's very easy to get started if you combine it with food. ;-)

Google has a weekly meeting called TGIF (Thank God It's Friday) to which the whole company is (virtually) invited. No matter the size of the company, there is always room for a huddle.

The huddle or all-hands meeting has many other names, too. Just remember that it should never degenerate into a broadcast from managers to workers!

We formed a guild across a number of small companies, which is great for the exchange of ideas and experiences across corporate boundaries.

Guilds can form their own hierarchies, similar to local sports associations self-organizing into national and global federations.

Agree with management on the amount of time you can spend per week on guilds and huddles.

Some people organize regular meet-ups in their city about Management 3.0. (Check out the management30.com website.) These are guilds, too!

If you don't like the word guild, call it what you want. Just remember that probably nobody has ever been inspired by the term *center of excellence.*

We always say: "Any person from another company should be able to attend our meetings and find them interesting." This makes sure we discuss our profession, and not specific projects, in our guild.

Creative workers' primary allegiance is often their specialization, not their organization. Supporting worker guilds is therefore in the interest of the company.

Get each guild member to organize at least one session themselves. This prevents them from expecting that the guild leader does all the work.

Support your guild with good collaboration tools for ongoing conversations. It's often not enough for people just to see each other face-to-face once per month.

Find more ideas at m30.me/business-guilds and m30.me/corporate-huddles.

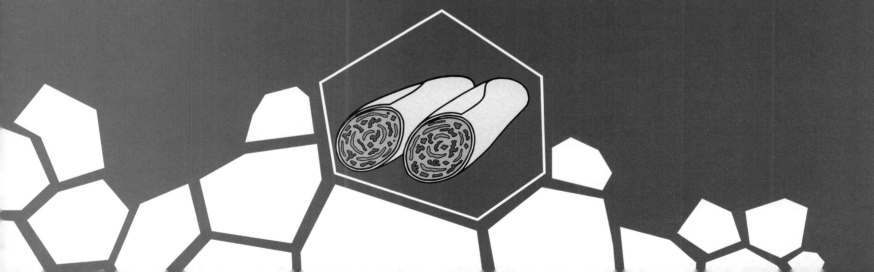

feedback wraps and unlimited vacation

Learn How to Offer Constructive Feedback

> Idealism increases in direct proportion to one's distance from the problem.
>
> John Galsworthy,
> English novelist
> (1867–1933)

More and more employees enjoy freedom in their choice of working hours, workplaces, and vacation days, while some even have complete freedom in a trust-only work environment. This means face-time between coworkers happens less often and we must learn to give each other constructive feedback in a way that is fast, easy, and . . . written.

The first time I became a manager at a small company I wondered about a number of things beyond just the size of my monthly salary. I wondered about the size of my end-of-year bonus, the size of my office corner, and how many vacation days I should negotiate with the business owners. One of them said to me, "Why should I care how long you are away from the office? I just want to see a profit at the end of the year." I remember feeling thrilled at the freedom, trust, and responsibility I was given. After my studies, which were all about achieving results no matter if I showed up in class or not, this was my first *trust-only* work environment.

Contrast that with the experience I had several years later at another company that had a time clock. All employees were expected to check in and check out at the start and at the end of every day. Proof that this clocked time was actually monitored came when the financial controller reprimanded me one day for "working" only 7 hours and 25 minutes the day before. Apparently it didn't matter that I had clocked at least 9 hours on other days. This is a clear example of a *time-driven* or presence-driven work environment.

You won't be surprised when I say I preferred the former to the latter.

Flextime

I was at the office for only 7 hours and 25 minutes on that particular day because I had an appointment with the dentist, whose opening hours were almost as narrow as our financial controller's mind. But compared to other workers, I suffered only a minor inconvenience.

Many employees have to juggle the challenges of dropping off and picking up their kids from school or day care, attending to their parents at an elderly home, visiting the hospital to see a loved one, attending yoga classes, learning a foreign language, evading or suffering traffic jams, working out at the gym, walking the dog, donating blood, or doing charity work.[1] It makes you wonder, if we want half the world to work from 9 to 5, shouldn't the other half be working from 5 in the afternoon to 9 in the morning?

Dividing the world into two groups of people (those who work "normal" hours and those who don't) is clearly unrealistic. That's why many organizations have introduced a *flextime policy.* Such a policy often defines a core time slot when everyone is expected to be at the office, while allowing flexibility for the other hours. Under this policy, employees can easily compensate for their 7 hours and 25 minutes on one day by ~~working~~ *showing up* at the office for 8 hours and 35 minutes on another day (often called *compensation time*).

It was a first step toward a more trust-driven work environment, which also meant a first step toward performance evaluations based on effort and results, not on time.

Remote Working

Fortunately, the "flexibilization" of work environments didn't stop there. In a number of organizations, employees are allowed to do part of their work at home, in remote coworking offices, while traveling abroad, at the day care center, or at the local Starbucks. A *telecommuting policy*  allows people to do their work where it makes the most sense for them, given their personal circumstances and the nature of their work. Multiple reports have indicated increased morale, better focus, higher productivity, reduced turnover, and lower expenses in environments with a flexible attitude toward the location of work.[2,3] Also, such organizations tend to draw more experienced, high-quality workers who prefer to work wherever they want.

Not unexpectedly, allowing people to do their work anywhere creates a bucket load of new challenges. What about privacy, security, and confidentiality? What about people's equipment, insurance, and travel expenses?[4] Most organizations feel the need to develop a remote working policy that clearly defines people's rights and responsibilities when they are working away from the office.

And then there are other issues. When people work on their own as telecommuters, there is an increased risk of loss of trust, collaboration, and social cohesion.[5,6] In other words, the organization may risk losing a healthy culture.[7] It's no coincidence that even the hippest and trendiest Silicon Valley companies often spend large sums of money on free food, games, massages, and fitness equipment in order to keep everyone together in the same office as much as possible.

Still, the option of doing useful work while away from the office seems like a second step toward a more trust-driven work environment. And it is also a second step toward feedback systems focusing on *how* people do their work, not on *where* they work.

Unlimited Vacation

We can even go another step further in making our work environments more flexible. Ever since people have worked away from the office, the line between work time and free time has started to blur. When an employee books a vacation from the office, should that be considered as the first hour of vacation time? And when the same person phones into an important meeting from the holiday resort, does that count as two missed hours of vacation?[8] What about writing a report while babysitting the neighbors' kids? What about walking the dog after lunch while discussing a project with a team member?

Smart organizations would rather not specify in detail what is and what is not allowed during specific times of the day, as long as people do enough useful work *and* take enough time off. Plenty of studies have found that time away from work, with regular vacations, improves people's performance and lowers their stress levels, which increases the quality of their output when they *do* work.[9]

> ## Time away from work, with regular vacations, improves people's performance.

For this reason, companies such as The Motley Fool, Netflix, HubSpot, Evernote, and Zynga have stopped defining how many hours per day people should work and how many days in the year they can go on a vacation.[10] The benefits of such an **unlimited vacation policy**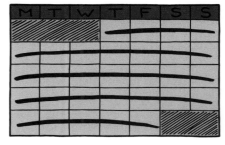

are similar to the ones I mentioned earlier: better morale, increased productivity, higher retention, and higher engagement.[11] And no tiresome discussions about banking vacation days, half days, bonus days, and other nonsense.

Surprisingly enough, with an unlimited number of vacation days and without any guidance on *how much* vacation per year is reasonable, it appears some people actually take less time off than they should. The reasons mentioned most often are not wanting to be characterized as a "slacker," not having the experience or courage to say "no" to extra work, and not being able to choose (also called "choice overload").[12,13] Taking into account these undesirable side effects of an unlimited vacation policy, some companies are strongly suggesting a *minimum* amount of vacation per employee, but no maximum.[14] (This also happens to be the law in many countries.)

Assuming that we can properly address these side effects, the responsibility for one's own free time sounds to me like a third step toward a more trust-driven work environment. At the same time, it is a third step toward performance feedback that must be based on actual work *performance* instead of work *presence*.

Developing Trust

"Trust people to get the work done."

Oh. Really? You believe in a results-only work environment?

Few topics are as widely misunderstood as trust. Everyone talks about it, but when I ask for clarification, nobody can properly define it. They all claim employees have a right to be trusted, but few are willing to trust a coworker to successfully perform open-heart surgery, build a rocket, or win the Olympics.

Trust is a rather complex topic. The model of trust that I trust most lists 10 factors that all contribute to the presence (or lack) of trust.[15]

Growing trust involves quite a bit more than "just relying on everyone to get the job done." Not everyone knows *how* to do a certain job (capability). This makes people uncomfortable with a limitless amount of freedom for themselves *and* for others (risk tolerance), which actually feeds their *distrust* of a results-only work environment, which worsens their collaboration (communication), which further breaks down trust, which nudges authoritative managers to "take action" and call everyone back to the office (power), which destroys another chunk of trust, which stops people from delivering on commitment (integrity), which evaporates the last bit of trust people still had. And that's just one possible outcome of a laissez-faire approach to a results-only work environment.

- **Risk Tolerance**
  Some people are risk takers, others are cautious.

- **Adjustment**
  Some people are optimists, others are pessimists.

- **Power**
  Some people have authority, others suffer from it.

- **Security**
  Sometimes the stakes are high, sometimes they're low.

- **Similarities**
  Some people are similar to each other, others aren't.

- **Interests**
  Sometimes interests are aligned, sometimes they aren't.

- **Benevolent Concern**
  Some are nice to us, others . . . not so much.

- **Capability**
  Some know what they're doing, others . . . not really.

- **Integrity**
  Some people deliver on commitment, others . . . forget it.

- **Communication**
  Some can communicate well, some . . . —uhm.

> There is no better way to build cross-group trust and offset initial skepticism than to establish a strong track record of delivering on commitments.

Robert Hurley, *The Decision to Trust*[16]

As an alternative, the spiral of trust could move upward. By allowing those with a *track record of delivering on commitment* (integrity) to work from home, you grow more trust in remote working. This reduces a manager's urge to "take action" (power), which generates more trust among everyone that they can indeed self-organize, helping them to collaborate better (communication), which creates yet more trust and helps even the most risk-averse people (risk tolerance) to see the benefits of a results-only work environment. The spiral continues until employees have earned freedoms they never had before and can do work in ways they never thought possible (capability).

Human organizations are complex systems. We can imagine many other vicious and virtuous cycles of trust, using any combination of the 10 trust factors. However, many authors believe that growing trust by focusing first on commitment (integrity) is a good bet.

Developing a track record of commitment and trust might take a lot of time and effort. Trust is like money. It can take years to earn it, and it takes only minutes to lose it. Authoritative managers who communicate (intentionally or not) that nobody in the office can be trusted to set their own time schedule, choose their own work place, and select their own vacation days do not develop trust. They merely *add* to the distrust that is already there in the organization's culture.[17] You may wonder at the long-term effects of such a message on performance and retention, but many experts already know.

On the other hand, I agree that merely trusting everyone, no questions asked and no strings attached, will often have the same results. Instead, you should start with the premise that trust (maybe not in your interests, similarities, or benevolent concerns, but in your capabilities, integrity, and communication) needs to be established first *before* you can do whatever you want. A focus on results not only follows but also precedes unlimited freedoms.[18] It appears that a results-only work environment is a right that has to be *earned*.[19]

Instead of focusing on results, I believe creative workers should focus on trust first. They should learn that trust is grown by delivering on commitments, communicating often and well, aligning interests, showing benevolent concern, and so on. When trust is established *first*, it is much easier to discuss and evaluate results *later*. Expecting trust to emerge automatically when just evaluating results is naïve and short-sighted. That's why I prefer to talk about a **trust-only work environment.** When there is trust first, there will be results later. Create a trust-only work environment *before* a results-only work environment. Trust me.

Developing a work environment in which we trust people to get their work done also implies developing a work environment in which we can give feedback about that work. We saw that the steps toward giving workers more freedom by removing the focus on *where* they work have also increased the need for evaluation about *how* they work. When work is something people *do*, not a place where they go, then feedback should also be targeted at what they do, not where they are.

When there is trust first,
there will be results later.

Performance Appraisals

As soon as managers think about the possibility of switching from a time-only or presence-only work environment to a results-only or trust-only work environment, the first question that usually pops up is, "How do we evaluate results?" After all, a fair consideration is, "If we are not supposed to measure the *input* (the amount of time someone is present at the office) we need to measure the *output* (the actual results produced) or else we won't know why we are paying that person a salary." And then they create yet another policy.

> In policies, we see at-will agreements and elaborate rules of conduct (so we can fire you easily when you screw up), elaborate policy manuals (we're in control and you're not a responsible adult), time clocks and leave approval slips (we don't trust you), attendance awards and incentive pay (you really don't like to work), suggestion programs ("If you have an idea, put it in a box"), and, of course ... the sacred cow, the Godzilla of them all—yes, the performance appraisal.

Tom Coens and Mary Jenkins,
Abolishing Performance Appraisals[20]

Traditionally, most businesses use a formal process involving **performance appraisals** as the main (or sometimes only) way of "evaluating" the performance of employees. The performance appraisal is described as a mandated process in which, for a period of time (often annually), an employee's work performance, behaviors, and/or traits are rated, judged, and/or described by someone other than the rated employee, and documented records are kept by the organization.[21] Managers and HR professionals believe they need this process in order to:

1. help employees improve their performance;
2. motivate employees with coaching and counseling;
3. enhance communication with valuable feedback;
4. find a fair way to distribute compensation;
5. have useful data for promotions and staffing decisions; and
6. collect a paper trail in case they need to fire someone.

Second only to firing employees, managers hate performance appraisals the most.

Regrettably, the practice doesn't work. Performance appraisals have a terrible track record.[22] While most companies appear to use them, a great majority of people find them completely useless and often counterproductive.[23] A significant body of research confirms that performance appraisals usually destroy intrinsic motivation and team collaboration.[24] This typically stressful annual ritual of appraisals almost always fails for a number of reasons: The employee and manager have opposite mindsets; pay often has nothing to do with performance; no manager can ever be objective; the performance checklists are too generic; the evaluations create distrust; and individual evaluations destroy teamwork.[25,26,27] Many managers seem to have at least an idea that something's wrong because, second only to firing employees, they hate performance appraisals the most.[28]

Nobody has been able to supply evidence that appraisals will help organizations improve their performance in the long term. Most managers and HR professionals just take them for granted without truly thinking about their many hidden assumptions.[29] If performance appraisals were themselves subject to a performance appraisal, they would be fired on the spot for complete lack of any concrete results. Worst of all, they reinforce the hierarchy that modern organizations should try to get rid of.

Fortunately, the world is slowly waking up. One by one, both small *and* big organizations are getting rid of performance appraisals.[31] One main reason is that the practice is unsustainable in light of the

Performance appraisal has become more than a management tool. It has grown into a cultural, almost anthropological symbol of the parental, boss–subordinate relationship that is characteristic of patriarchal organizations.

Tom Coens and Mary Jenkins,
Abolishing Performance Appraisals[30]

emerging globalized creative economy. Remote working, contract workers, agile and lean methods, and many other trends make it more and more difficult to organize formal performance evaluations between "superiors" and their "subordinates." (Case in point: My spouse hasn't had any recent performance appraisals because he's always away from the head office!) Better to get rid of this useless ritual completely and replace appraisals with something that makes more sense in the twenty-first century.

So, what *should* we do?

I believe the first thing we must learn is how to offer *written* feedback to our colleagues in an easy, honest, and *friendly* way. I would like to emphasize friendly because research shows that a "treat 'em mean, keep 'em keen" approach undermines morale and motivation in organizations, which destroys collaboration between employees as well as their performance.[32] It sounds obvious, but sadly, it seems necessary to remind managers of this fact. When feedback is honest, however, research shows that engagement goes up.[33]

With more and more employees working remotely instead of at a central office, we need a way to provide frequent, honest, and friendly feedback on each other's work via e-mail and other online tools instead of only relying on face-to-face conversations. We cannot wait with our evaluation of someone's new design, report, software app, or quality process until the next time we happen to run into them at the office. (That could take a while!) Considering they don't want us to monitor their working times, workplaces, and vacation days, creative workers have a right to receive useful feedback on their results and they need it *fast*. Feedback needs to be part of our work every day. Feedback should be *normal*.[34]

> Creative workers have a right to receive useful feedback on their results and they need it *fast*.

Step 1: Describe Your Context

The purpose of feedback is to help people improve their work.[35] It is crucial to realize that your goal is not to make them feel good about themselves. Your goal is to make them feel good about your feedback. When people appreciate constructive feedback, you increase the chance that they will act on it.[36]

As a first step, it is useful to start any attempt at giving feedback by describing your context. ☺ Briefly mention the environment you find yourself in, your state of mind, and the expectations and assumptions you have, which may all influence your evaluation in some way.[37] For example, "I am reviewing the new website from my hotel room in Shanghai, feeling a bit tired after a long conference day, but I don't want to keep you waiting. I work with the assumption that the website I'm looking at is the beta version, which implements all features we discussed in the last sprint." Another example: "I'm giving you this feedback early in the morning, after a cup of tea and half a bottle of vitamin pills. I think I caught the flu! :-(I have the third draft of Chapter 4 in front of me now, as a PDF on my Android tablet. I understand it still needs to be copyedited."

By starting with a description of your personal situation, you enable the people on the receiving end to notice any similarities between them and you, which can generate trust. ("The flu? I feel sorry for you. My husband is suffering from it right now!" "In Shanghai? Cool, I was there last year!") You also allow them to appreciate your attempt at communicating well and they will better understand the context of your evaluation. Instead of "your Twitter feed on the homepage doesn't work!" they will read "your Twitter feed on the homepage doesn't seem to work from my hotel room in Shanghai!" This would allow them to correctly identify the Great Firewall as the source of the problem. (Yes, this is a real, personal example.) And if you want to say the work looks horrible, this could be easier for someone to accept knowing it sucked from the perspective of someone suffering a crappy Wi-Fi connection, an old smartphone, bad coffee, three screaming babies, and a terrible hangover. This allows the creative worker to keep believing the work actually looks great in the worker's own safe environment, but offers the additional challenge of making it look good for someone in a less favorable context.

Step 2:
List Your Observations

The purpose of the second step is to explain the things you observe, in terms of facts and experiences as if you have the eyes of a researcher. ● Do *not* give your opinion on what's wrong or right about the person's traits, knowledge, or professionalism. Only focus on the things you can actually see about the work or behaviors.[38,39] Make sure that anything you report is a plain fact. It should be as if the feedback is coming from a scientist's mind and, therefore, hard to deny or ignore. By just listing plain observations instead of emotional outbursts, you communicate your competence, which adds to the generation of trust.

For example, the feedback "the Twitter stream on the home page doesn't work" can be easily dismissed with "it works fine on *my* computer." Instead, you could say, "Under the Twitter header on the home page, I see an empty gray box. I expected to see the three or four latest tweets from our corporate account." Whether things "work" or not is an interesting topic for a philosophical debate in a hotel bar. The *fact* is you are looking at an empty gray box. This cannot be denied, unless you have a track record of poor eyesight.

By keeping observations and facts separate from evaluations and judgments, you can avoid unhelpful generalizations. The comment "nothing you delivered has ever worked as promised" might *feel* true to you, but is less likely to inspire improvement than the comment, "A cryptic error message (see attached) prevented me from accessing the application. It looked similar to the error message I reported last time and the time before." When you decouple observation from evaluation, you decrease the chance that people hear harsh, unfair criticism, and you increase the chance that they are willing to improve.

Do not fall into the trap of only pointing out things that are below expectations. You *must* also point out the things you noticed that are beyond what you expected. For example, "I was surprised to see the e-mail address was validated in real-time," or, "The joke in the first paragraph made me laugh unexpectedly, and I sprayed my cappuccino all over my notebook." Encouraging people to grow their strengths is not just useful for novices: Even experts and top performers appreciate recognition of their talents every now and then.[40,41] It also makes problems and issues easier to act on for those on the receiving end when they see there is a genuine appreciation for the things that were done well.

The result of step 2 should be an unsorted list of things you noticed while reviewing the work, both below and above expectations, as if you have been giving the commentary to a live sports event you had been eagerly awaiting.

Step 3:
Express Your Emotions

Now that you have your list of facts and observations, it is time to evaluate the impact they had on you. Yes, feel free to get emotional!

By expressing the emotions you felt when reviewing someone's work, it is easier to connect with the other person, and it can help you prevent or resolve conflict. You use it to express your benevolent concern for good results, which again adds to the growth of trust. For example, you can report that you felt *slight annoyance* when you saw no results in the Twitter box on the home page, and you felt *great amusement* at the joke in the first paragraph. The automatic e-mail address validation made you feel *happy* at the competence level of your coworker, while you felt *anger* when seeing the cryptic error message for the third time.

Don't be tempted to make assumptions about what *other* people might see or feel when reviewing the work. "No user will ever understand the icon on this button" is not good feedback because it expresses frustration. It is *not* a fact augmented with a feeling. A much better comment would be, "I saw a shower icon on the wall, but it took me a minute to understand that it was actually the light switch for the bathroom. It made me wonder if other users would make that connection more easily than I did." (Yes, being respectful often requires a few more words than responding like a jerk would.) What is reported here is a misunderstanding (fact) and the expression of puzzlement (feeling). You can argue for hours about what other people might or might not understand, but nobody can deny your own observations and your own feelings.[42]

If you want, you can emphasize the separation of facts and feelings by adding emoticons to the observations you reported in the previous step:

Observation	Feeling
"Under the Twitter header on the home page I see an empty gray box. I expected to see the three or four latest tweets from our corporate account."	:-/
"A cryptic error message (see attached) prevented me from accessing the application. It looked similar to the error message I reported last time, and the time before."	>:-(
"The joke in the first paragraph made me laugh unexpectedly, and I sprayed my cappuccino all over my notebook."	:-D
"I was surprised to see the e-mail address was validated in real-time."	:-)
"I saw a shower icon on the wall, but it took me a minute to understand it is actually the light switch for the bathroom. It makes me wonder if other users will make that connection more easily than I did."	((+_+))

Explicitly listing the words *annoyed, angry, laughing, happy,* and *confused* probably makes your report a bit easier to comprehend, but I think there's value in playfulness. Personally, I appreciate people being serious about not taking work *too* seriously. {8-)

Step 4:
Sort by Value

In the fourth step, you might find it useful to sort the observations by the value that you recognized in the work.  Usually, most of the things that resulted in a positive feeling will have a positive value for you, and the observations that led to a negative feeling will have a negative value. But it doesn't have to be that way! For example, someone could have made a hilarious mistake that made you laugh out loud (a positive emotion) but the embarrassing error must certainly be corrected (negative value). On the other hand, some other issue could have made you feel annoyed (a negative emotion), but maybe this helped you discover something crucial that would have cost you an arm and a leg if it had not been discovered early enough (positive value).

Assuming that people read your feedback from top to bottom, it will be helpful to put the most valuable observations at the top and the least valuable ones at the bottom. This makes sure people first learn how their work has *added* value for you; and only after that, they learn how their work has *subtracted* value. It seems like the equivalent of starting with compliments before dealing with criticism, though it is actually not the same thing.

In my opinion, it is misleading to talk about "positive feedback" (compliments) versus "negative feedback" (criticism). As we've seen, your *feelings* can be described as positive or negative, and the *value* of what you observed can also be positive or negative. But your feelings about discovering negative value can be positive, and vice versa. Therefore, your feedback as a whole should be called neither positive nor negative.[43] It is merely a list of factual observations, positive/negative emotions, and positive/negative value. The end result communicates that your interests are aligned with the other person's interests, and this creates more trust.

Step 5:
End with Suggestions

OK, it's time to wrap up! You've spent some time describing your context, listing your observations, expressing your feelings, and sorting items by value. Now it is time to end your feedback on a high note. You can do that by offering a couple of helpful suggestions.

Assume that everyone wants to do well. If people don't perform well, the fault should be found in the system around people that is preventing them from doing a great job.[44] Therefore, any evaluations of performance should reveal systemic problems, not personal failure. Your suggestions for improvement should reflect that mindset. For example, you could end with, "If you find this useful, I would love to help review the design process. Maybe we can discover why some error messages keep occurring." Or you could say, "If you want me or other people to test the Twitter box on other computers and other browsers, let me know." Or you could make an offer such as, "I attached some examples of icons that you might find helpful. They are just sketches, of course."

Remember that your suggestions are . . . just your suggestions.[45] Professional creative workers may disagree with you. That's why we call them professionals and creatives. But when you practice the separation of facts from feelings, feelings from value, and learn to wrap your report inside a context, spiced up with some suggestions, I'm sure most creative workers will be delighted with your approach to giving feedback.

It is said that experts usually look for things to improve, while novices usually look for confirmation that they're doing well.[46] With the method described here, you can serve both groups. In fact, you don't even need to know if someone is an expert, a novice, or anything in between. What you offer are observations, feelings, and value. It is up to them to decide how to consume your healthy feedback wrap. What they will certainly appreciate is that you can deliver a feedback wrap fast, which communicates integrity and commitment, the first and foremost prerequisites for trust.

The praise
Sandwich

One well-known method for constructive feedback is called the "praise sandwich." It suggests that any criticism should be wrapped between positive comments before and after the criticism.[47]

However, many authors have problems with the praise sandwich. Some claim that people hear only the positive parts of the praise sandwich and tend to ignore the bad stuff offered between the compliments.[48] Other authors claim the opposite, saying that human brains are wired to respond to negative information, meaning they ignore the compliments.[49]

I believe both are true, depending on who is listening (or reading). Research confirms that novices prefer support and confirmation while experts prefer honesty and valuable information.[50] Therefore, novices who feel insecure about their capabilities may seek confirmation they are doing a good job and might only pick up the compliments. Experts who desire honest evaluation, however, focus only on the criticism and may dismiss the compliments in the praise sandwich as insincere flattery.

Written Feedback

With employees and other creative workers continuously moving between projects, working both inside and outside the office, and enjoying free time and vacations whenever they think they can, it is crucial for employers and coworkers alike to develop the capability of giving and receiving honest, constructive feedback on results. Trust-only work environments should be feedback-rich.[51] This means there should be frequent feedback about the same products and processes from different people.[52]

In agile software development communities, when the release of a product is painful and time-consuming, it is often said it should be done *more often* so that people are forced to learn how to make it painless and easy. With constructive feedback, it's the same. Traditionally, performance appraisals are done once a year in a big, painful, and time-consuming way. For a creative worker, the challenge should be clear. How can we give feedback *every day*? The feedback wrap will help you do exactly that. With a bit of experience, you can send a feedback wrap in less than 15 minutes. And a feedback wrap is also easy to *ask* for.

Obviously, because this is all about *written* feedback, your words must be picked carefully. Written language must often be softened with "maybe," "a little," and "it seems that." And what you cannot communicate in body language will have to be translated into respectful sentences. Never forget that, unlike face-to-face conversations, written conversations are easily retrieved and reproduced, sometimes long after you had forgotten about them. Assume all your e-mail is read by the NSA, leaked to the press, analyzed by your enemies, and forwarded to your mother-in-law. In other words, write nicely.

Even then, you *still* have little control over other people's interpretations. But let's not pretend that people are any better at offering and receiving verbal feedback. I believe people's response to feedback, whether written or verbal, is mainly determined by their inner state of mind and any conflicts they have with themselves. When a person's thinking is dominated by self-criticism, regret, pride, or some other very common human mental state, the response to your feedback may be unexpected and may seem illogical.[53] No amount of tweaking of words, whether verbal or written, can prevent an outburst of being human.

And yet, though I am among the first to admit that face-to-face discussions are crucial in all human relationships, I am convinced that the health of such relationships can be improved significantly with respectful written feedback on each other's work in a trust-only work environment. Written feedback also helps you to keep proper documentation, to think more carefully about delicate issues, and to report on observations, feelings, and value in a well-balanced manner. And most important of all, feedback wraps can be delivered *fast* and *often*, and nobody needs to wait for scheduled face-to-face performance appraisals (which shouldn't happen anyway).

> Assume all your e-mail is read by the NSA, leaked to the press, analyzed by your enemies, and forwarded to your mother-in-law.

Wrapping Up

Among systems thinkers, it is well-known that 95 percent of the performance of an organization is the result of the whole system, not the individual people. It makes little sense to have performance appraisals with individual employees when most of their performance is the emergent result of the interactions between clients, tools, processes, and other parts of the environment over which they usually have little control.[54]

What organizations need is a *trust*-only work environment. By purposefully creating trust, people will be more eager to find and solve any performance issues. Who cares about the performance of individual parts when those parts are directly responsible for only 5 percent of the outcome? What you should care about is how the parts interact with each other, which includes how they give and receive feedback, because the other 95 percent of the performance in the system is found in the interaction among the parts!

The feedback wrap will help people focus on personal improvement *and* systemic improvement. At the same time, the practice generates trust through good communication, benevolent concern, aligning interests, increasing competence, and delivering on commitment. This growth of a *trust*-only work environment clears the path for a results-only work environment, where people can have flexible working hours, remote workplaces, and unlimited vacations, and, indeed, *maybe* some collective goals and targets.

Last, but *definitely* not least, I feel it's necessary to emphasize again that the feedback wrap can *never* replace face-to-face conversations, nor can it be an alternative for coaching and personal development. You still need to address those in other ways. But I'm sure this simple little practice grows trust among coworkers; it helps people improve the performance in the system; it motivates them with good communication and feedback; and it allows you to keep documented records of results, in case you ever need them. But I trust you won't.

Example

To: Jason Little
From: Jurgen Appelo
Subject: Feedback on Lean Change Management, Introduction chapter

Hi Jason!

I'm reviewing your TXT file in Notepad++ while having lunch at home. I'm in a slightly annoyed mood because my music system was not delivered by the reseller this morning. Again! Hope it won't affect my appreciation for your writing. Fortunately, the sun is shining outside. :-)

Feedback:
- I appreciate the "rocket surgery" joke. I actually wondered if you wrote this intentionally, but I assume you did. I hope there will be more of these. (Feeling: amused)
- I appreciate the hotel story. It's very visual. (Feeling: interested)
- I like the mention of "pesky humans" and putting "change resistance" in quotes. It shows you appreciate people. (Feeling: appreciation)
- I like the mention of "nonsense." It gives you an attitude. (Feeling: appreciation)
- I like "the crème brûlée will come out nicely toasted". Metaphors are great. Keep using them. (Feeling: appreciation)
- Style issue: "to manage uncertainty better through lean startup." I miss a qualification here. Do you mean the book? The movement? The concept? (Feeling: puzzled)
- I noticed a number of style issues where in my opinion the sentences don't flow well. It confirms to me the text is not yet edited for style. (Feeling: none)
- I noticed a number of typos, including: "the my experience," "as a being a," "none of it stuff." I stopped marking them because I think a spelling and grammar checker could do this better than I can. (Feeling: slightly annoyed)

Suggestions:
- Always use a spell and grammar checker before sending texts to reviewers.
- Also, what helps me a lot is reading a text out loud. That way you find your tongue will be struggling with sentences where your brain doesn't. And this helps you catch the style issues.

I think the text is ready for editing for style, and I will be interested to see how that will change it.

Cheers,

Jurgen

How to Get Started

You can start developing your remote communication skills using the feedback wrap exercise right now.

1. I noticed there is always something I can give feedback on, whether it's a new software app I'm using, an article I'm reading, a text I'm reviewing for a friend, a website I'm testing for a colleague, a new hotel I'm staying in, or the delivery service of a product I just ordered. Just pay attention to the things you are involved in today, and pick one or two to give feedback on.

2. Ask people if your feedback wraps were valuable for them and if they see ways in which you could further improve them.

3. Pay attention to the people you sent your feedback to. Are they making changes to address the constructive feedback you gave them?

Tips and Variations

Check out the book *Nonviolent Communication*,[55] which offers a very similar approach to giving feedback.

When I intend to offer someone constructive feedback face-to-face, I practice the feedback wrap two or three times before we meet.

In any situation where you're talking face-to-face, step 1 (describing the context) can probably be omitted.

Don't forget to use the same feedback technique to point out the great things that people did.

Don't pad your constructive feedback with fake compliments before and after. Most likely, you will only confuse people.

I use the same feedback technique on my children. I am now a much calmer parent! :-)

Feedback is best served hot. If you are unable to meet with a person face-to-face (directly or remotely), it's often better to write than to wait.

Instead of ending with a *suggestion*, nonviolent communication prefers ending with a *request*: "Now that you know the facts, my feelings, and my needs, can I ask you to do the following thing?"

For me, writing a good feedback wrap can easily take half an hour. But it's time well spent because I get better results than with a praise sandwich.

I used a template of the feedback wrap for evaluation forms. People found it quite convenient to write evaluations using the five simple steps: context, observations, feelings, needs, suggestions.

Save the feedback wrap for later, even when you gave it face-to-face. The documentation might come in handy if the situation does not improve.

Try to combine the feedback wrap with another practice, such as kudo cards or a happiness door.

Find more ideas at m30.me/feedback-wraps.

metrics ecosystem and scoreboard index

Measure Performance the Right Way

The way people measure performance in organizations is often just plain wrong. Everyone should learn the 12 rules of good metrics. This would help establish a culture in which people see measurement as a way to learn and improve, and create an organization where all workers participate in the metrics ecosystem.

Measure not the work until the day's out and the labor done.

Elizabeth Barrett Browning,
English poet (1806–1861)

I had a slice of banana cake accompanied by a small latte in my favorite coffee bar just before I wrote this sentence. That's another 300 kilocalories (or "calories" for our friends in the United States) that I just added to my fitness tracker. I allowed myself this transgression because we ran out of fruit juice at home, which meant I only drank water with my breakfast and my lunch. I was far below my calorie target for the day. Well, until I saw the banana cake.

Besides my daily calorie intake, there are many more things I could measure about myself and my work. Page views per blog post, unique visitors per month, Google rankings, Net Promoter Scores of my workshops, evaluations of my conference sessions, subscribers to my mailing list, stakeholders in Happy Melly, licensed Management 3.0 facilitators, revenues and profits, liquidity and solvency, book sales per month, steps I walked per day, and much, much more. Sometimes, it seems as if I spend half my time looking at numbers and searching for better ways to measure things. Maybe I should consider a measure for the number of metrics I'm working with and kick myself for going over target!

If there's one thing I've learned about measurement in my professional career, it's that the set of metrics being used is always changing. That's not because I can't seem to make up my mind about good measurement. It's because I believe a business can be much happier and healthier when it's not always doing the same thing.

Health and Happiness

Scientists seem to agree that happiness is one of the major goals in a human being's life.[1] That sounds reasonable. And if happiness is the purpose of the mind, then I would suggest that health is the purpose of the body. Indicators of happiness and health are necessary for us to investigate problems and to make decisions about how to improve. We measure to understand how to live a better life, both mentally and physically. For organizations, it's no different. As managers, we want to know, "Do we take the blue pill, or the red one, or the colorful ones with the letter M on them?" Such decisions require insight. And insight requires measurement.

> **We measure to understand how to live a better life, both mentally and physically. For organizations, it's no different.**

"But measurement is hard, and numbers are boring, and the outcomes are depressing, and the cow is sick, and the horse is dead. . . ." Bah, these are all bad excuses! Most people have no idea how to measure well. They make their organization run a marathon with a thermometer up its rear end, and then they wonder why it's running so slowly (and awkwardly). In that regard, it's no wonder that an organization which measures very little and just runs around blindly usually goes much faster, until it runs into a tree, hopefully not with a thermometer in its mouth.

Measurement can be easy, fun, and motivating, and it's one of the most important activities for any organization. What gets measured gets managed, and what gets managed gets done. It's a cliché because it's true! I measure the number of words per book, blog posts per week, and chapters per month because my purpose is to be a full-time writer. Happy Melly collects stories of happy and healthy companies because its purpose is to help people have better jobs. Google has a transparent system that enables *all* employees to define and track their own objectives.[2] When organizations end up in the wrong place, it's often because they didn't use the correct measures to discover where they were going.[3]

Comparing organizations with human bodies is actually not such a good idea. Except when in the vicinity of an attractive person, body parts usually make no plans and decisions on their own. The human body is called an *animated system*, while an organization is a *purposeful system*.[4] Cities are better metaphors for organizations. A city is a community of people, many of whom have their own ambitions. The whole city is managed by a few people on everyone else's behalf and is usually endowed by its managers with its own purpose. It's basically the same with an organization, except that the geographical boundary that defines the city is replaced with an economic and legal boundary that defines the organization. But no matter whether we talk about humans, cities, or organizations, there's one thing we recognize among all of them. We measure things in order to make decisions toward a purpose.

- **Rule 1: Measure for a purpose**

Proxies and the Unknown

A single number indicating health does not exist. Neither does one single value for happiness, or for most other qualities, for that matter. It is often said, "Not everything that counts can be counted." Usually, the best we can do is work with values that are only surrogates or proxies for the real thing. As a result, our measurements are imperfect. We don't measure love by tracking the number of phone calls.[5] And yet, a complete lack of phone calls from a loved one should indicate at least *something*. It is still useful information, as long as we don't jump to conclusions by confusing the lack of phone calls with a lack of love. (I just got my call two minutes ago, no kidding! My happiness increased, a little bit.)

Jumping to conclusions with incomplete information, and not understanding that there's a gap between what is *measurable* and what is *desirable*, is one of the biggest problems with humans. For example, for many decades, governments have used gross national product (GNP) as an indicator of the health of their economies, but this well-known metric ignores the cost of natural resources. It only indicates sales. The metric does not attribute any value to plants, animals, or human lives! When a natural disaster wipes out a number of living things or even an entire species, the GNP of a country usually goes *up* because of the increased labor and sales of materials. But we'd be stupid to believe that the health of the economy increased as a result of the disaster.

The real health of an economy, like the happiness of a person, is not measurable. But that doesn't mean measurement is a lost cause. On the contrary, there are plenty of things we can measure![6] We can at least reduce our ignorance by using multiple imperfect metrics. For example, there are many competing indices that all claim to measure the

> Just as a human being needs a diversity of measures to assess its health and performance, an organization needs a diversity of measures to assess its health and performance.
>
> Peter F. Drucker and Joseph A. Maciariello, *Management*[7]

happiness of people across countries.[8] All of these measures have their own intricate methods, variables, and formulas. They're all imperfect, but together they give the best possible picture we can paint of happiness in the world at large. In organizations it should not be any different. It is one reason why Google lets employees measure their progress toward their objectives by using multiple *key results*.[9]

Your job is to find the best possible (combination of) proxies that get as close as possible to the thing you *really* want to know. Your measurements should never lead you to ignore the unknown or give anyone else a false feeling of confidence. Unknowingly relying on an imperfect metric could be even more dangerous than knowingly proceeding without one!

The most important information we need is either unknown or unknowable,[10] but this is no excuse for not measuring at all.[11] We have a responsibility to refrain from jumping to conclusions and to keep pushing back the boundary of the unknown.

- **Rule 2: Shrink the unknown**

Big Data, Small Progress

We live in an age where having too little information is less often a problem than having too much of it. In many businesses, people have data covering the number of employees hired, number of training programs implemented, number of help desk calls, number of machines repaired, number of inspections, number of audits, number of invoices processed, number of sales calls, number of clinical trials, number of patent applications, and so on.[12] **Big data** is all the rage these days.[13] All this data can make people feel good because it makes it clear that a lot is going on. "Look at us being busy!" And there are always at least *some* numbers going up.

But not all metrics are created equal. For any football (or soccer) team, the statistics reporting percentage ball possession, corner kicks, total fouls, key passes, attempted passes, or top salaries are all very nice and interesting, but the only thing that really counts is whether the team wins![14] For any organization without a clear goal, it is tempting just to report the numbers that say, "We're going fast!" Such numbers have been called **vanity metrics** because they make businesses look good.[15]

I know what I'm talking about! I've prided myself on the large number of page views on some of my blog posts, which turned out to be completely irrelevant to my goal of writing books. I've been smug and felt pleased because of the high ratings for my workshops, but my real goal was to enable *other* trainers to facilitate my courses successfully. To become happy and healthy as an organization, a bit more is needed than just looking busy and looking good. What you need is a sense of *progress* toward your purpose or goal. What you want is for your measurements to enable you to learn and improve.

- **Rule 3: Seek to improve**

Everything Depends on Everything

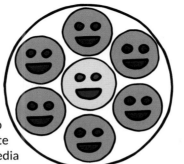

It's relatively easy to measure the performance of a writer. All mistakes in this book are mine. But how do you measure the performance of those who contribute to a TV program? Or a software product? Or a social media marketing campaign? For a number of decades, the interdependence of work processes has been growing. With more and more people working together in teams, groups, and networks, and with an increased diversity of contributors, it gets harder and harder to measure who contributed how much to which part of the results. Performance measurement of the parts in a network becomes impossible when everything depends on everything else. Is a hospital's rating a measure of its management, or the doctors and nurses, the patients, or the average standard of living in its region? Do school exams measure the performance of the pupils, the school, the exam board, or all three?[16]

The only way to deal with this complexity is to acknowledge that the performance of a part must be evaluated across its dependencies. This means the efforts and results of one person should not only be evaluated against that person's own purpose, but also against the needs of all of the stakeholders. Yes, workshop trainers should measure their progress according to their ambitions. But they should also understand the needs of their students, peers, the training organization, courseware creator, venue owner, government, trainer's guild, and even spouses. Those are the ones enabling the trainer to pursue those ambitions.

> ### There's no shortcut to an optimized whole, and no complex system will ever really be optimal.

Some authors claim the only purpose that really counts is to delight the customer, and performance optimization across all stakeholders is mathematically impossible.[19] I agree with that last part. It is one of the messages of complexity science! There is no way to calculate the global optimum for a system in a complex environment. In fact, we'll never know where that optimum is! All complex adaptive systems seek their best performance possible by continuously repeating an **adaptive walk** across an invisible fitness landscape.[19] It is never a straight path. There's no shortcut to an optimized whole, and no complex system will ever really be optimal. That's how the brain works. That's how nature works. That's how the economy works. That's how the Internet works.

It's naïve to optimize conditions for one client (the customer, the shareholder, the employee, or any other) *assuming* what's good for one will automatically be good for all the others. Arguing that optimizing for all clients is "too hard" should not be an excuse. Try raising a family!

- ### Rule 4: Delight all stakeholders

> A system's performance is the product of the interactions of its parts.
>
> Russell L. Ackoff, *Re-Creating the Corporation*[17]

Subjectivity and Reflexivity

I once organized a workshop for a company where I discussed a happiness index with its employees. They told me their management measured happiness in the organization every three months through the use of elaborate forms that had to be filled out electronically by everyone. After a lot of work, management was able to report that happiness in the company had dropped from 3.8 to 3.5. I asked the employees, "How do you feel about this measurement?" Someone from the back of the room said, "I hate it!" and some of the others started nodding their heads. Apparently, the way management measured happiness in that organization was *destroying* people's happiness. It could be that this metric made only the managers very happy!

An alluring aspect of measurements is that people associate them with research and science. Observation is a crucial part of the scientific method, and it's no coincidence that business improvement methods, such as the lean startup, kanban, scrum, and others, rely heavily on measuring work. Measurement is considered by many to be an inherently neutral activity that involves analysis, objectivity, and understanding.[20] Unfortunately, in a social context, these lofty ideals are hardly ever achieved.

Measuring people's productivity causes them to pay more attention to their work, and their productivity goes up. This phenomenon is often referred to as the **Hawthorne Effect.** The introduction of a happiness index can make a team feel good (or bad) about management, which influences the team's happiness. The attempt to estimate the size of a project causes people to add more requirements, which results in the estimate going up. A quality test at the end of a production line can introduce a sense of safety and subsequently more risky behaviors and lower quality among workers.

> The act of measurement is neither objective nor neutral. It is subjective and, of necessity, biased. It changes both the event and the observer. Events in the social situation acquire value by the fact that they are being singled out for the attention of being measured.
>
> Peter F. Drucker, *Management* [21]

This is referred to as **risk compensation.** A news item about an increase in book sales will further increase the sales of that book. And the announcement that a number of colleagues are stealing office supplies might not be the safest approach to protecting the remaining office supplies since, according to the **broken windows theory,** this could lead to more stealing. In all these examples, the observer influences the system and the system influences the observer. In complexity science we call this **reflexivity**. The only weapon against the **observer effect** is common sense and a skeptical mind toward any "scientific method" in a social setting.

- ## Rule 5: Distrust all numbers

Management by Objectives

There's nothing wrong with targets, as long as you don't bother anyone else with them.

While I was writing this book, I set myself a target to write two chapters per month. I did not always succeed, but I knew I would never achieve my purpose if I didn't force myself to make some progress. I also have a target for sleep (at least 7 hours), calorie intake per day (less than 2,500 kcal), and blog posts per week (at least three). We measure ourselves and give ourselves targets to help us stay on track toward the goals that we've committed to.

Peter Drucker offered his **management by objectives (MBO)** method for exactly this purpose: to help managers define the purpose of their organization, set targets *for their own work*, and measure progress toward their goal. There's nothing wrong with targets, as long as you don't bother anyone else with them. Drucker specifically said that if managers continuously fail to fulfill *their own* commitments and never reach their objectives, they should make room for others.[22] I agree. I should also find myself another career (or at least write *other* books) if I continuously fail to inspire people to improve their organizations.

Sadly, MBO has often been misunderstood and badly implemented. Managers set targets for *others* and fire *others* for doing work that is measured incorrectly in order to reach goals that are badly communicated.[23] For example, call center employees are sometimes pressured into reducing the duration of their calls instead of helping solve customers' problems.[24] Managers often do this because the wrong metric (call length) is easier to obtain than the right one (happy customers), and it is tempting to measure the things that are easiest to quantify. By adding targets into the mix, employees do what is counted (reducing call length) instead of doing what counts (helping customers). This perverse style of MBO leads to a decrease in people's motivation and the destruction of the organization, which is exactly the opposite of what Drucker intended.[25]

Targets are dangerous. There is no way to set a perfect target. As soon as you set a target for others, they will pursue the target instead of the original purpose. According to **Goodhart's law**, "When a measure becomes a target, it ceases to be a good measure." The best you can do is to keep targets vague, and keep them to yourself. Instead of single points, work with imprecise targets, ranges of values, or merely a direction.[26] Google has solved this by asking its employees to set multiple *difficult* targets for themselves with the strong suggestion that it should *not* be possible to achieve them all. The effect is that the targets become merely a range and a direction instead of one fixed point.[27]

Instead of aiming to sell exactly 100,000 copies of this book, I could aim for an imprecise six-digit sales figure. Other good enough targets for me would be to sleep better, to burn more calories than I consume, and to write more instead of less. I know it's too hard for me to achieve all of this, and I won't make the mistake of imposing any of these targets on you.

- **Rule 6: Set imprecise targets**

Judgment and Control

It's a pity managers in American management literature are so often compared to sports coaches, and creative workers are then compared to players and athletes. The metaphor simply doesn't hold when we look at the way results are measured across these domains. The very purpose of professional sports is to be *measured* (by computers, referees, arbiters, or juries) in terms of number of games won, points scored, weights lifted, meters run, or seconds completed, in order to decide who *wins* and who *loses*. They are always **zero-sum games**— only one can win! In many organizations, possibly inspired by the data analytics capabilities of the NBA, the NFL, and FIFA, managers are also seeking better ways to quantify team performance.[28] However, judging creative workers based on projects completed on time, lines of code written, tests passed successfully, or new customers acquired is the *last* thing you need in an organization. Creative workers play a **non-zero-sum** game. *Everyone* can win!

Professional organizations, such as Toyota, don't use measurements as a way for managers to judge the performance of their workers. The metrics are available for people's self-improvement rather than for managerial coercion and control.[29] At Google it's the same; all workers only set objectives and key results for themselves.[30] For organizations that truly desire to be transformational, measurement must be separated as much as possible from judgment.[31] As long as metrics are abused as a tool for control, measurements will give rise to power play, fear, and politics. To any manager who is trying to find the "best" performance metrics for measuring teams, I say, "Before you try to measure someone else's performance, please explain how you measure your own."

> **Before you try to measure someone else's performance, please explain how you measure your own.**

Judging people is the perfect recipe for *measurement dysfunction*: Bad organizational behaviors emerge as a result of metrics and targets. These behaviors then interfere with the stated purpose of the metrics.[32] This phenomenon is referred to as *Campbell's law*: "The more any quantitative social indicator is used for social decision making, the more subject it will be to corruption pressures and the more apt it will be to distort and corrupt the social processes it is intended to monitor." [33]

It is easy to see that all metrics should be owned by their users and should only be used by them to judge themselves.[34] It is crucial that creative workers see measurement as a positive thing, as something that empowers them to improve their work and their outcomes in the areas under their control. For managers it is no different. The objectives of managers are their own objectives. The performance measured by managers across their scope of control is their own performance. Everyone who is held accountable for something needs metrics to improve their own work. The scope of accountability may differ between managers and workers, but the conclusion is the same. We all measure ourselves.[35]

- **Rule 7: Own your metrics**

Rewards and Punishments

My life as a robot was brief and depressing. I was about 12 years old, enjoying a vacation with the family in a tent at a French camping site. The owners of the camp had invited all the kids to come to the central building dressed in self-made costumes. I had spent an hour or two raiding our tent and my mom's kitchen supplies, pulling a grey garbage bag over my head, cutting buttons out of wine corks—there are always plenty of those available in France—covering my ears in plastic cup holders, and sticking a part of the tent on my head. Robocop, the Terminator, and smartphone operating systems had yet to be invented. I was the ultimate android. My brother and sister happily joined in the merriment with their own (much less cool) costumes, and everything was great until the organizers picked a winner. A winner? Yes, a winner. And it wasn't me. I was very disappointed. The robot outfit quickly disappeared and I went back to solving my Rubik's Cube.

I have addressed the issue many times in my books and on my blog, and I will do it here once again: Incentives bring problems. Rewards may briefly motivate people who win them, but they also seriously demotivate those who don't. The net result is often more negative than positive. For every person you make "employee of the month" you turn dozens, hundreds, or thousands of colleagues into "losers of the month." A creative work environment should not be an Olympic game.

The danger of rewards is that they work! They motivate people to win the rewards.[36] But what is rewarded (and can be measured) is never exactly the same as the true purpose of the organization (which cannot be truly measured). Google does not use people's objectives and targets as input for promotions.[37] This makes perfect sense because, when workers feel the targets and results are of the greatest importance, they lose sight of their original objectives, and each of their

> If your parent or teacher or manager is sitting in judgment of what you do, and if that judgment will determine whether good things or bad things happen to you, this cannot help but warp your relationship with that person. You will not be working collaboratively in order to learn or grow; you will be trying to get him or her to approve of what you are doing so you can get the goodies.
>
> Alfie Kohn, *Punished by Rewards*[38]

decisions will be a little worse than what is really needed for the company.[39] We refer to this as the *law of unintended consequences,* or the *law of oops-my-bonus-just-destroyed-the-company.*

Rule 8: Don't connect metrics to rewards

Gaming the System

A **pay-for-performance** environment with metrics, targets, and incentives is the perfect place to work for people who like playing games. A system that rewards workers for achieving certain outcomes is an explicit attempt at manipulating their behaviors. We call that gaming. Management is playing a management game with the workers using rules and numbers. But the actual game is different from what the managers expect. A system designed explicitly to manipulate people's behaviors is an open invitation to everyone involved to use that same system for their own advantage. The actual game being played is the game the workers decide to play with that system. If it's OK for management to manipulate workers with a pay-for-performance system, it is also OK for workers to use that same system to manipulate management. Game theory and complexity theory can predict who will win that game.[40]

can I manipulate the system today?" An *opportunity* to play the game is not enough. People also need a *motive*.[41] I am convinced people are only motivated to act this way when they have no sense of purpose, no values, no integrity, or no sense of community.

Shared values and transparency can reduce the desire to game the system. Everyone should be aware of each other's integrity and good intentions. That means everyone has a right to know all the numbers, all the rules, all the metrics, and all purposes. At Google, employees add their objectives and targets into the employee directory, and everyone can see each other's results, including those of the top managers.[42] It makes sense because Google has a grand purpose to organize the world's information and make it accessible and useful for everyone.

I've heard of people scheduling e-mails to be sent late at night so that they get rewarded for "working late." I've heard of people repeatedly tapping the spacebar on their keyboards during lunch time, because they got paid for "number of keystrokes." I've heard of people traveling to work twice per day, once to "clock in" and once to "clock out," so that the computer registered "8 hours of work." But why should any creative worker do this? How many of us go to work in the morning, looking forward to our daily targets and incentives, wondering, "How

Instead of playing dirty games with metrics, targets, and incentives, we should aim for everyone to be internally motivated, and with transparent values and measures, people will have enough self-assessment information to improve their work while playing nicely.

• Rule 9: Promote values and transparency

Dehumanization

I admit I love numbers, but sometimes, they can be a bit . . . lifeless. Many managers get their information in the form of figures, which cannot carry any emotional weight. With numbers, someone's hard work becomes merely a statistic. Blood, sweat, and tears are transformed into spreadsheets. Personal passions and tragedies become mundane graphs and tables. Metrics allow us to morph joy and pain into squares and digits, with the help of pivot tables and chart wizards, at the mere touch of a button. The essence of work gets lost with measures. Instead of looking at what is really happening with the employees, management looks at what's happening with the figures.

For every healthy organization, it is imperative that management includes "people management," "floor management," and "visual management." Space in work areas could be set aside for daily meetings, charts, graphs, boards, and color-coded information. When the infrastructure allows it and the people are collocated, the information is placed as close as possible to the people and their work.[43] Improving the organization with metrics is good, important even, but measurements are even more helpful when you can see, quite literally, what is happening behind the data.

And numbers are often not even needed. Sketches, scribbles, and colors can convey more meaning than digits. People's faces on magnetic buttons have more visual impact than names on sticky notes. It is precisely for these reasons that nicely designed infographics on the Internet have become a very popular alternative to boring tables and graphs. And have you ever wondered why you like business books much more when they have lots of colorful illustrations in them?

- **Rule 10: Visualize and humanize**

> **Measurements are even more helpful when you can see, quite literally, what is happening behind the data.**

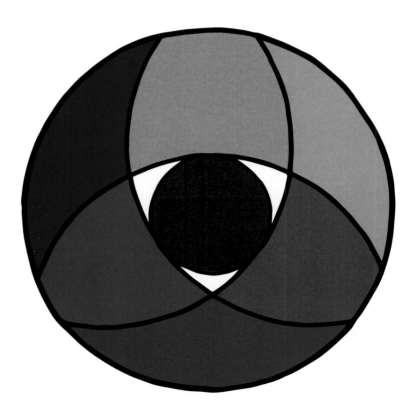

Too Little, Too Late

How often should you have a cardio test? How often do you check your watch when trying to catch a flight? How often should you have the tires of your car checked? How often do you check if your spouse is still happy? There is only one good answer to these questions: "Often enough to ensure problems don't grow too big and risky, and probably more often than you're doing now." Don't delay measurements until symptoms of problems are popping up. If you don't have regular checkups, your diagnostics and interventions might be too late.

Agile and lean communities around the world have learned that it makes sense to measure things more often. Customer needs are evaluated not only at the start of a project; they are discussed every week. Progress on a project is reported not once per month but every day. Quality tests on products are not performed once per yearly quarter; they are done continuously. And the happiness of employees is certainly not measured only once every three months; it should be monitored all the time.

Measuring well usually means measuring more often than you're doing now. It also means finding leading indicators that precede lagging indicators. A great chef doesn't need to sample the food every second (a leading indicator), but he certainly needs to do this *before* serving the outcome to the guests and waiting for their feedback (a lagging indicator)![44]

In my experience, this means setting up reminders and triggers for myself because, if I don't, I will forget to measure. Without checklists, alerts, and notifications, I will only do what's urgent, not what is important. That's why I have recurring tasks that remind me to check *total and average problem time* on the Happy Melly task board, *number of licensed workshops per month* for the Management 3.0 brand, and

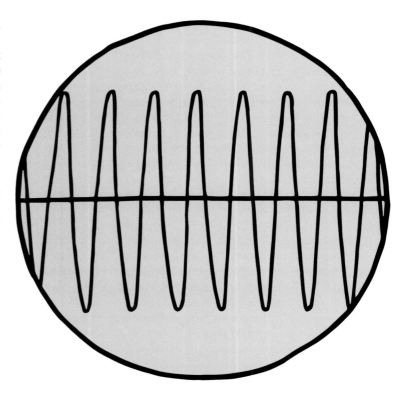

useful quotes I read in nonfiction books. I check *cash flow, profits, debtors,* and *creditors* on a monthly basis; I do the same with *book sales* and *blog statistics.* Each completed book chapter is, for me, a trigger to count the *number of words,* and each business trip with my car is a trigger to make a note of its *mileage.* Oh, and I also have a daily reminder to check if someone should get a *kudo card* or *thank-you note.*

- # Rule 11: Measure early and often

Stagnation and Complacency

So far, we have covered 11 challenges and rules for metrics, which is rather annoying because I don't like the number 11. I set myself a target of coming up with 12. Eleven is dumb, 12 is good. It's probably a leftover religious streak in me. Fortunately, I am happy to report that there's one other issue we haven't covered yet with our investigation of measurements. We haven't covered the problem of stagnation.

Many managers are on a never-ending quest to find the "best metrics" for their organizations. They don't seem to realize that measurement is part of the work we do. Measurement *is* work. Considering that the environment always changes, and our work always changes with it, why shouldn't the same thing be true for our metrics? They need to change as our business changes. It is useful to see them as tools for *diagnostics*. We measure to understand things *before* and *after* our analysis of symptoms and our attempts at improvement. We can do that a number of times, until the metric isn't helpful anymore, and then it's time to use something else. There is no holy grail of measurement.

Nobody should hesitate to try out new measures and experiment with different metrics.[45] People, teams, and organizations will adapt and get used to their own measurements. That's when stagnation and atrophy have a chance to creep in. It's good to try something else after a while. Replacing your metrics not only helps you cover other perspectives and uncover different unknowns, but it also keeps you from being lulled into a false sense of complacency. And for every complex adaptive system that prefers to stay happy and healthy, a regular change in stimuli is a good thing.

- **Rule 12: Try something else**

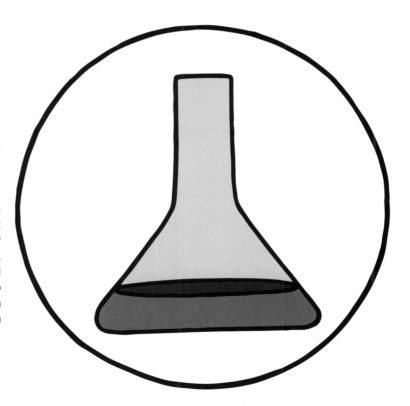

Rules for Measurement

Yay, we did it! We found ourselves 12 rules for good measurement.
Let's review them before turning what we've learned into a concrete management practice.

Rule 1: Measure for a purpose

You must always understand why you are measuring. The metric is not a goal in itself. Never forget that it's just a means to an end. It all starts with *why*.

Rule 2: Shrink the unknown

A metric is just a surrogate for what you *really* want to know. Don't jump to conclusions. Always try to reduce the size of what is still unknown.

Rule 3: Seek to improve

Don't only measure things that will make you look good. There is plenty of data around, but you must focus on what enables you to do better work.

Rule 4: Delight all stakeholders

Your work depends on others, and others depend on you. Never optimize for just one stakeholder. Instead, measure your work from multiple perspectives.

Rule 5: Distrust all numbers

Observers usually influence their own metrics, and they suffer from all kinds of biases. Have a healthy, skeptical attitude toward any reported numbers.

Rule 6: Set imprecise targets

When people have targets, they have an inclination to focus on the targets instead of the real purpose. Avoid this tendency by keeping your targets vague.

Rule 7: Own your metrics

Everyone is responsible for their own work, and metrics help us improve that work. Therefore, everyone should be responsible for their own metrics.

Rule 8: Don't connect metrics to rewards

Rewards often kill intrinsic motivation and lead to dysfunctional behaviors in organizations. Don't incentivize people to do work they should *like* doing.

Rule 9: Promote values and transparency

Human beings are smart and able to game any system. To prevent gaming, be transparent about values, intentions, and the metrics everyone is using.

Rule 10: Visualize and humanize

Numbers tend to dehumanize everything. Replace digits with colors and pictures, and keep the measurements close to where the actual work is done.

Rule 11: Measure early and often

Most people don't measure often enough. Measure sooner and faster to prevent risks and problems from growing too big for you to handle.

Rule 12: Try something else

It's rarely a good idea to do the same things over and over. The environment changes all the time. The same should apply to how and what you measure.

Integration and Scaling

Now we arrive at the gates of a huge problem that business consultants and management experts have been struggling with for decades, if not centuries. How does it all come together? How do *your* metrics connect with *mine*? How do we choose metrics as a *team*? And how do we make sure the metrics of multiple teams integrate nicely into a shiny *framework* for the whole organization?

At this point, it's crucial to remember that organizations are complex, adaptive systems, like cities and communities. The parts have their own purposes, identities, values, and ambitions, and at the same time, they contribute to the whole system, which also has its own purpose and identity, just like the system next door. And together, with a few other systems, they form an even bigger whole at the next higher level. And so on, and so on. Everything is interdependent, both horizontally and vertically.

Scaling of metrics fails because people don't understand complexity. The integration of metrics is a lost cause when people treat the organization like a machine. The whole system is not improved when we simply replace or improve all the individual parts. On the other hand, we also cannot just instruct everyone to "improve the whole" instead of the parts because there are wholes on many different levels. As a result, nobody will agree on what exactly "the whole" is. These are two different problems, and I should clarify them separately.

We find an example of the first problem (optimizing the parts) in the common use of the famous **balanced scorecard**.[46] The good thing about balanced scorecards is they require managers to analyze performance from different perspectives with multiple metrics. The bad thing is that descriptions of balanced scorecards have relied on the metaphor of a pilot looking at the dashboard of a cockpit in an airplane; in other words, a manager is operating a machine.[47]

> There is no right mix of metrics that will result in an optimization of the whole, so don't even try.

This metaphor would only be correct if the parts of the airplane all had minds of their own, and were in a position to control what information to feed back to the pilot and what to hold back. The airplane parts would also need to be able to quit their job and merge with another airplane, all in midflight. The wings would report that they were "right on schedule" while trying to make the performance of the jet engines look bad. The engines would be on nonspeaking terms with the wheels, and the tail would secretly be planning to split off and start its own skydiving business. Instead of having a dashboard full of objective measurements, the pilot would be looking at a series of green lights while flying straight into a mountain. Obviously, the machine metaphor for metrics is flawed in a social context. (Sadly, the pilot metaphor sells extremely well to traditional managers.)

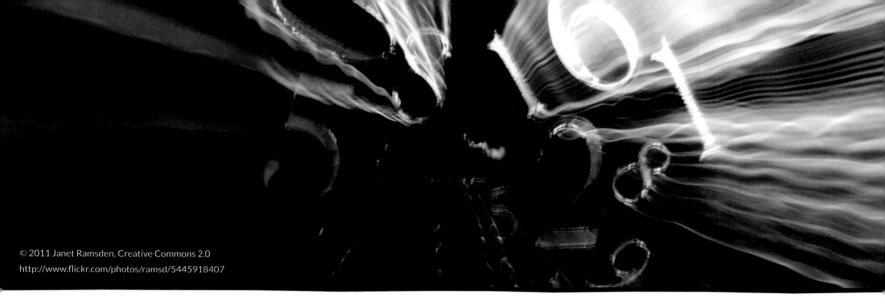

Examples of the second problem (optimizing the whole) often result from comparing organizations with individual organisms that are trying to survive and thrive as a whole. Checking a person's heart rate, blood pressure, MRI scans, and stool samples can be useful for investigating symptoms and finding problems, and all of this *could* help a person become healthy and happy. But the comparison of organizations with organisms would only be complete if the heart could decide to become a third foot, the left lung had the ambition to take over from the brain, the two eyes were not motivated to synchronize work with each other, and the sexual organs insisted on working remotely. Optimizing the whole is a great idea, and doctors can obviously contribute to the health and happiness of a whole patient, but in the fuzzy multileveled context of an organization, simply giving everyone the instruction to "optimize the whole" is naïve. There is no right mix of metrics that will result in an optimization of the whole, so don't even try.[48]

Organizations are purposeful systems. The parts have their own purposes, and the whole has its purpose. This pattern repeats itself in a fractal way, with individuals being part of (sometimes multiple) teams and communities, which are part of (often multiple) departments, which are part of (or defined across) business units, which are part of companies, which are part of cities and industries, which are part of countries.

There are purposes and metrics *everywhere*, and they are all conflicting, coordinating, colliding, and cooperating with each other in a never-ending game of competition *and* collaboration. This is not a failure of integration. It is a feature of all complex, adaptive systems: They evolve and transform as networks of interdependent parts. Think of a biosphere. Think of the Internet. Think of the gene pool. Treating a business like a machine, and optimizing the parts, is a big mistake because machines don't evolve by themselves—yet. Treating a business like one organism and attempting to optimize the whole is also a mistake, because one organism usually cannot transform itself. You must treat your organization like a community. The community may have its purpose and metrics, but so do all its members.

Dashboards, Scorecards, and Frameworks

The *last* thing we need in a networked, self-organizing, complex system is a "comprehensive hierarchical organization of measures that fit together according to a logical structure."[49] What is *logical* is science, and science suggests that things should grow and evolve bottom-up. So let's ignore any suggestions for top-down, intelligently designed measurement frameworks.

We need a philosophy of metrics that can help organizations evolve and transform. Individual metrics between parts and between levels can be both competing and collaborating. They can be in conflict and they can be in harmony. There is no way to create a comprehensive hierarchy of metrics, so we won't even go there.

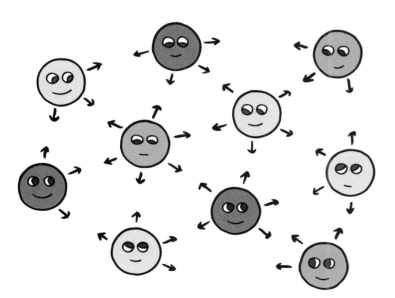

The solution is for all individuals in the organization to have their own metrics. All workers are given the responsibility to measure whatever is important to them within their own scope of control and given their own purpose (Rule 1). Empowering all workers to create their own information will motivate them to improve their metrics (Rule 2) and improve their work (Rule 3). At the same time, they should measure their work on behalf of their direct clients, covering all interdependencies and their scope of concern (Rule 4). Being responsible for their own metrics should mean people will be more mindful of how they and their clients are influencing the measurements (Rule 5). Maybe some people will even want to set some targets (Rule 6), but neither the metrics nor the targets are created for anyone else but themselves (Rule 7). This also means there are no incentives (Rule 8); and because it is all transparent, everyone can observe each other's intentions and metrics and respond to them (Rule 9). This will help to prevent dehumanization (Rule 10). Finally, when people have full control over their own metrics, it is easier for them to measure as often as they feel is needed (Rule 11) and to change the metrics whenever they feel like it (Rule 12). In other words, what you need to grow is a metrics ecosystem.

Because all metrics are different, with different frequencies of updates and different styles of visualization, it makes little sense for each person to create a scorecard or dashboard of metrics. Why should I put *calories per day* on the same dashboard as *profits per month*? As long as all information is easily available, I don't see the point of designing a framework.

The Scoreboard Index

		unhappy	happy
customer engagement	(objective)	low bound	high bound
ratio active customers	(metric)	0%	100%
profiles up-to-date	(metric)	0%	100%
scheduled events	(metric)	0.0	2.0
network growth	(objective)		
total users	(metric)	75	250
acquisition ratio	(metric)	0%	10%
practitioner growth	(objective)		
practitioner stories	(metric)	0	100
practitioner certificates	(metric)	0	10

One of the most difficult things for managers is coming up with good metrics that are an indication of the performance of the business. After all, that's what **key performance indicators** are supposed to be, right? But if no measure is perfect, what can you do?

It's actually not that difficult. The problem has been adequately solved in several other contexts. For example, what is the most commonly used key performance indicator of any market? Easy! It is the stock market index: a weighted average or total of many individual stock prices. Within the context of your business, you can do the same.

First, start with some qualitative objectives, such as "more engagement among customers" and "more activity on the website." Some people may want to focus on only a few objectives at any moment. Others will prefer to list all stakeholders and their needs so that nobody is neglected. For this practice, the difference doesn't matter.

Second, define a few quantitative metrics per objective (or stakeholder), such as "page views per week" or "blog comments per week." Each objective and stakeholder should be represented with multiple measures because it's always good to look at a

challenge from different angles. Never rely on just one metric!

Third, for each individual metric, define a lower bound and an upper bound: the number at which you would feel quite unhappy and the number at which you would feel very happy. For example, I would feel unhappy when this book sells fewer than 10,000 copies. I would be ecstatic when it sells 100,000 copies or more. Obviously, these lower and upper bounds are subjective choices. But that's fine. What you need is a range against which to evaluate your performance as a worker, a team, or a business. And that self-evaluation is always subjective.

The next thing to do is to collect measurements on a weekly basis. Of course, you may want to monitor some things daily, and maybe some data is only available once per month. But I find that a weekly moment of reflection is (for me) just the right cadence for the (re)prioritization of my work.

Once you have all measurements, you can use the lower bounds and upper bounds

	9-Nov 15-Nov	16-Nov 22-Nov	23-Nov 29-Nov	30-Nov 6-Dec	7-Dec 13-Dec	14-Dec 20-Dec
customer engagement						
ratio active customers	47%	47%	48%	47%	47%	48%
profiles up-to-date	47%	46%	46%	47%	47%	49%
scheduled events	0.84	0.81	0.82	0.73	0.75	0.82
network growth						
total users	133	135	136	139	144	146
acquisition ratio	3.8%	3.7%	3.7%	9.4%	9.0%	8.9%
practitioner growth						
practitioner stories	22	27	28	29	34	35
practitioner certificates	0	0	1	1	2	2

mentioned earlier to express every measurement as a point between 0 and 100. For example, when I find that we sold 25,000 copies of the book, my score on this metric will be 27.8 percent. (The number sits at 27.8 percent between 10,000 and 100,000.)

Last, but not least, calculate a weekly index of the metrics. Having converted all measurements to points between 0 and 100, it is easy to take the average and call it your weekly performance index. Even better, you can plot the results of individual measures with colorful lines in a graph, with the index shown as one thick black line. It is almost like a stock market, with one index (hopefully) showing a positive trend across the entire system.

Summarizing, start with a scoreboard of metrics, across all objectives or stakeholders, that are not too difficult to obtain on a regular basis; find a way to normalize and weigh them; and then calculate the average. This is what I call a **scoreboard index**. You evaluate your performance with scores depicted on a board and turned into an index. It enables weekly prioritization of work; it is neutral toward specific measures; and it's easy to comprehend the visualization.

One benefit of this indexed approach to performance measurement is that it's much easier to replace metrics without fear of discontinuity of the main measure. In all stock market indices, individual stocks are replaced quite regularly. Nobody cares about that. What people care about is the index: Does it go up or down?

One index created out of many metrics, acting as a proxy for total performance, offers the best of both worlds: Workers get *one* thing to optimize while they can stay flexible with

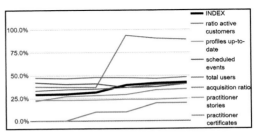

regard to the individual component metrics. (Granted, you need someone with a knack for numbers to transform different types of measurements to similar scales. But that's easily delegated to someone's Friday afternoon.)

No metric is perfect. The danger with individual key performance indicators is that people easily become fixated on optimizing just one or two of them, particularly when they are financially incentivized to do so. This endangers the performance of the business in other dimensions. But by measuring performance using a scoreboard and calculating and communicating an index, gaming the system gets a lot more difficult.

I found that the scoreboard index satisfies at least seven of the 12 principles for good metrics. (Can you tell which ones?) No practice is perfect, and I'm sure there are ways to either improve this one or to augment it with other complementary good practices. At the very least, the scoreboard index is an *indicator* that reflects *performance*, and it could be a key practice for your business, too.

	9-Nov 15-Nov	16-Nov 22-Nov	23-Nov 29-Nov	30-Nov 6-Dec	7-Dec 13-Dec	14-Dec 20-Dec
INDEX	29.4%	29.8%	31.6%	39.6%	41.6%	42.6%
customer engagement						
ratio active customers	47.4%	46.7%	47.8%	47.5%	46.5%	47.9%
profiles up-to-date	23.3%	23.0%	23.2%	23.7%	23.6%	24.7%
scheduled events	42.1%	40.4%	40.8%	36.7%	37.5%	40.8%
network growth						
total users	33.1%	34.3%	34.9%	36.6%	39.4%	40.6%
acquisition ratio	37.6%	37.0%	36.8%	93.5%	90.3%	89.0%
practitioner growth						
practitioner stories	22.0%	27.0%	28.0%	29.0%	34.0%	35.0%
practitioner certificates	0.0%	0.0%	10.0%	10.0%	20.0%	20.0%

How to Get Started

Anyone who has ever performed fitness exercises knows that *measuring yourself* is a crucial part of all workout programs. In organizations, it's no different. Start measuring the right way and then lead by example.

1. Learn about my scoreboard index or Google's objectives and key results (OKR) system for performance measurements and start experimenting with a similar system yourself.[50]

2. Evaluate the things you measure regularly and see if they help you learn to improve toward your purpose.

3. List all your stakeholders (which includes the teams and groups you belong to) and check if you measure your performance for each of their perspectives.

4. Visualize your metrics in a way that makes them interesting, and keep them close to where the work actually happens.

5. Be transparent about your metrics. Show them to others and ask the same courtesy from them. Discuss it all together, and feel free to collaborate and compete on measures.

6. Now scale this to the whole organization, where everyone maintains responsibility for their own measurements.

Tips and Variations

The scoreboard index is similar to OKRs, a practice popularized by Google. You can easily make a mashup of the two practices.

Those with a knack for numbers may prefer more realistic exponential scales instead of linear scales for their measures.

You should make the results visually interesting and abundantly available, or else the measures won't make any difference.

Every person, team, and unit can create its own scoreboard index or OKRs. All are responsible for their own measures.

I configure my spreadsheet to show all numbers in shades of red or green. This way, it's easy to see which measures are doing well and which are not.

Some people like a quarterly cadence of choosing objectives and targets (OKRs); others prefer a continuous flow of changes (scoreboard index). Pick what works for you.

Make sure that objectives and measurements are transparent and available to everyone else in the organization.

The objectives on our scoreboard are also available as tags on our workflow board so that all our tasks are connected to one or more objectives.

Feel free to change objectives and metrics whenever it makes sense. Your goal is to learn and improve, not to become a slave to your measures.

With your objectives, always think "from the outside in," meaning a stakeholder must find what you are trying to achieve valuable.

Briefly discuss the index (and the individual measures, where needed) in a weekly meeting with your team.

Find more ideas at m30.me/metrics-ecosystem and m30.me/scoreboard-index.

Instead of one lower bound (unhappy) and one higher bound (happy), you can experiment with more happiness levels.

9

merit money

Pay People According to Their Merits

Money can't buy happiness, but it can make you awfully comfortable while you're being miserable.

Clare Boothe Luce,
American author
(1903–1987)

Paying people for work, without destroying their motivation, is one of the most difficult challenges for management. Regrettably, most compensation systems are considered unfair by employees and unscientific by experts. That's why it would be wise to consider some lesser-known alternatives that are based on real merits instead of imagined performance.

Jojo runs a business. His revenues are good, but the income varies significantly. One month he wonders if he will be able to survive the slowness of summer; another month he wonders if his bank account can survive the next stampede of customers. And yet, Jojo pays himself the same somewhat conservative salary every month. It's enough to pay for his food, mortgage, and novels, but not enough for that vintage Eames lounge chair he has always wanted.

However, today he wants to allow himself something extra. The exports to Norway last month earned him twice the amount he makes in Germany. His Chinese customer *finally* paid the invoice he had already written off. And hurray! After two years of ignoring his marketing, the Americans have now discovered his services, too. Jojo thinks this all calls for a little celebration and a pat on the back. After all, *he* did all the work, didn't he? He considers a transfer of a little *extra* money to his private account, just for once. Maybe he can read his next novel in a new chair.

Why not? He earned it.

Earning Money

What if Jojo is not a one-person company but a bigger organization? Should it be any different? In many organizations, employees get a steady monthly salary that is conservative enough for the organization to survive and enough for people to pay their bills.

But what if the business climate is favorable and there's some *extra* money available? Increasing everyone's salary is often not an option. You should only do that when you know it is sustainable. Spending the money on improvements in the office is fine, but usually this benefits some workers more than others. And keeping the money in the organization's bank account is virtually the same as giving it to the business owners.

I believe that creative workers should be given what they *earn*. It is not enough to say that workers aren't primarily motivated by money (which is true) and that they prefer to pursue a greater purpose (which is also true). "Money doesn't motivate people" is not a useful answer to the question, "How do we pay employees fairly for their work?" Whatever purpose they pursue, there is probably still money involved in making things happen. Making money is good; making a difference is better; but making money while making a difference beats all.

What people earn is a result of an organization's interaction with its environment. An organization's income cannot be fully predicted; therefore, what people earn should be the sum of their (predictable) salaries and any (unpredictable) extras the organization can afford to hand out.

Earnings = salaries + extras

Making money is good;
making a difference is better;
but making money
while making a difference beats all.

Bonus Systems

> We recruit a person into what we proudly claim to be a knowledge organization boiling over with interesting tasks and challenges. We offer a fair base salary, but then add that "We really do not expect you to do your best. The tasks and the environment we can offer is probably not motivating enough. We will therefore put you on a bonus system. Only then do we expect you to go that extra mile." Unintentionally, this kind of message says quite a lot about the company and our new colleagues.
>
> Bjarte Bogsnes, *Implementing Beyond Budgeting*[1]

A practice that has infiltrated the business world like a pestilence in a shantytown is the **annual bonus system**.  (Also see Chapter 1.) The idea of this practice is that managers give workers targets and calculate annual bonuses that usually depend on people's performance ratings, job position, salary, overtime, age, shoe size, and a host of other variables. The common rationale behind the bonus system is to incentivize performance. But actually, it stinks.

Traditional bonus systems rarely have a positive effect on people's performance.

Decades of research has confirmed, again and again, that traditional bonus systems rarely have a positive effect on people's performance when they are involved in creative knowledge work.[2,3] On the contrary, the effect is just as likely to be negative.[4,5] There is so much wrong with traditional incentive programs that it is impossible to list all the problems. But I feel incentivized to give you the most important ones here.[6,7,8]

1. People get addicted to regular rewards, and if they don't get their anticipated reward, they will feel disappointed or punished. This ultimately destroys motivation and thus performance. (See Chapter 1.)

2. Individual rewards disrupt collaboration, which is crucial in creative knowledge work. Individual rewards stimulate competition and cheating, which destroys the relationships between workers, and also between workers and their managers.

3. Traditional bonus systems rely on objective measures, but reality is far too complex to capture in numbers. The metrics often ignore the soft side of good performance, including teamwork and collaboration. (See Chapter 8.)

4. Research shows that rewards distract people from complex work, disrupt creative thinking, and increase people's stress levels. This causes them to play safe and prefer easy tasks, while innovation requires the opposite: taking risks and doing complex tasks.

5. The research also shows that bonuses undermine intrinsic motivation and altruism. As soon as rewards are handed out, people start to think, "They pay me extra for this work; thus, it cannot be fun, interesting, or good."

It should also be noted that bonus systems are usually based on company profits. But creative workers cannot directly relate their work to their company's profits, because most of what influences profits—a combination of systemic effects and environmental factors—is beyond their immediate control.[9]

Flat Systems

Some people argue that organizations should get rid of their bonus systems entirely. They say most of an organization's performance is in the system, not in the people, and therefore it's best not to differentiate between employees. Everyone should get a steady salary and (maybe) an incidental bonus that is the same for everyone. Some even go as far as to suggest that there shouldn't be any incidental bonuses at all. Only Christmas bonuses seem to be appreciated, but those count as anticipated (and therefore promised) bonuses; they are not intended to redistribute unexpected extra income of the organization. In other words, these people are all in favor of a **flat system**, without any unanticipated extras.

I believe a flat compensation system doesn't address the challenge of paying employees what they really *earned*. First of all, there is the problem that roughly 80 percent of all people think they perform better than average,[10] and thus, when everyone gets paid the same as everyone else, 80 percent of workers will feel underpaid. (It won't be true, but you can't argue about feelings without real data.) Second, while bad fortune in business is usually absorbed with conservative salaries and incidental layoffs, good fortune should likewise be enjoyed through extra payouts and by hiring new people. When you don't pay any extras to workers, the workers share the burden of setbacks, while only the business owners reap the benefits of success. This is probably not motivating to most people. It has certainly never motivated me.

A flat compensation system doesn't address the challenge of paying employees what they really *earned*.

Merit Systems

In an organization that is operating in an uncertain environment, I believe workers should have a steady salary that is predictable and slightly conservative. On the other hand, they should also get extras depending on the unpredictable part of the environment. Both salaries and extras should be brutally fair and based on merits, not equality.  This has led me to suggest the following practical constraints for better compensation systems based on the five problems listed earlier:

1. **Salaries should be expected, but bonuses should not.**
Always keep bonuses a surprise. When bonuses become frequent and anticipated, they ought to be converted to regular salaries.

2. **Earnings should be based on collaboration, not competition.**
When determining how much people should earn, the main criteria should be their collaborative work toward a common goal.

3. **Peer feedback is the main performance measurement.**
Contributions to a shared purpose are best detected and evaluated by peers, not by managers. Only the whole system knows all the details.

4. **Use creative thinking to grow the compensation system.**
Expect that people can (and will) game any system, and tap into that creativity by inviting and supporting it, instead of driving it out.

5. **Use compensation to nurture their intrinsic motivation.**
Make money a reflection of people's curiosity, honor, acceptance, mastery, and all other intrinsic motivators.

Of course, implementing these suggestions for a compensation system is not a trivial thing, but I have discovered different ideas that seem to work rather well for various creative organizations. These ideas also turn out to be quite compatible with each other as well as with the science of behavioral economics.[11]

Virtual Currencies

Any manager in an organization can start a merit-based earning system—covering people's extra income, not their regular salaries—and for the remainder of this chapter I will assume you are a manager. (As an individual employee you could do this as well, but when your span of control covers just your own money, it makes little sense to re-distribute your bonus to yourself.) The distribution of money is a sensi-tive topic; therefore, you have to treat this practice with proper care.

The first thing you do is set up a *safe-to-fail environment*. You can con-sider reserving just 10 percent of the current annual bonuses for the new system. It is not necessary to ignite a company-wide revolution either by yourself or by disgruntled employees. Take it easy. Start in a way that allows you to fail and learn.

The second thing you do is create a virtual currency to represent the merits that people can accumulate over time. 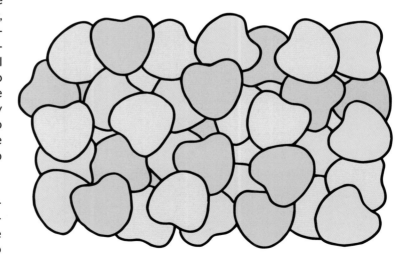 You can use *credits, points, coins, hugs, beans, candies, bananas,* or anything else to repre-sent recognition of people's contributions to the network. It is impor-tant not to use real money because the monetary value of the virtual currency is *zero* until management decides there is a good reason to convert the virtual money into real money. For virtual coins, I will use the term *hugs* in this chapter because a hug clearly has no monetary value, and we generally give hugs to others, not to ourselves. (I tend to hug myself when I'm sleeping, not when I'm working.) The exchange rate of a hug to a euro, dollar, yuan, or other official coinage is 1 to zero.

The third thing you do is decide which organizational units can collec-tively receive hugs besides getting them individually. Within a self-or-ganizing team, recognition of merits is a relatively easy thing. People all know each other personally, and they have a good sense about who contributed what to the team's collaborative work. I have a good idea which of my team members helped me get an article published before a deadline. I know who paid for coffee last time. (It certainly wasn't me.) And I know who stole my socks. (Yes, I know where they are!!) On the other hand, I get good service from my accountant, but I don't know if it's really him or the team behind him doing all the work. More generally, when organizational units work with representatives, oth-ers in the organization usually cannot distinguish between the work of the representative and the work of the entire unit. As a manager, you should therefore decide whether entire units could also be the beneficiaries of hugs.

Peer Recognition

Now we get to the core of the merit system. The next step is for you to define the total amount of hugs available, and how often they will be passed out. My suggestion would be to do this once per month, but I'm sure other frequencies (weekly or quarterly) are possible, too.

And then the fun starts.

The single most crucial aspect of a merit system is that every individual can only recognize the contributions of other people, and that the opinions of all individuals have equal weight. Therefore, everyone in the organization gets an equal share of the hugs, but **all employees must give away *their* hugs to others.**[12]

> Nobody can claim to have the best definition of what performance is and what collaboration means. We should, therefore, use everyone's opinion equally.

You have just created a market for merits, and like any other market, you can expect to witness unpredictable and amazing creativity. One worker may decide to share her hugs equally among all team members. Another worker can use a personal metric, such as compliments received or productivity observed, for the distribution of hugs to peers. Another worker might receive half a colleague's total hugs after helping out when that colleague was feeling depressed and on the verge of quitting. Workers are also allowed to give away hugs to people or units outside their own team. After all, good working relationships don't limit themselves to formal organizational boundaries.

The central idea of the merit system is that nobody can claim to have the best definition of what performance is and what collaboration means. We should, therefore, use *everyone's* opinion equally. This can be viewed as the **wisdom of the crowd.**[13] Instead of *claiming* rewards, which is usually the case in salary negotiations and annual bonus systems, all merits have to be *earned*. After all, social science says human beings are keen observers of other people's behaviors, but very poor at evaluating their own.[14] Therefore, the *claimed hugs* (everyone claiming an equal share) only become meaningful by converting them to *earned hugs* (through peer feedback and recognition by others).

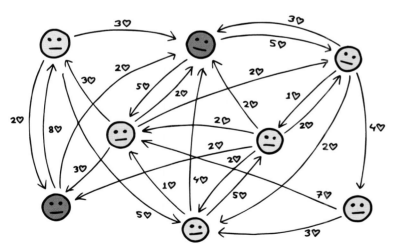

What happens to people who get less than expected?

It is said that 80 percent of all people believe they perform better than average. However, depending on the distribution of hugs, roughly 50 percent of the workers will get more hugs than the average. This means that an estimated 30 percent of the workers could feel disappointed that their work is not recognized by their colleagues, or at least not as much as they had expected. These people have a choice. They can either learn how to do better, accept the fact that not everyone can win gold in the Olympics, or else find another place where they believe their contributions will be better appreciated.

The criteria for passing out hugs should be related to a shared purpose as well as values and principles that inspire people. For example, the question that people could ask themselves is:

What did others do that helped us to engage people, improve work, and delight clients? Did someone get us a step closer to achieving our purpose?

Given that a healthy organization will have a mixture of individual goals, team goals, and organizational goals, it will be up to the individuals to find a healthy balance between the needs of employees and units. No written policy or procedure can calibrate intrinsic desires in an organizational network. That task is better left to the most complex device in the known universe: the human brain. All available brains, in fact.

Cashing Earnings

After a number of iterations and people's earned hugs have accumulated over time, there will (hopefully) come a time for hugs to be cashed in, using a certain exchange rate.  There are different ways for doing this.

Every month, management could set aside a bonus, with a total value depending on business profits. They could then ask the newest employee (or someone else who has the least to gain from a possible payout) to roll two dice. Management will only allow hugs to be cashed when the number rolled is four (or some other favorite number). If any other number comes up, the bonus will simply roll over to the next month. This means the bonus money becomes available only once per year on average, accumulating each month, but paid out at random intervals. This would make people feel less stressed about anticipated bonuses. Less stress is important for creative thinking.

The financial value of hugs can be published like shares on a stock market. It will depend on the bonus money available and the number of outstanding hugs. When the hugs become cashable, people could have a choice. Either they convert their hugs to real money now, or they save their hugs for the next round, in the hope that the value will go up. (An additional idea is to have an expiration date on earned hugs, similar to frequent flyer miles with airlines. Another idea is to limit the total number of hugs people can save, similar to upper limits for unused vacation days.)

Several alternative programs can be conceived, depending on the culture of the organization, the kind of business it is in, and the bonus money available. But whatever specific implementation an organization comes up with, merit systems in general are much more likely to help people focus on shared purpose and collaboration than traditional programs with numerical targets and annual bonuses.

Six Rules for Rewards

The merit-based system as described here satisfies the five constraints I listed earlier. The system keeps any big rewards unexpected; it emphasizes collaboration instead of competition; it relies on peer feedback; it invites rather than destroys creative thinking; and it aligns rewards with various intrinsic motivators such as honor, acceptance, mastery, freedom, relatedness, and goal (see Chapter 10).

Depending on how you implement a merit system, you could also satisfy the six rules for rewards that were outlined in Chapter 1:

1. **Don't promise rewards in advance.** People know what salary they get every month, but (in the ideal version of this practice) they don't know if and when there will be something extra. Bonuses should depend on the environment, not on a calendar.

2. **Keep anticipated rewards small.** Monthly salaries are anticipated, of course. However, since workers receive their salaries whether they achieve good results or not, this anticipation will not interfere with their stress levels and performance.

3. **Reward continuously, not once.** The merit system has a regular cadence because workers reward each other frequently. Feedback is not put off until the end of the year; therefore, the chance of forgetting things is small.

4. **Reward publicly, not privately.** In the ideal version of this practice, the hugs are earned publicly. Transparency makes sure that everyone knows what is going on and what is appreciated by others, so they can adapt accordingly.

5. **Reward behavior, not outcome.** People will give hugs for the things they did for each other and for the organization. This rewards behaviors. The final outcome will depend on the environment, and people cannot be made responsible for that.

6. **Reward peers, not subordinates.** Management switches focus from managing the earnings of people to managing the constraints of the system. The recognition that people get is from peers, not from management.

Like any useful recipe, the rules for rewards should be considered as guidelines, not laws set in stone. Nevertheless, it is encouraging to see that our merit system is in line with these guidelines, particularly since they were derived from motivational literature.

But...
thinking about money is distracting!

Correct, but *someone* has to do it. Not paying workers any money is not an option. They are creative workers, not unpaid volunteers. Paying everyone the same amount all the time is also not an option for various economic reasons. A moderate level of income fluctuation is necessary to keep the system anti-fragile. So, who will decide *how* the money flow in the system will fluctuate?

Simply thinking about money has an influence on people's behaviors.[15] Therefore, it is tempting to leave this dreaded responsibility to one manager so that everyone else can "just focus on the work." Of course, what usually happens is that, besides focusing on their work, people complain about their compensation and how badly the manager is doing his or her job. After all, everyone feels entitled to more!

Shifting responsibility for the money flow to the workers through the use of a peer recognition system is similar to introducing capitalist democracy. We can discuss all the risks and dangers of this system and how to improve it, but there's one thing we can agree on: It will probably work better than getting paid as if through a dictatorship.

Experiment and Customize

The system described in this chapter is a generic practice for earnings based on merits. It can (and should) be customized in many different ways. For example, instead of hugs or beans, the creatively challenged organizations may prefer a term such as credits or points. And instead of a fully open process, the transparently challenged organizations may want to keep part of the process anonymous and reveal only a small part of the results to the participants (such as the "top 10 recognized people in the organization"). The system can also be introduced gradually. At first, you could do this for a small part of the traditional bonus. Later, with more experience and more buy-in from employees, you can increase the percentage and the impact of the system.

Money and emotions are tricky things; therefore, any system that involves both will have to be set up in a way that is safe-to-fail. With small increments (such as weekly or monthly experiments instead of quarterly or annual outcomes), the feedback cycle is shorter and people will learn faster how to improve the system. The use of a valueless virtual currency instead of real money will allow people to experiment more comfortably; it will be easier for them to decide that a chosen path is not working and change direction or start from scratch. We must also realize that creative people *will* game the system. The trick is to exploit this creativity to make the system more resilient. The short iterations and valueless currency should help people to adapt to each other's strategies and allow management to tweak the constraints, all in favor of increasing collaboration and working towards a common purpose.

When central authority is replaced with distributed decision making, things can and will go wrong. One only needs to consider the countries where a dictatorship has been replaced with a democracy.

This is rarely a straightforward process. Likewise, switching from a traditional bonus system to a merit-based bonus system will probably involve the need to address a number of problems. I received some reports about employees making deals with each other, about cheating leading to more cheating, and about rewards being given for unhealthy behaviors. If you ask me how to *prevent* these problems, I will tell you that you can't. I can only suggest that you set up a system that is safe-to-fail, and that you learn what other organizations do to make things better. This is similar to the way democracies learn from each other how to have better elections and better institutions. After all, the only alternative is either dictatorship or anarchy.

> **Creative people *will* game the system. The trick is to exploit this creativity to make the system more resilient.**

Finally, it is hoped that the merits market described here will grow into a more collaborative culture within the organization. But one thing is certain: when recognition of merits (and allocation of money) is transferred from management to workers, it absolves management of performance reviews and bonus calculations. This means that managers can start leading and servicing people instead of managing everyone's money.[16]

What if . . . ?

In various discussions I have had about the merit system, people are always positively interested, while at the same time being genuinely concerned about several variants of the "what if" question:

- "What if two people decide to give each other all their hugs?"
- "What if people demand hugs in return for good behavior?"
- "What if extroverts get more hugs than introverts?"
- "What if people are just pretending to be interested in collaboration?"
- "What if intrinsic motivation is destroyed when someone gets no hugs?"

I don't have ready-made answers to all these questions. The way I see it, any merit system has flaws that will surely come to the surface; nevertheless, it will always be better than the dysfunctional financial reward systems most organizations have institutionalized now. Why worry too much if a new system might demotivate 10 percent of the people, when the current system demotivates 90 percent of them?

With simple rules, fair governance, and sufficient transparency, people will be able to adapt to each other's behaviors (both the good ones and the bad ones). Ultimately, the only remedy to self-organized misconduct and emergent unfairness will be the positive creativity of peers, not the addition of extra rules and procedures. The best way to deal with problems is to turn the financial stuff into a real, complex, adaptive system.

A crazy idea that works

"I am the CEO at Fonte Medicina Diagnóstica, a molecular pathology center that deals with cancer tests. One of the problems I ran into as a new CEO was our salary system. In my opinion, the people that made the most effort should be entitled to some extra money, but I had no idea how to measure employee performance. One of the company's key values is collaboration, and I wanted this to play an important role in our compensation system.

For a while we had a bonus system based on 360-degree evaluations, but that process took way too long. We then decided to implement a merit money system. Every month everyone at the company receives the same bonus with a fictional currency. There's just one rule: You can't keep the money for yourself. You can give it all to the same person, or you can distribute it in small amounts. Can't think of someone? Just give it away next month. As a manager, I can only see part of how people are performing. But with this system, employees decide for themselves whether their peers do their jobs well. We also have a trade market with a conversion rate. People can choose to exchange their fictional currency or keep their money and wait for a better rate.

I now have far fewer things to deal with. All kinds of arguments and other things that I needed to handle have now appeared to solve themselves. People just know good behavior will pay off. Dysfunctional behavior will be dealt with: You won't get any extra money. The best part is, I explained it to the people in 30 minutes and it worked right from the start!"[17]

Cláudio Pires, *Brazil*

Cashing stars

"I've seen a practice similar to merit money at a client's business in Romania. They have two visual boards: On one board there are the pictures of all company members (roughly 20). On the other board they have a catalog that lists various physical items, starting with a pack of beer and going all the way up to a PlayStation. Other artifacts include books, monitors, or fancy office chairs. Each physical item has a price in stars: 1 star for the pack of beer up to 100 stars for the PlayStation.

During each project, whenever a team member feels a colleague helped him, he is free to award a star to that colleague. There's no limit imposed by management on the number of stars you can award. At any time, the team members can 'cash in' their stars by asking management to purchase the desired physical item for which they have enough stars. The CEO told me that, initially, he was afraid people might exploit this system unfairly, but in fact nothing like that happened. Nobody abused the system and everybody acted like a trustworthy adult."

Flavius Ştef, *Romania*

How to Get Started

Let's see if your organization is ready to introduce its own merit system.

1. With this practice, it is very important that you first create a safe-to-fail environment. For example, announce the new program by saying you first want to gain experience through a trial period of a couple of iterations, and that you will surely do a reset of the whole system after that period.

2. Think of the logistics, such as the name of the virtual currency and how it will be awarded. Will it be introduced physically or electronically? Can people reward entire teams and business units? How much of the system will be transparent?

3. Get commitment from key leaders in the organization. Allow people to get involved voluntarily so that they can first watch the effects on other people and on the business as a whole.

4. Evaluate the trial period with all stakeholders before doing a real introduction.

Tips and Variations

The money part of merit money is actually optional. If you leave it out, you simply have a great, continuous 360-degree feedback tool.

Some people have suggested using an opt-in approach for merit money: Only those who want to join will do so.

Some suggest reducing available points for people who work only part-time, but we believe everyone should have equal votes.

Initially, we gave away all our points once per month. But we switched to a monthly budget of points that we can give away in small amounts any day of the month.

Similar to an options system, you can have people choose a voluntary cut in their monthly salaries in exchange for a (potentially higher) merit money payout.

Instead of money, you could get people to exchange the points they earned for perks and prizes.

We throw one die each month and we pay the cumulative bonus when 6 comes up. Our team finds it great fun.

We reset the system each month so that people lose their points if they don't use them. It's also possible to carry people's points over to the next month.

Out of our entire team, only one person doesn't want to use the tool. That's OK, but it also means she hardly receives any points.

We keep things simple: We only give points to individual people, not teams or units, and only to people working for the company.

We tag all points that we give to each other with one or more company values, such as #transparency, #commitment, or #kindness.

Try to be as transparent as possible. But no matter the transparency level, make sure that management gets the same information as the employees!

Find specific tools and more ideas at m30.me/merit-money.

10

moving motivators

Discover Real Engagement of Workers

> It's a great mistake, I think, to put children off with falsehoods and non-sense, when their growing powers of observation and discrimination excite in them a desire to know about things.
>
> Anne Sullivan, American teacher (1866–1936)

The goal of each organization is to motivate people to be productive together. Most companies achieve this by paying their workers. But extrinsically motivated people aren't necessarily intrinsically engaged. Use the moving motivators exercise to find out what drives your workers and how to make engagement a built-in property of the organization.

It is Sunday when I write this. My spouse has been away for the weekend, which means I've been enjoying me-time for two days. I could have binge-watched a TV series, organized my music collection, or explored the forest on my mountain bike. But I didn't. Instead, I took the opportunity to finish a PowerPoint slide deck. It involved researching terminology, designing slides, positioning images, polishing texts, and fine-tuning colors. Why? Because I enjoy *making* things. The moment I clicked *Save as* PDF late yesterday afternoon and reviewed the final version of my slides may have been my happiest moment of that day. I *created* something! That, and I emptied a bowl of chocolate-covered almonds.

I have always had a great appetite for understanding things about the universe. When I was 16, I was probably the only kid in my class who was trying to grasp Einstein's theory of relativity. And when my classmates were outlining body parts on the walls of our city's shopping malls, I was drawing molecules and four-dimensional space-time continuums at home in my room upstairs. Science has often been more important to me than fun. No, scratch that. Science *is* fun. I still remember how much I was in awe when reading Richard Dawkins' *The Selfish Gene* and talking to my spouse about evolutionary strategies and the idea that we're little more than lumbering robots, spreading our genes around the world. Amazingly, our relationship held.

Nothing can come out of a creative process when there's nothing going in. That's why I didn't spend my time yesterday on what other people might call leisure activities. Learning how the universe works and turning that knowledge into creative expressions, with models, texts, and illustrations, is much more enjoyable. In fact, *leisure* is usually defined as "time when you can do whatever you want to do" and "enjoyable activities that you do when you are not working." I find this a sad definition. It seems to imply that people, when they are working, cannot do what they want and will not enjoy the activities, either. How different would the world be if everyone found their jobs motivating and engaging.

Employee Engagement

It probably comes as no surprise to my readers that many people around the world usually don't associate the word *enjoyment* with the word *work*. Time and time again, research programs and survey reports have shown that employees don't feel engaged with their jobs. (The same applies to their managers, by the way.) Most companies admit that they have an employee engagement problem; most companies feel they don't have engaging work or an engaging brand; and most companies have no idea how to change this.[1] Reports confirm that business leaders and human resource managers consider tackling the lack of employee engagement one of their top priorities.[2] Judging by the sheer amount of data available on this topic, it seems that those who publish such employee engagement documents are quite motivated to churn out report after report.

In a way, the lack of engagement among employees is strange. The innate goal of an organization is to get people to produce things collaboratively. Together they make products and services that they otherwise wouldn't create by themselves. This means that *motivating people to be productive together* is a built-in property of every organization. Without motivation, nothing would be produced.

Business leaders and human resource managers understand this. There is no production without motivation. But a *motivated* worker is not necessarily an *engaged* worker.

> A *motivated* worker
> is not necessarily
> an *engaged* worker.

Payment is the traditional way organizations motivate their employees. And it works (quite well, actually). But managers get even higher productivity when, besides the money, people also feel motivated by something that is more meaningful to them. We call that *engagement*. And in most organizations, it's lacking. Leaders and managers should try to turn mere motivation into true engagement, even when the mundane reason is higher productivity. The big question then is, "How do we make engagement (or *meaningful* motivation) a built-in property of the organization?"

> **Firms exist to coordinate and motivate people's economic activity.**
>
> John Roberts, *The Modern Firm*[3]

Can We Really Motivate People?

I lied. Yesterday, I briefly watched a couple of YouTube videos of Ruby Wax, Jennifer Saunders, and Dawn French, some of my favorite comedians. They make me laugh. They make many people laugh. Actually, they get paid to make people laugh. Maybe they can make people cry too, but I'm sure they're not paid to do that. Politicians are.

Sometimes, I hear consultants or coaches say, "You cannot really motivate people, they can only motivate themselves." This often annoys me. What nonsense! Do these coaches and consultants also believe that we cannot really make people laugh? That people can only decide for themselves to start laughing?

> It is a mistake to talk about motivating other people. All we can do is set up certain conditions that will maximize the probability of their developing an interest in what they are doing and remove the conditions that function as constraints.
>
> Alfie Kohn, *Punished by Rewards*[4]

Yes, yes, I know. Technically, it is incorrect to say that "someone is making people laugh." All that comedians can do is set up the right conditions that maximize the probability of audience members becoming amused, to such an extent that they start making involuntary noises with their vocal cords, and remove any conditions that might prevent this from happening. In laymen's terms: They make people laugh. Some are so good at maximizing those probabilities that they get paid for it. Success, however, is not guaranteed. Ask Tony Blair.

With motivation, it is the same. Technically, we cannot make people feel motivated. But we can certainly set up the right conditions that maximize the probability that it will happen, even though success is never certain. Managers should manage the system, not the people. This means that managers are responsible for making motivation a built-in property of the organization. Some managers are good at that. Many are not. But they can learn!

Intrinsic and Extrinsic

Social scientists have come up with various ideas to divide motivation into different categories and dimensions. I have mentioned this before, but let's look at it a bit more deeply this time.

- **Intrinsic motivation** is the desire to do something because of an interest in the topic or enjoyment in the task itself. It exists within the individual and can be validated by studying both animal and human behaviors. We can recognize that organisms spontaneously engage in playful and curious behaviors without others asking or telling them to do so. It is why we say that intrinsic motivation is a natural tendency of an organism.

- **Extrinsic motivation** is the need to do something to achieve an outcome that is desired by something or someone outside of the individual and obtained by offering rewards (for showing the desired behavior) or dealing out punishments (for lack of the desired behavior). Quite often, extrinsic motivation is used to incentivize behavior of people (or animals) that one wouldn't normally get from their intrinsic motivation. Money, grades, and trophies are examples of extrinsic rewards.

You can easily check whether the people in your organization are intrinsically or extrinsically motivated by canceling payment of their salaries. Those who stop working—because they require and expect the money—are extrinsically motivated. Those who keep working—because they enjoy the work—are intrinsically motivated. (I suggest you make this a thought experiment only!)

The distinction between intrinsic and extrinsic motivation is useful but rather simplistic. There are few systems in the world more complex than the human brain. It would be a bit naïve to believe that the complexity of human psychology and sociology can be reduced to just two simple categories of motivation.

> The distinction between intrinsic and extrinsic motivation is useful but rather simplistic.

Complexity thinkers might agree with me that reality works the other way around: There is intrinsic motivation among humans to make phenomena much simpler than they really are. We have *created* the mutually exclusive categories of intrinsic and extrinsic desires because our brains have a strong need for simplification, abstraction, and reduction. For example, we speak of men versus women as two genders and easily forget about the alternatives, such as genderqueer (in between), bigender (two genders), trigender (three genders), agender (gender neutral), third gender (something else), and pangender (a bit of everything). Likewise, we speak of day versus night and easily ignore that dusk and dawn are both, neither, or somewhere halfway. And we speak of life versus death and then find ourselves struggling how to classify what is lifeless, undead, resurrected, self-organizing, autopoietic, or just plain weird.

It won't surprise you that, according to some researchers, the diverse range of human motivations cannot be forced into just two categories.[5] For example, many people would say that I am intrinsically motivated to research literature and creatively transform the things I learned into presentations and books because these activities bring me joy. However, I also experience enjoyment when I receive compliments, awards, and money for the products that I offer to the market. Granted, I often started these projects without anyone's suggestions or incentives, which indeed hints at intrinsic motivation. But I certainly *imagined* the incentives, and I have also stopped many creative experiments due to a lack of interest and encouragement from the environment, which would suggest extrinsic motivation. So, am I intrinsically or extrinsically motivated? And do we really need to make a binary distinction?

Complexity thinking requires us to acknowledge that there are many shades of gray between the two extremes, and different people are motivated in different ways. Some people need little or even no encouragement to do things. Others need a bit more, even when they truly enjoy the activities. And quite often, it is hard to decide what is intrinsic and what is extrinsic. Does someone enjoy cooking because of an intrinsic need for food? Or because of the encouragement (and possibly a late-night reward) from a loved one? Do people go to the gym because their bodies make them feel good? Or because the response of other people makes them feel good? Am I working on this chapter because I want to write it? Or because you want to read it? How about pan-motivation? A bit of everything?

CHAMPFROGS

I offer my own CHAMPFROGS model to anyone who wants to dive a bit deeper into the topic of worker motivation. This model draws from several other models.[6,7,8] However, CHAMPFROGS limits itself to motivational factors in a business context. In this model, I choose to ignore intrinsic motivators such as food, love, and vengeance. Obviously, we should not ignore such needs permanently, but—with some exceptions—I find the following 10 motivators more relevant in my discussions with managers and workers around the world:

I have no idea what the word CHAMPFROGS means. It's nothing more than a nice mnemonic that enables me to remember the 10 intrinsic motivators for team members.

Before we have a look at each of the 10 motivators, remember that we are looking for meaningful motivation and true worker engagement—not only because an engaged worker is more productive than someone who is merely motivated by payment, but also because meaningful motivation is the right thing to strive for. You'll see.

Curiosity People have a variety of things to investigate and to think about.

Honor People feel proud that their values are reflected in how they work.

Acceptance Colleagues approve of what they do and who they are.

Mastery Their work challenges their competence, but it is within their abilities.

Power There's enough room for them to influence what happens in the world.

Freedom People are independent of others with their work and responsibilities.

Relatedness People have fulfilling social contacts with others in their work.

Order There are enough rules and policies for a stable environment.

Goal Their purpose in life or need for direction is reflected in the work.

Status Their position is good and is recognized by the people they work with.

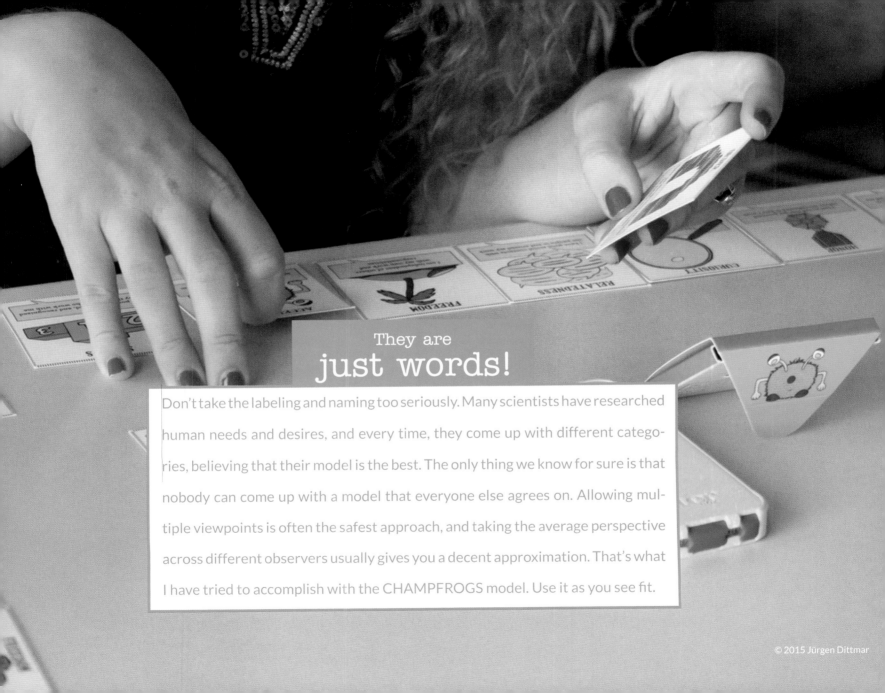

They are
just words!

Don't take the labeling and naming too seriously. Many scientists have researched human needs and desires, and every time, they come up with different categories, believing that their model is the best. The only thing we know for sure is that nobody can come up with a model that everyone else agrees on. Allowing multiple viewpoints is often the safest approach, and taking the average perspective across different observers usually gives you a decent approximation. That's what I have tried to accomplish with the CHAMPFROGS model. Use it as you see fit.

Curiosity

Curiosity is the first of 10 meaningful motivators that can help you take your workers from merely (extrinsically) motivated to (intrinsically) engaged by the work, the people, and the organization. Curiosity is about the joy of learning what is true or false and understanding how things work. Laboratories, research centers, and universities are the kinds of organizations that thrive on people's innate drive for exploration. For such organizations, curiosity is the reason they exist.

Human beings are inquisitive creatures. For example, research has shown it is more effective to motivate children with stories about strange animals than with simple colorful stickers.[9] Invention and exploration are wired into our brains. As children, we didn't know that we were being creative. We just knew it was exciting for us to try new things.[10] And this didn't stop when we grew up. Curious workers will show up at work to learn stuff, no matter whether they are rewarded for it or not. The knowledge they acquire is their reward.

As a manager, you can use this motivator in your organization by ensuring that discovery and invention are an essential part of everyone's job. Get people to try new tools, experiment with different processes, and invent their own solutions to their team's problems. Granted, this could be harder to achieve for an accountancy firm than for a laboratory group, and some people are by nature more curious than others. Nevertheless, I believe that any organization can become a research center for its own products and services.

Honor

Religious institutions and the military are typical examples of organizations known for their sense of *honor*. Honor is about loyalty to a group of people and integrity of one's behaviors according to a moral code or a system of values.

While writing this chapter, I was reading a fantasy novel in which a soldier was struggling with an ethical decision. His personal need for honesty and commitment required him to betray his friend to an enemy. And sure enough, that's what he did. Remaining true to his values weighed even heavier on him than a longtime friendship.

We all have stories of conflicting priorities in our personal lives, where we have to balance values such as honesty and friendship, rationality and kindness, or ambition and tranquility. Literature is riddled with such examples, not necessarily limited to friendships, religions, or wars. Self-discipline is often mentioned as a requirement for a person to keep a sense of honor. For example, I never negotiate individual discounts with customers for my services because my sense of fairness says that any discount I offer to one customer should also be offered to others in similar circumstances. Therefore, my honor and self-discipline require me to have rules for discounts or else I feel guilty for not being fair to people.

Can you apply this motivator in your organization? Of course! Develop and grow a clear code of conduct or value system in the organization. This will motivate people who see their own values reflected in the organization's values. And there is no need to start a religion or a war to achieve this.

Acceptance

When I researched the need for *acceptance*, the main theme I found was people's intrinsic need for self-esteem and a positive self-image. It is something that all of us share. As children, we need it most from our parents; later in life, we need it from our partners and peers.

Interestingly, the need for acceptance is often associated with people who are *lacking* in their sense of self-worth. It is said that such people are motivated to purposefully avoid conflict and criticism. They fear rejection and will do anything to seek the approval of parents, partners, or peers. Given this background reading, it would be tempting to say that, for such people, acceptance functions as a demotivator and not as a motivator. It is the lack of it that drives them toward certain behaviors.

However, we don't need to refer to clinics and self-help groups as the primary examples of organizations that have acceptance of people built into their systems. It is insufficient only to repair people's self-esteem. We can also boost it and strive to have a diverse group of people feeling great about themselves, regardless of their background and their physical or mental nature.

Diversity of workers is the key to innovation in organizations.[11] As a manager, you can do more than just be respectful toward minorities. You can ensure that people get hired because they add distinctive qualities to the social system. You can ensure that teams are organized in such a way that diversity in all forms is not merely tolerated as being acceptable, but embraced as being crucial. I can imagine no better way to motivate those who feel the need to be accepted for who they are.

Mastery

Consultancy companies full of specialists come to mind when I think of organizations driven by *mastery*. But one could also think of law firms, martial arts schools, and other organizations that, in order to survive, depend on growing people's level of competence in certain disciplines.

It is interesting to note that Professor Reiss considers mastery to be part of the need for power in his 16 basic desires theory because power motivates efforts to pursue challenges, ambitions, excellence, and glory.[12] However, Professors Deci and Ryan consider competence such a crucial human need that they promoted it as one of only three motivators in their self-determination theory. I prefer a position in the middle.

Mastery is about the challenge behind the work that people do. Some people are perfectly happy with easy tasks that come with good compensation. Others have the need to feel challenged so that they can grow their skills and make progress toward excellence. For example, the pursuit of mastery is the reason that all my projects are time-limited and different from the previous ones. Doing more of the same is just not challenging enough for me.

As a manager, you should make sure that repetitive and boring tasks are stripped from your business model and either automated or handed over to another business where people know how to thrive on that kind of work. You are responsible for offering people work that feels challenging to them but is still within their abilities.

POWER

There's enough room for me to influence what happens around me

Power

When I think of *power*, the first types of organizations that come to mind are political parties, secret service agencies, and government departments. In literature, power is often associated with dominance behavior, leadership, and imposing one's will on others. Supposedly, the need for power is intrinsic to humans and animals because of our desire to survive. Researchers have even linked the craving for power to other addictive behaviors, such as sex and cocaine.[13]

Personally, I prefer to see power as the need to have *influence* in the world, which feels like a more positive and enlightened description. Many would agree with me that there is little evidence of His Holiness the Dalai Lama showing dominant behavior and imposing his will on others. And yet, he is considered to be quite an influential figure. Therefore, he has power. Power is about being able to change things around oneself and make a difference in the world. Unlike Reiss, I believe it is quite different from mastery. Artists may care much about personal excellence and yet have little interest in the number of people whose hearts and minds are moved or changed with their work. These would be people seeking mastery, but not power.

It is no coincidence that the word power is encapsulated in the word *empowerment*. As a manager, you can set up the environment in such a way that people feel empowered to take responsibility and become leaders and change agents, without having to ask someone's permission. A stifling hierarchy and bureaucracy will be demotivating for people with a high need for power. In a social network, people are empowered by being connected to the network. Power as empowerment means facilitating this connectedness.[14]

Words and meanings

I realize that the word *influence* might be less controversial than the word *power*. Likewise, people might prefer *autonomy* over *freedom*, *purpose* over *goal*, or *competence* over *mastery*. However, it is important to realize that words matter less than meaning, and people should have the freedom/autonomy to construct their own mental models of motivation. Besides, **CHACIAROPS** doesn't resonate as well as **CHAMPFROGS**. All models are wrong, but the one described in this chapter is certainly useful.

Freedom

Without a doubt, start-ups and other entrepreneurial organizations are among the best examples for the motivator of *freedom*. I have always liked running my own businesses, and when I was employed I preferred small organizations. Why? Because they made me feel freer.

Independence and autonomy are well-known motivators for many people in the world. It's just a hunch, but I think introverts are more likely to be motivated by independence than extroverts. (I dare say it is the most important motivator for me!) People who are motivated by freedom usually dislike being dependent on others. They don't want assistance to get things done and would rather do everything themselves. It has happened many times that people offered me help with something, but asking for help rarely even crossed my mind!

Like power, freedom is closely connected to empowerment of workers. In a hierarchical setting, there is an implied dependence of employees upon management in which employees feel they need authorization for just about anything they wish to do. This is the reason I left a company of 5,000 people after just one year.

Freedom is also about empowerment in the network. People must feel free in the self-organizing teams in which they are working. When some team members insist that all decisions are made collaboratively and that rules are necessary to keep order in the team, those who are motivated by freedom may feel that their environment is suffocating them.

Relatedness

If freedom is appreciated by introverts, then *relatedness* is surely one of the main motivators among extroverts. Again, I'm just guessing. But some people thrive on social contacts with other people. They need family or friends to chat, play, and have a good time together.

Do not confuse means and ends when people like hanging out with others. There are those who socialize with peers mainly because of the effect it has on their position in the social network. Such people could be motivated by power or status, not by relatedness. With relatedness, we clearly refer to those who like socializing for the sake of not being alone.

One could say that every organization lends itself to having this motivator built in because every organization consists of people working together. However, the motivator might be more difficult for virtual companies compared to traditional ones. And remote, distributed teams will find it harder for their team members to socialize than collocated ones. (It is ironic that I'm writing this while skipping a hangout with my remote team. I decided I needed me-time more than we-time today.)

What can you do as a manager to have relatedness motivate your people? My thinking is that social interaction between them happens easily, unless it is somehow blocked by the environment. For example, it's easier for people to socialize in a relaxed, open office space than in a noisy room full of cubicles and corner offices. Likewise, you can take care that the work environment does not stop at the exit but that there is plenty of opportunity for people to engage beyond the company's office walls. And with remote teams, there are also many options for chat and play. Your challenge is to give workers a good reason not to skip their team hangouts! As I just did. Oops.

ORDER

There are enough rules and policies for a stable environment

Order

All human beings need a sense of *order* and *certainty*. This is wired into our brains. There's a reason that managers and leaders often complain about employees resisting change—people mostly like to keep things the way they are. (Conservatism is the political ideology based on this intrinsic human need.)

The typical organizations that we may associate with certainty and stability are fast-food chains and traditional factories. Any organization that needs to run like a clock, where employees know what is going to happen when and who is responsible for what, is an organization that thrives on order.

In an agile context, with organizations facing accelerated change and more frequent disruption, it is not easy to offer people a sense of certainty. With the average lifetime of companies shrinking every year, *nothing* is certain for anyone.

So, what can you do to satisfy people's need for order and stability? The solution is in the details. Job security is an illusion, but we can still achieve a bit of certainty in other ways. For example, many people don't like working at a different desk every day, so give them the option to have a preferred desk if they so desire. Many people don't like variable pay, so offer them a monthly income that is stable (even when they are freelancers). Many people dislike not knowing what is expected of them, so make sure you agree on a work profile or job description, preferably that they created themselves. The future of the company might be uncertain, but you can work to decrease the number of unpleasant surprises that people are confronted with every day.

GOAL

My purpose in life is reflected in the work that I do

Goal

Charity organizations. Those are the first groups that come to mind when I think of the motivator of *goal* and *purpose*. Many people want more out of their work than just a job or a career. They would like their work to be part of their calling. This nicely coincides with Maslow's hierarchy of needs, which says that self-actualization is the fifth and highest level of intrinsic motivation. The first two levels, physiological and safety needs, correspond to having a job, while the third and fourth levels, belonging and esteem, correspond to having a career. An ordinary job or an exciting career may be what people had before they found their calling. (It took me 20 years.)

Not only charity organizations have idealism woven into their raison d'être. Great organizations can (and should) have an inspiring purpose that goes beyond making money and pleasing stockholders, customers, or other stakeholders. If you can't define the why of your company, the rest doesn't really matter.

Motivate your employees by clarifying what the company stands for and what it tries to achieve in the world. People appreciate recognizing that their personal goals are reflected in the work they do. For example, the purpose of my company is to help people be happier in their jobs. This motivates my fellow workers because the purpose resonates with their own goals. In some cases, the company's purpose is the reason they joined!

Status

When I think of *status*, I think of sports, fashion, royalty, and exclusive networking clubs. And being listed on three Top 50 leadership lists on Inc.com. Right. There is a good reason many people want to decorate themselves with awards, titles, badges, brand names, silver linings, and golden medals. It increases their social standing. The pursuit of wealth is in many cases an indicator of someone's desire for status, but there are other ways of earning status, too.

Privilege, recognition, and exclusivity come in many forms. The vertical structure of traditional organizations is an obvious candidate: those at the top decide who else is allowed to climb higher on the corporate ladder. The desire for status leads to long job titles, favored parking spaces, spacious corner offices, and sometimes even a special elevator for upper management. But we can find status in social networks as well. Apart from climbing upwards in hierarchies, people also enjoy accumulating connections in networks. I cannot deny checking my Klout score every now and then, just to see how well I'm doing as an influencer compared to my peers.

As a manager, you can nurture people's need for status by offering them opportunities to make progress in the directions that matter to them. But you should aim for company-wide recognition of people's achievements in a fair and transparent way. The social standing of employees should correlate to their capabilities for production and innovation, not their talent at playing political games.

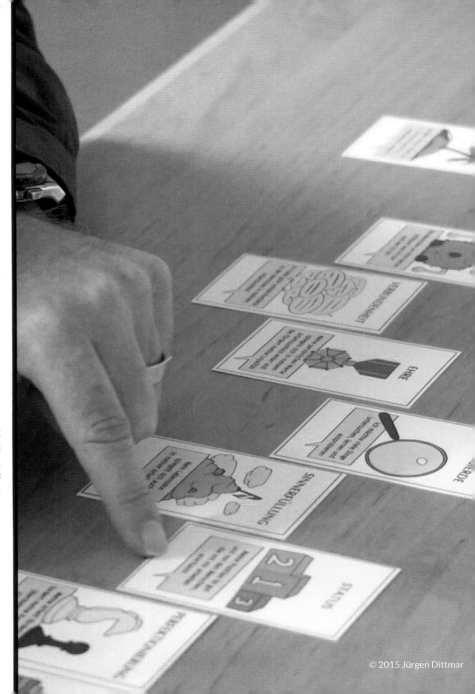

Manage the System

It is the goal of a firm to motivate people to be productive together. Therefore, motivation is a systemic property of the firm. Sadly, in many organizations, workers are motivated only by their financial compensation, but there is no real engagement with the work and the people because other intrinsic motivational properties are missing.

> **Managers must seek ways for curiosity, honor, acceptance, or any of the other motivators to become systemic properties of the firm.**

Managers must seek ways for curiosity, honor, acceptance, or any of the other intrinsic motivators to become systemic properties of the firm. That means, even when you're not paying attention to the system for a while, the system's properties are still affecting the engagement and behavior of workers. The proverbial carrots and sticks (incentives and punishments) don't fall into that category. They may work for you, but they require your continuous attention to have them be effective. And before you know it, the business fails to work without them.

> If people worked for years in a system that essentially relied on targets and pressure from above to prevent them from slacking off, then slacking off is exactly what might happen when bosses and targets are removed all of a sudden.

Frédéric Laloux, *Reinventing Organizations*[15]

Engagement of people should be woven into the fabric of the organization in a systemic way. This means you shouldn't waste your time trying to motivate individuals. If you do, you're operating in failure mode. You won't be able to keep that up indefinitely. Use your time to understand why the system, the organization itself, is not engaging them. That means, even with the simplest, most mundane kinds of jobs, organize the system in such a way that people find some of their 10 intrinsic motivators satisfied. Manage the system, not the people.

> Being an engineer or a carpenter is not in itself enjoyable. But if one does these things a certain way, then they become intrinsically rewarding, worth doing for their own sake.

Mihaly Csikszentmihalyi, *Creativity*[16]

Employee Engagement Programs (Don't Work)

Considering that engagement of people should be a built-in property of the organization, you now understand why employee engagement programs oftentimes don't work.

> Most so-called employee engagement programs are misbegotten, unwieldy, ineffective rolling caravans of impractical or never-going-to-be-implemented PowerPoint presentations.

Les McKeown, "A Very Simple Reason Employee Engagement Programs Don't Work"[17]

Almost all employee engagement programs focus on specific activities undertaken by managers or consultants to directly "motivate" people, using team-building exercises, outdoor activities, charity contributions, or games and parties. But no amount of motivational activities can hide that the system itself is not engaging. And—admitting that this paragraph might be bad for my annual revenue—hiring a motivational speaker is not going to make a difference either. It would be the equivalent of hiring a clown at a funeral to do something about all those sad faces.

If you check any organization where people are genuinely happy and engaged, you will find that the work and the organization trigger their intrinsic needs for curiosity, honor, acceptance, mastery, or any of the other motivators. You will most certainly not find a business leader or human resource manager spending a good chunk of time keeping the workforce motivated with an employee engagement program.[18] What you will find is that people are engaged because of the work and the people around them.

And that brings me to the only genuine employee engagement program that I am aware of: figuring out how people in your organization are intrinsically motivated and changing the organization in such a way that people's intrinsic needs are satisfied by the system. You could start by playing the moving motivators game.

Moving Motivators

The moving motivators exercise is played by arranging 10 motivational cards in order of importance (from a personal perspective) and then moving them up or down depending on a person's context, usually their work environment. By shifting cards to the left or to the right, the player indicates that specific motivators feel either more or less important than others. By moving cards up or down, the player indicates that a change in the environment is having either a positive or a negative effect on motivation.

For example, I consider *freedom, status,* and *curiosity* to be my most important motivators, while I find *acceptance* and *relatedness* the least important. When I quit my daytime job a number of years ago, my *freedom* and *curiosity* motivators (important for me) went up, because I became independent and was able to explore a new work life. My *relatedness* motivator (less important) went down, on the other hand, because I left many nice colleagues behind. Still, the net effect was positive overall. It was a good decision.

The moving motivators game can be played by one person, as a personal reflection tool; by two people, in a one-on-one setting; or even by a team of peers, as part of a retrospective or team-building exercise. I have facilitated the exercise many times with hundreds of people all around the world. The results have always been quite inspiring. Here are some of the usual takeaways for the players:

- There is no right or wrong in this exercise. Everyone is wired differently. Some people are motivated by freedom, others by relatedness. The beauty of the game is that it reveals these differences and makes people aware that we often misjudge each other by assuming that everyone is just like us. (I have assumed many times in my life that freedom is as important for other people as it is for me. I have learned that I was wrong.)

- There is often some disagreement about terminology, and that's OK. Even the scientists don't agree with each other. The meaning of power and status for me can be slightly different from your interpretation of those words. What is more important is that the cards help us explain how we feel and what we need.

- Many things are context-specific. For example, in some countries, ordering cards from right to left makes more sense than ordering them from left to right. Some people prefer prioritizing things vertically instead of horizontally. And the observer has an influence as well. It makes a difference whether you play the game with your spouse, your best friend, your colleague, or your manager!

- The importance of motivators may be different depending on whether work environment or personal life is the context of the exercise. Likewise, some motivators may become more or less important to a person, depending on changing circumstances.

- Last but not least, because results among players are always different, the game highlights diversity and alternative perspectives. And that is always a good thing.

FREEDOM

CURIOSITY

I am independent of others with my own work and responsibilities

© 2015 Jurgen Appelo

Much
easier

The moving motivators game makes it a lot easier to ask the question, "What motivates you?" For many people, this question is itself too vague and abstract to answer. But when they have 10 cards on a table, with nice pictures on them, and they are asked to move them around spatially, left to right and up and down, a discussion about motivation suddenly becomes a lot easier.

The moving motivators game also offers a great opportunity to assess the impact of an organizational change. How do people feel about an upcoming merger, a change of department, a job promotion, a new business strategy, or a new team of colleagues? With moving motivators, you can find out how the change affects people's intrinsic motivation. In many cases, you will find mixed results. Some motivators go up, others go down. Work life is rarely simple!

Finally, many people find the game itself motivating. It triggers people's need for curiosity, relatedness, and order. Beyond your own team members, you may even want to consider including stakeholders and management, if possible.[19] And no matter the exact layout of the cards on the table, people usually find the discussions during and after the exercise the most valuable.[20]

As managers, we ask people what motivates them because we want to answer the question, "What's in it for them?" The goal of the organization is to engage people for productivity. We seek proof that this is indeed happening. And if we can't find any evidence, we have work to do.

The work we do is about introducing experiments with good practices. We can boost people's need for curiosity and exploration with celebration grids. We can satisfy their sense of honor with value stories. A feeling of acceptance may be achieved with personal maps, while mastery could be nurtured through feedback wraps or a metrics ecosystem. To increase power, freedom, and order, we can obviously introduce delegation boards, while relatedness and status may be satisfied through the use of a kudo box. Finally, a worthwhile goal is evidently communicated with a culture book. But those are just my suggestions. You may know better alternatives.

> The goal of the organization is to engage people for productivity. We seek proof that this is indeed happening.

Engage!

I am writing this conclusion on a Friday night. Many people will be having dinner in a restaurant or watching a movie in the cinema, and I'm sure that a good number of them will be glad that their work week is behind them, because *finally* they have time for leisure activities and enjoying their lives!

Not me. I feel happy that I signed the contract for the publication of this book just an hour ago, which means *more* work for me: researching, writing, editing, reviewing, illustrating.... I'm rubbing my hands eagerly in anticipation of the development of my production and marketing plans. I'll probably do that on Sunday. My work-life is just too engaging

Discovering motivation

"I used moving motivators with various teams and companies. The game helps every team member to reflect on [their] own drivers for motivation and assess their current status and necessary changes to further increase their engagement. They share their learnings, and this new level of transparency helps teams to create a common understanding, increase trust, and discover new ways to collaborate.

One team member figured out that another environment would better suit his needs, which meant relocating and starting in a new company—OK, that was a tough outcome.

One manager and his team learned more about their problems and about the needs of one another, which had been hidden for years but were uncovered by playing moving motivators and sharing their observations. Another team experienced the team's diversity and learned more about everyone involved, which led to funny new ways of interpreting past situations. 'So, *that's* why you always ask for more documentation!' (the need for order) and 'Therefore, you connect with so many people outside our team' (the need for relatedness)."

Sebastian Radics, *Germany*

to let things go for more than a day. (This also means that I easily go for a stroll in a park on a Tuesday afternoon, go shopping for new shoes on Wednesday morning, or spend some time producing vacation videos during my work week. There is no work-life balance for me, because work and life are one big blur. It is work-life fusion.)

What about your workers? Are they looking forward to the next workday? If not, what's preventing them from feeling intrinsically motivated? Why is your system not working for you? As a manager, that's *your* job. Find out. Engage!

Moving motivators as a hiring technique

"I was working in a small company when my boss approached me and asked me to help expand our team by hiring new members. Although I had never been on the interviewer's side of the table, I gladly accepted the challenge. I had read from great sources that the people you hire are the people that will grow your company's culture, so I needed to focus on values. But how?

One morning, while I was taking a shower (the most inspired moment in my day), I realized that I had the perfect tool to do this: moving motivators. So, I decided to use it during my interview sessions with the job candidates by asking the following question: How would you value your move to this company?

I got two takeaways: The first was to compare the intrinsic needs and values of the candidate with what was most important from the company's perspective; the second was how his or her needs and values would change when he or she moved to our company. We were then able to understand if that person was a good match for our company.

I don't know if I will ever be asked to work in HR, but at least the people that we hired fit well with our company's culture."

Gerardo Barcia Palacios, *Spain*

How to Get Started

Now it is time for you to start experimenting with moving motivators.

1. Download the free PDF with the 10 motivational cards from the Management 3.0 website (m30.me/motivators) and ask your kids or your neighbors to cut them for you.

2. Find someone to do this exercise with: your spouse, your colleague, your best friend, or the pizza delivery guy.

3. Be the first one to start so that you gain trust and set a good example. (The other person starts by being an observer.) Order the cards horizontally. What's most important to you goes on one side; what's least important goes on the other side; the rest end up somewhere in the middle.

4. Now imagine some kind of change or event that would have an impact on your motivation, such as moving to a new home, changing workplaces, getting a job promotion, or extending your family.

5. Imagine the impact of this change on your 10 motivators. When the impact is positive, move the card up; when the impact is negative, move the card down.

6. While you're moving your cards left and right and up and down, tell the other player what you're doing and why. Just try to think out loud, describing what the words and pictures mean to you and why you're moving them.

7. When you're all done, switch roles. And then, evaluate!

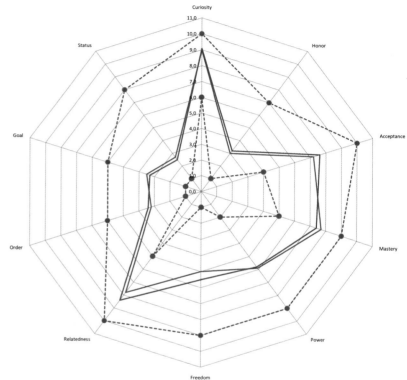

© 2014 Dave Brands

Tips and Variations

It helps some groups to start with a brief discussion of the 10 motivators to get a narrower understanding and interpretation of each.

When playing moving motivators, it helps some people to think out loud by talking to a (silent) observer.

For many players, it is important to know the context. Try to assess motivation according to a specific change in a specific environment.

You are free to leave out cards (or maybe even add some others) in any way you like.

Take a picture of the results so you can look back later on, and maybe even share the outcome with others.

We collected the outcome of all team members and we depicted the results in heat maps, showing motivation across the whole team.

I used the game to guide people's emotions when one of them was promoted to team leader. It helped the others to express and resolve feelings of uncertainty and disappointment.

Ask people questions, such as "is your outcome different from what it was a year ago?" and "what do you want it to be three years from now?"

As a personal coach, I played the game with a CEO who was wondering for months if she should have children. Amazingly, the game helped her to reach a decision!

Always plan to have a discussion after playing moving motivators. That's where the most value is.

Our team loved creating a radar graph with calculations of the variation and differentiation per card. That was really motivating for them. ;-)

We have the results of our team on the wall, so that we can always point at it during a team meeting and say, "That will or will not motivate us!"

Find specific tools and more ideas at m30.me/moving-motivators.

11

happiness door

Aim for a Happier Organization

> Happiness is not a station you arrive at, but a manner of traveling.
>
> **Margaret Lee Runbeck, American author (1905–1956)**

Some people believe that happiness is something they will achieve when they are famous or successful, or when they acquire enough money. But research tells us that happiness is more a decision than a destination. And it is something you can simply decide to achieve in the workplace as well. Apart from reviewing and implementing the 12 Steps to Happiness, I suggest that you measure happiness in a playful way with a happiness door.

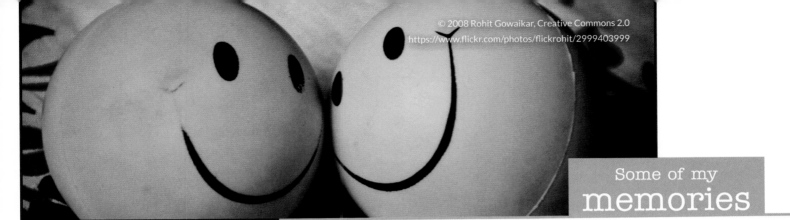

Some of my
memories

A book called *Managing for Happiness* would not be complete without a chapter specifically dedicated to the happiness of workers. It is a topic much discussed and often misunderstood. This makes it all the more relevant to give you a quick overview of what researchers have figured out about happiness and how we can apply their findings to the workplace. It all starts with a simple thought exercise.

Think about this: Can you recall some happy moments that you enjoyed when you were at the office, doing work, or just spending time with your colleagues? Are there any memories from your past that generate a warm feeling or a smile on your face? Go ahead, think about it for a moment. I'll wait.

Dum-tee-dum-tee-dum…

Did you find something down in the basement of your brain? I'm sure you did! If not, keep reading. This chapter will show you how to generate some more happy memories.

I remember the exclamations of joy and appreciation for the courseware that I spontaneously (and without permission) redesigned at the first company where I worked after completing my studies. I remember racing around with reindeer and snow scooters (not simultaneously) with my coworkers on a day out in northern Finland. I remember winning a business plan contest and having pictures taken by journalists of me and my team. I remember playing a very successful April Fools' prank on some team members that had them puzzled and laughing for a whole day. I remember playing Settlers of Catan in the basement of our office on "Games Night," a regular event that was organized by my colleagues. I'm glad to say I have plenty of memories of times when I enjoyed doing work, getting credit for my work, or just having fun with my colleagues during or after work. I assume you have some cherished memories yourself as well.

Engagement or Satisfaction?

Several times in this book, I have referred to low engagement levels of people at work. According to Gallup's *State of the Global Workplace*, one of the best-known reports on employee engagement, only 13 percent of people worldwide are actively engaged, while 24 percent are actively disengaged. And the rest of the workforce finds itself in a depressingly large no-man's-land somewhere in between.[1] In earlier chapters of this book, we've seen various practices that can increase people's engagement levels. However, employee engagement is only one part of the story.

Despite *engagement* levels being quite low globally, *satisfaction* levels appear to be quite high. According to a LinkedIn/Adler Group report, a whopping 72 percent of employees worldwide feel either somewhat or very satisfied in their jobs, while only 14 percent say they feel somewhat or very unsatisfied.[2] This leads us to the fascinating, paradoxical conclusion that many workers are quite satisfied with their work but at the same time not very engaged. How is that possible? Apparently, worker engagement and worker satisfaction are not the same thing.

Engaged workers feel motivated to be productive in the organization. They try to deliver their best possible work and keep all their stakeholders happy. But when an engaged worker is not also a satisfied worker, we should wave a red flag for a possible burnout situation: giving it one's all but completely ignoring one's own needs. Fortunately, such cases are rare and I've only ever known one close friend who fell victim to a job burnout.

By the same token, a satisfied worker is not necessarily an engaged worker. Satisfied workers feel content in their work environment because it satisfies all or most of their needs. But when the person is not

engaged and productive for the organization, we should be wary of the problem of slacking off: being not very productive and focusing only on one's own needs. Sadly, I have personally known and seen quite a few more of these cases.

So, where does happiness sit in this picture?

Happiness is most commonly defined as a mental state of well-being supported by positive or pleasant emotions ranging from relaxed contentment to intense enjoyment. This means that happiness can be a long-term positive feeling and attitude that has nestled in the subconscious of your brain, but it can also be seen as a short-term burst of joy induced by oneself or by the environment.

I can imagine a happy person with a long-term positive attitude who nevertheless feels not engaged in the job, and I can imagine a similar worker who, despite a positive long-term outlook, feels unsatisfied with a specific work environment. This lack of engagement or job satisfaction will probably have a temporary effect on the person's short-term happiness level. Likewise, an unhappy person who has negative feelings in general may nevertheless feel engaged in the job and satisfied with the work environment, temporarily. But the person's long-term unhappiness will probably make itself felt across both engagement and satisfaction levels at some point.

As always, things are complex. Engagement, satisfaction, and happiness are hard-to-define concepts that are correlated but not fully overlapping, and everything is connected to everything else.

Engagement, satisfaction, and happiness are hard-to-define concepts that are correlated but not fully overlapping.

Happiness First, Success Later

It is best when people feel happy, in any organization, regardless of the type of work and the kind of industry. Happiness, engagement, and job satisfaction are intimately entwined, and it's a fact that happy workers are more productive than unhappy ones.[3] But what can a manager do to contribute to the happiness of workers?

For many people, happiness is an end goal. But researchers tell us that happiness has much more to do with a person's state of mind than with the person's success in life. Quite often, happiness is the precursor to success, not merely the *result* of it.[4] Granted, successes can contribute—temporarily—to a boost of your short-term happiness. But if you aren't enjoying long-term happiness already, it is less likely you will achieve those successes in the first place!

Happiness is a decision, not an outcome

Therefore, despite what most people think, happiness is the means and not the end. The smart thing to do is to allow happiness to take us on a path to success.[5] We should all reserve some time to take concrete steps to be happier workers. In the wake of happiness, progress and success are more likely to follow. Happiness is a decision, not an outcome.

People want to be happy, and all the other things they want are typically meant to be means to that end.

Daniel T. Gilbert, *Stumbling on Happiness*[6]

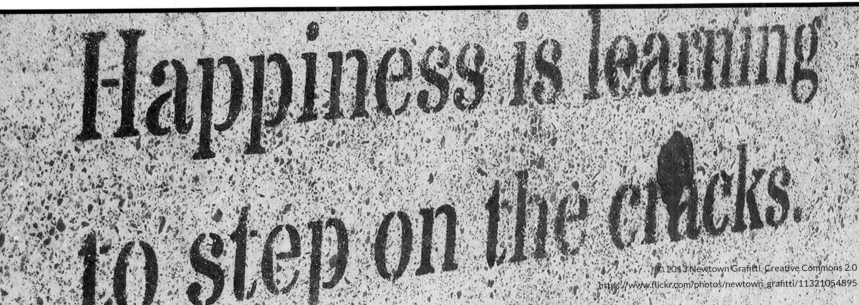

© 2013 Newtown Grafitti, Creative Commons 2.0
https://www.flickr.com/photos/newtown_grafitti/11321054895

Twelve Steps to Happiness

I've said it before: I love doing a bit of research. I remember doing this particular research when I was enjoying a vacation in Buenos Aires, Argentina. While in a happy mood, I thought to myself, "What are the things, according to science, that usually make people feel happy?" So, while sipping a drink or two, I spent a few hours browsing the Web for scientifically backed articles on happiness, and I noticed that the same things were mentioned again and again across many articles and research reports. I ultimately arrived at a list of 12 items that I refer to as the **12 Steps to Happiness** because I want to emphasize that happiness is a path, not a destination. There are no keys, roads, or flights to happiness because happiness is not some place where you can arrive. It is what you experience when you take steps in the right direction.

Here is the list of 12 steps. As a manager or team member, take each one of these into account and try to apply them wherever possible. Your aim is not only the increased happiness of your colleagues but also more happiness for yourself. In fact, just trying to contribute to other people's happiness is almost guaranteed to contribute to your own at the same time. We all deserve a bit of happiness each day.

> **The very good news is there is quite a number of internal circumstances . . . under your voluntary control. If you decide to change them . . . your level of happiness is likely to increase lastingly.**

Martin E. Seligman, *Authentic Happiness*[7]

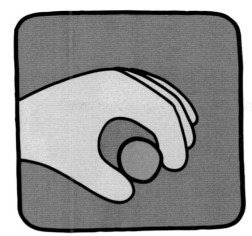

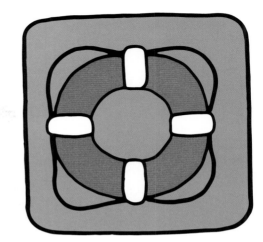

Thank your coworkers and always try to be appreciative.[8] Showing your gratitude to colleagues and appreciating who they are and what they do won't cost you more than writing them a simple note or giving them a thumbs up, warm handshake, or honest hug. I have "thank someone" as a daily recurring task on my task list. My most recent thank-you note was for a team member who convinced me to join an online meeting, even though I actually wanted to be alone to think and write. I truly appreciated her attempt to keep me involved. I've heard of other teams enjoying a regular "thank you round" where everyone is invited to explicitly thank one other person at least once per week.

Give a little present to a team member or make it possible for them to offer each other gifts because gifts make both receivers and senders happier, and happier people send more gifts, in an endless virtuous cycle.[9] You can make it as simple as the introduction of kudo cards (see Chapter 1), incidental gifts around birthdays or anniversaries, or more elaborate gifts as a one-per-year celebration, perhaps around Christmas time or another national holiday. The best gifts are unexpected, though. I recently brought my team members a crunchy cookie spread from Belgium. They loved it. They even posted photos of it on Facebook. Warning! Be careful to always keep the gifts small so that they don't get interpreted as financial incentives and destroy people's intrinsic motivation.

Help someone out who needs a bit of assistance or give team members time and space to lend each other a hand because altruism makes people feel good.[10] For example, you can institutionalize people helping each other out with regular pair working sessions (pair coaching, pair developing, pair writing, or even pair managing). You can invite workers to become mentors or coaches of their peers. And you can use one-on-one sessions to both ask for help and offer help, in two directions. I still find it amazing that so many people volunteered to help me out with this book by reviewing drafts or submitting their stories, even if I couldn't use everyone's input. Never forget that even when you don't need everyone's help, you can increase other people's happiness by allowing them to help you.

Eat well and make good, healthy foods easily available for everyone in the workplace. After all, there is a strong correlation between food and mood.[11] It is amazing how commonplace sweets, cookies, snacks, carbonated drinks, and pizzas have become in the workplace. If managers really cared about people's happiness and productivity, they would push for access to healthier alternatives, such as fruit, nuts, veggies, and fresh water. And not only during lunchtime but throughout the day. With this particular topic, I must plead guilty. I'm not known for my eagerness to plunder any salad bar. But we should all keep some room for personal improvement, right?

Exercise regularly and allow your coworkers to take proper care of their bodies. Physical exercise is touted as a cure for many ailments and as a great boost for happiness.[12] This is certainly something you should think about as a manager. Of course, I'm not suggesting that you should construct an in-house gym at the office, but a small contribution to a health program of their choice will be appreciated by many employees. And don't forget the possibility of organizing a weekly run, long walk, or bike ride with your colleagues. I know several of my friends who enjoy such regular workouts with their coworkers. Likewise, ergonomic chairs, standing desks, and software that offers people advice on the proper use of computer equipment and healthy stretching exercises can be a great way to minimize the risk of stress and depression.

Rest well and sleep sufficiently. A good night's sleep is one of the most often suggested tricks to enjoy a long and healthy life.[13] In the context of a work environment, it would be wise to offer people a place to recharge throughout the day. Repurpose one of your meeting rooms and make it a "zen room" with reclining chairs, pillows, and soft, relaxing music. Be an advocate of rest and relaxation breaks and be suspicious of anyone who claims not to need them. Make sure that "standard office hours" don't force-fit people into straitjackets of productivity. Different people need different activity levels throughout the day. I once found someone lounging on a sofa in the office basement—and gave her a compliment for taking good care of herself.

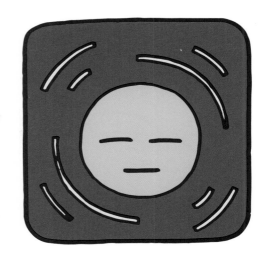

Experience new things because the happiness you derive from experiences is longer lasting than the happiness you get from things.[14] Make every day an opportunity to learn something new, try something out, and run an experiment. Innovation mostly comes from creative workers, not from management, and it is best achieved when people enjoy the freedom to be creative together. For example, many years ago, my fellow software developers spontaneously organized a "Pink Friday," which meant that they asked all their coworkers to wear something pink on that day. There was no particular reason other than colleagues having fun and creating a new experience. Such memories mean more to me now than any number of gadgets and trinkets that we bought or received as employees.

Hike outdoors, enjoy nature, and get people to escape their office environment every once in a while. Being outside and connecting with nature leads to an increased sense of vitality that goes beyond mere physical exercise.[15] Not coincidentally, I'm writing this while still feeling a bit tired from my 20-kilometer bike ride in the forest an hour ago. It is one of the ways in which I make sure that I'm not glued to my desk and computer all day long. My daily city walks, to fetch myself a nice coffee and do some reading, are another example in this category. Push yourself and your coworkers to get some fresh air as well. Next time you get yourselves an afternoon coffee, go and get it from that great brewer 2 kilometers down the road. Or, as I did some years ago, get your team out of their caves to enjoy a team meeting in the sun.

Meditate every day or adopt regular mindfulness practices, because there's evidence that better awareness of oneself and one's surroundings and improved inner peace and quiet are useful ingredients for greater happiness.[16] Our busy work schedules and hectic private lives easily dominate our minds while the world keeps changing faster and faster, not making things any easier. But our minds were not created for the twenty-first century. Like our bodies, our brains need some care and attention, too. Forward-thinking companies introduce mindfulness programs to their employees or offer them dedicated meditation rooms because this helps improve people's focus and clarity, as well as their overall well-being.[17]

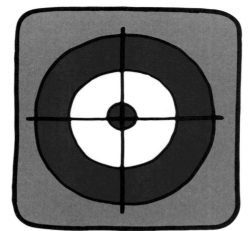

Socialize with people and make it easy for your coworkers to develop connections, not only with each other but also with other stakeholders. The longest study on happiness that was ever carried out found that the number one factor that determines a fulfilling life is our relatedness to family and friends.[18] That means it's the people around you, not your work, that make you happier in the long term. Organize team lunches, after-work drinks, or—as I have done in the past—invite coworkers to your house and get them to cook dinner together. Another time, I convinced my colleagues to show their vacation photos on a projector in a meeting room during lunchtime. They loved it. When you get people to learn about each other's hobbies, families, values, and ambitions, small talk comes much easier to everyone, which helps them appreciate each other and strengthens the social ties.

Aim for a defined purpose as an organization and help people to develop, communicate, and realize their own goals. Paradoxically, one should never attempt to pursue happiness itself because it is elusive. Don't strive to be happy. Instead, strive to do something meaningful. It is the pursuit of meaning that generates happiness.[19] There's no better way to make workers happy than to show them there is a good reason for their participation and that they contribute to a worthy purpose. (With the purpose to indirectly increase other people's happiness, my company Happy Melly found a sneaky way around the paradox.) But let's not forget that it's not only the work of employees that should add to the organization's raison d'être; the organization should also strive to support its people in achieving their goals.

Smile to make everyone feel better. My high school years were the darkest of my life, but I recall with pleasure the few moments when I made everyone in the classroom laugh with some of my silly jokes. Even when you feel there is little reason to do so, it's still a smart idea to try and smile. Happiness makes us smile, but it also works the other way around: Smiling makes us happy.[20] Research confirms that painting a fake smile on your face can have a positive effect on your mood because you're tricking your brain into thinking that you're happy, which means that the chance of smiling for real increases, which in turn is good for your levels of engagement, satisfaction, and productivity. Of course, it's far better when most of your smiles are genuine and sincere. To achieve that, I suggest the judicious use of harmless humor and savvy silliness.

The Happiness Door

It was during the very first Management 3.0 workshop, in early 2011, that I came up with the idea of the **happiness door**. I was trying to find a way for participants in my workshop to give me feedback in a manner that was not only safe and respectful but also fun and engaging. I was already familiar with the concept of the **feedback wall**: asking people to write comments on sticky notes and collecting them publicly on a wall. I was also familiar with the idea of a **happiness index**: a scale of (usually) one to five that people use to indicate how happy they feel about something. In my car on the way home, after a stressful but also successful first workshop day, I came up with the idea to combine those two practices into one.

The method is very simple. You ask participants to give you immediate feedback during or after a presentation, training session, business meeting, pole dance, or any other type of social interaction. You want that feedback quickly because, in most people's brains, first impressions dissolve faster than European credit ratings. You also want it soon so that you can act on the feedback and minimize the suffering caused by your embarrassing mistakes. People write their feedback on sticky notes and they put their notes on a door where you've drawn a happiness index with a scale of 1, or bad (at the bottom), to 5, or great (at the top). The higher people place the sticky notes, the happier they are. People are even allowed to leave their sticky notes empty and just use them to indicate their level of happiness. The method is easy to explain in 30 seconds and it's a great way to quickly capture people's (anonymous) feedback while they leave a room.

Sometimes participants just write "awesome exercise" or "I love the discussions." That's great. It will help you feel happier as the manager or organizer of the event. Sometimes people leave just a smiley or a blank note. Other participants have more specific feedback to share, such as "too many quotes," "use more pictures," or "too much theory" and "add more theory." (Yes, I once received the last two at the same time.) The happiness door has always worked well for me.

Happiness doors were used with various degrees of success at a small number of conferences that I attended. In every case, I was unaware of the organizers' brilliant strokes of thievery until I actually saw the doors. I noticed tweets and comments of participants appreciating this way of collecting feedback by organizers, which was similar to the comments I receive from attendees of my workshops.

Feedback wall and
happiness index

I take credit for inventing the happiness door even though I called it a feedback door in the beginning, which led to some confusion. Several workshop trainers told me they had invented the "feedback door" years before me, but it turned out none of them did what I described here. Usually, they only collected optional feedback on a wall, window, or coffee machine. It is important to remember that the happiness door is a feedback wall *and* a happiness index in one. Its purpose is to generate written feedback (comments) *and* numerical feedback (ratings).

> The happiness door is a feedback wall *and* a happiness index in one.

A few things are important to consider for a successful implementation of the happiness door:

- The happiness door (or wall, flip chart, or whiteboard) should be strategically placed, for example, next to the exit of the room. Preferably, it should be a place everyone walks past when a meeting, a conference talk, or a training session has ended.

- All participants must understand the scale of the happiness index. Usually, a rating of 5 means good and a rating of 1 means bad. But in some parts of the world, people more commonly associate 1 with good and 5 with bad, which is confusing when you have participants with different backgrounds in the room.

- I prefer drawing smiley faces instead of numbers, not only to avoid confusion over the meaning of numbers, but also because such illustrations make the door itself more engaging for people.

- Organizers may want to consider distributing sticky notes in a not-very-subtle way. At some events, I saw organizers attach sticky notes to the backs or seats of all the chairs. At other events, there were people offering stickies right next to the door.

- It is easy to collect and save the results of a happiness door. I always take a picture of the door first and I save the notes in envelopes. If you want to keep the scores, just write the numbers on the notes before you take them from the door, as I saw some organizers do. You can also use five numbered envelopes, as I often did.

There are other ways of collecting feedback from event participants. Some organizers collect feedback on whiteboards in hallways, but I like the request for input to be quicker and more "in-your-face," near the exit of the room, so that it's hard to ignore. Some event managers use paper forms and closed boxes, but I like the feedback to work as an information radiator. I have seen organizers collect feedback in three colors (red, yellow, and green) but I think the happiness index (1 to 5) is a more useful scale. And some workshop facilitators collect only comments as qualitative feedback, but I've noticed some attendees are more comfortable with numbers, not text.

The happiness door combines the best of many feedback mechanisms that I have seen. But you may put a note on my door saying "you're somewhat biased."

Feedback and Influence

One interesting side effect of the happiness door practice is that it is reflexive. The information radiator not only *collects* people's feedback but also *influences* it. People can see what others are doing before them, therefore they will be influencing each other. When some people give low ratings, it is possible that others will do the same—or maybe some will attempt to compensate by being *more* positive. If the door only shows high ratings, it is possible that other people will think, "Well, there were parts that I didn't like, but maybe it's just me." Don't ever think that a happiness door would survive scientific scrutiny. As a measurement tool, it is unlikely to become popular among researchers.

The cleaning crew

A playful feedback method generates happiness among your coworkers.

"I tried to introduce a happiness door for the first time in my company during a three-day workshop. Since people in my company are not used to seeing this type of initiative during workshops, I spent some time explaining why there were smileys on the door and what the purpose was of the sticky notes. At the end of the morning session, the first note on the wall was my own. I put it there after people left the room, visible for all when they came back in. In the afternoon, some additional notes appeared slowly. By the end of day one, we had two hands full, and we went over them one-by-one.

Coming back on the second day, we discovered we had made a mistake. . . . We left the notes on the door, hoping to get more, but we forgot to leave a message for the cleaning crew. All the notes and smileys were gone! The lesson learned here is that the cleaning crew also has an important role to play in the success of a workshop. Include them, too!"

Patrick Verdonk, *Spain*

The happiness door is meant to *improve* happiness. Many people appreciate a social event even more when the approach to feedback is open, transparent, and engaging. The fact that there is a happiness door in the room means people are less likely to put anything near the bottom of the door! I sometimes joke that I intentionally place the bad area of the scale inconveniently near the floor, which will hurt your neck when you put a sticky there. It always makes people laugh, which is one of the 12 steps to happiness. The door is *supposed* to make people happier. Plus, the useful feedback that you receive, together with nice appreciative comments, will make you feel happier, too. Mission accomplished.

Next time you organize a meeting, workshop, or other kind of event, I suggest you try the happiness door, not only because the feedback is very useful for you as the manager of the meeting, but also because a playful feedback method generates happiness among your coworkers.

Better feedback with a happiness door

"As an agile coach, I regularly train staff. To improve my trainer skills, I gather feedback from my participants. I used to do this verbally, but this turned out to be unsatisfying:

- Giving honest, verbal feedback straight in the face was hard for my participants.
- Many seemed to feel a barrier to exposing their individual thoughts about the training in front of the group.
- Very few provided valuable feedback.
- I likely forgot some of the feedback by the time I could reflect on it.

I expected fewer problems with written feedback. This led to the idea to use a happiness door. What has changed is that I received more valuable, honest, and individual feedback because my participants felt safe to express their thoughts in written form. It also provided an instant overview of my performance and helped me to remember a feeling for the session. Finally, it was impossible to forget any feedback.

The only drawback I have identified so far is that the written feedback can be sometimes hard to interpret and you need to ask for nice handwriting. ;-) Anyway, the happiness door is great and there will definitely be more in my future trainings!"

Stefan Wunder, *Austria*

How to Get Started

At the start of this chapter, I shared some of my fondest memories with you. Now it is time to generate some of your own.

1. Download the **12 Steps to Happiness** poster from m30.me/twelve-steps.

2. Organize a meeting with your team and put up a happiness door in the room.

3. Review the 12 steps together and come up with an action plan to implement most or all of them.

4. At the end of the meeting, ask everyone to place a sticky note with some feedback on the happiness door.

5. Read the notes and smile.

© 2013 Jurgen Appelo

Tips and Variations

Draw smiley faces and thunder-clouds (or other pictograms) instead of numbers. It is easier for people to understand what they mean.

Write "HAPPINESS DOOR" in colorful letters above all the stick-ies and maybe draw a nice frame around the feedback area, too.

I always make it clear to partici-pants that I actually read all the sticky notes. I even read some of them out loud.

People appreciate that I immedi-ately take action after reading their feedback on the happiness door.

Tell your attendees that empty notes are OK. A rating without a comment is still better than no feedback at all.

Remind people that anonymous feedback is fine.

I combined the happiness index (vertical) with a return on invest-ment indicator (horizontal). This way, we could correlate happiness with value!

Some encouragement to give feed-back is often necessary. Don't let them wonder silently, "Should I put this on there?" Get them to do it!

In workshops, I usually ask for feedback once or twice per day. More often is overdoing it.

Ask people to write clearly. Sometimes, it's very hard to read people's tiny scribbles.

You can invent ways to combine the happiness door with other visual practices, such as delegation boards or kudo walls.

We combined the happiness door with the perfection game method. We asked for two stick-ies: one for happiness and one for improvements.

Find more ideas at m30.me/happiness-door and download the 12 Steps to Happiness poster from m30.me/twelve-steps.

12

yay! questions and celebration grids

Learn from Successes and Failures

It's important that someone celebrate our existence . . . People are the only mirror we have to see ourselves in. The domain of all meaning. All virtue, all evil, are contained only in people. There is none in the universe at large.

Lois McMaster Bujold,
American author
(1949–)

Does your organization appreciate the things you've learned? Do you applaud colleagues who do their jobs well? All too often, organizations live day by day, from one crisis to another, and they forget to take note of the good things that happened. By asking two important questions and drawing a celebration grid, you can look for things to treasure.

A few years ago, I discussed some organizational challenges with my former CEO. I noted that the employees in our company rarely took time to enjoy their successes. People were always working hard and never seemed to celebrate the things that went well. I suggested that maybe we should have a big bell in the office so that we could ring it whenever there was something to celebrate. The idea of a bell came to my mind because I wanted something that would be visible, inviting, and impossible to ignore when used.

One week later, to my surprise, the CEO brought me a copper ship's bell and said, "Here's your bell. Now do something useful with it."  I convinced the office manager to hang it in the middle of our big open office space, and I let everyone in the company know that every employee was allowed to ring the bell if they had something to celebrate. (I later heard of a similar practice with a cow bell instead of a ship's bell, in other organizations.[1])

From that moment, every few weeks or so, someone would enthusiastically yank on the rope. The bell would be rung for signing a government contract, for deploying a Web application, or for doing something less strenuous, such as running a marathon or giving birth to a baby. Any reason was valid. (I once rang the bell for having more visitors on my blog than the company had on its website. It was just an excuse to enjoy another celebration.)

When the sound of the ship's bell chimed through the office, all employees immediately got together for a 10-minute celebration. Our people knew that the bell was often a signal for free cake or cookies, which probably contributed to the quick gathering of the entire workforce around the coffee machine. The person who rang the bell then usually took a few minutes to explain what was being celebrated, followed by enthusiastic applause. Yay! And then the eating started. The last time I heard the bell was when the CEO announced that I was quitting my job.

Every employee was allowed to ring the bell if they had something to celebrate.

Experimental Learning

Some writers claim that "we only learn from failure" or that we should "allow ourselves to fail."[2] Some say we should celebrate mistakes because they help us to be more creative and innovative.[3] There are even congregations of people with the sole purpose of applauding each other's mistakes and failures.[4] Interestingly enough, other writers claim that we should "focus on successes" and that "success breeds success."[5] This raises the question whether we should celebrate successes *and* failures—in other words, celebrate everything. The truth is, quite literally, right in the middle.

Information theorists have discovered that systems learn most when failure rates are around 50 percent.[6] In other words, when your experiments have a good chance of succeeding *and* a good chance of failing, they generate the most information for you to learn from.

We learn the most when we can't predict whether our experiments will lead to good or bad outcomes. Apparently, failure and success are both needed for learning. What we learn from the most are the experiences we've never had before. When all we do is repeat established practices, it is hard to know if we could do any better. Likewise, if all we do is make the same mistakes, then we're not learning much either. Optimal learning happens somewhere in the middle; it happens when you frequently think, "I didn't know this, but I'm glad I found out because now I can do better!"

> Either excessive or insufficient probability of failure reduces the efficiency with which we generate information. . . . Avoid oversimplifications, like "eliminate failures" or "celebrate failures." There is an optimum failure rate.

Donald G. Reinertsen, *Principles of Product Development Flow*[7]

> No amount of examples of successes or failures is indicative of one's potential performance. It all depends on your own effort and understanding of your own problems.

W. Edwards Deming, *Out of the Crisis*[8]

A learning organization should not aim to minimize the amount of failure. Reducing failure would reduce learning. Of course, maximizing failure also makes no sense. What we should maximize is the *understanding* of our problems. This understanding happens by experiencing both successes and failures. There is an optimal learning rate when you think "wow, I'm brilliant!" and "my God, I'm such an idiot!" roughly in equal measure. Therefore, we should celebrate learning, not successes or failures.

Good Practices

In many working environments, people usually focus on fixing problems. This makes sense because continuous improvement allows organizations to survive and thrive. However, a focus on things that could be improved usually comes down to a focus on failures and mistakes, and this mindset can have some serious side effects. Being a perfectionist, I have sometimes been guilty of this myself. I have "raised the bar" for me and for others until the bar was so high that Godzilla could do a limbo dance underneath it while carrying a space shuttle.

However, I noticed a strange thing when I urged people to stop screwing up. I found this didn't motivate them at all! I realized getting better isn't just about reducing what goes *wrong* (making mistakes). It's also about increasing what goes *right* (using good practices). And every now and then, people need a reminder that they're doing just fine.

It's no wonder the culture in many organizations feels negative when the focus of discussions is mainly on mistakes and problems. Workers feel they are held accountable for not being perfect. Instead of having a constructive view of improvement, people end up with a defensive frame of mind. They avoid taking responsibility, and for every perceived problem, they point at others who must have caused it. Because people's minds are focused on self-defense instead of improvement, things will not get any better and the organization will just make more mistakes.

> ## We should celebrate good practices, not punish mistakes.

I believe we should emphasize the good practices over the mistakes because you get more of what you focus on.[9,10] If you focus on mistakes, people will make more mistakes. If you focus on good practices, people will invent more good practices.

By emphasizing good practices, and even ritualizing them, you also make it possible to free up people's mental power so they have more time for the more complex and uncertain aspects of their work. For example, quality checklists often have beneficial effects for creative workers, not only because they help to keep the quality of products and services high, but also because they enable workers to think of more interesting problems to solve and experiments to run.[11]

It seems evident to me that we should emphasize the good behaviors, not the bad ones. We should celebrate good practices, not punish mistakes.

Am I allowed to offer people
some criticism?

Yes, you are! Constructive criticism can be quite useful (see Chapter 7); though, research has shown that negative feedback is more effective for experts than for novices.[12] It's OK to let novices know when they made a mistake, but their performance will increase much faster when you focus on their good behaviors. It appears that experts will usually have more appreciation for knowing where they went wrong, but they welcome a pat on the back every now and then as well.

Two Questions

We've now seen that there are two possible reasons for celebrations. We can celebrate when we have *learned* something, regardless of whether the outcome was a success or a failure, and we can celebrate when we repeat *good practices*, probably resulting in a predictably good outcome. I call the accompanying illustration a **celebration grid**. 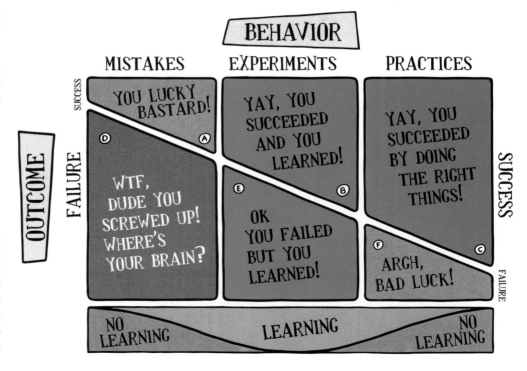 In this diagram, the areas of potential celebrations are colored green (regions B, C and E). This area is called the *celebration zone*.

As a great management exercise, you can help people to focus on the proper areas in the celebration grid by asking them these two "yay!" questions:

1. What did we do well (by following practices)?

2. What did we learn (by running experiments)?

Instead of questioning things that went wrong, it's often better to ask what worked well.[13] This emphasizes that you want to share good recipes, not mistakes. It's OK for people to discuss practices that are already widely known. Reinforcing good recipes makes it more likely that others will apply them, too (region C). Even when, despite

people's best efforts, the outcome of a good practice was a failure, you may still consider celebrating that at least they did their best (region F).

The second question is about the tests and experiments that people performed where they couldn't easily predict the outcome. It is important that both successes and failures are discussed in equal measure because, while it is true that you can learn much from failure, it's also true that you learn a lot from success. That's why your attention should be divided equally between both (regions B and E).

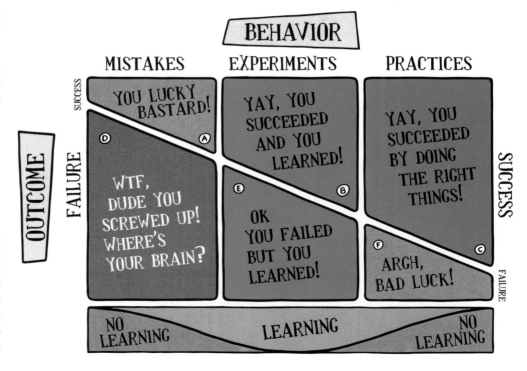

The two questions are both reasons to celebrate. You celebrate to reinforce good behaviors, and you celebrate to reinforce learning. Both are necessary when your aim is to motivate your team.

When you have regular meetings with colleagues, such as one-on-ones, stand-up meetings, retrospectives, or weekly Skype calls, I suggest you make a habit of starting with these two "yay!" questions.

Starting conversations with these questions has several benefits. First, it gives people permission to brag a little about their good work and what they learned. This helps them feel good about themselves. By emphasizing positive things, the atmosphere will improve, and people will feel more at ease so they can talk about some of their failures and mistakes later on.

Second, it motivates people to be mindful about the good recipes they applied and the things they learned, so they have something to share in the next conversation. Everyone should understand that their job is not just to reduce mistakes and failures. It's also to learn good practices and share them with their colleagues.

Actually,
this all sounds quite familiar!

Indeed, the same questions exist in other contexts too. For example, change management experts know that one of the first questions to ask in any change program is, "Where are things going well?" closely followed by "How do we get feedback?"[14] They are very similar questions, but in a different format. Another example is the *perfection game*, a useful feedback technique for trainers and facilitators. It asks people "how well do you like what we did?" followed by "if it's not perfect, how can we do even better?"[15,16] Again, they are two similar questions but with a slightly different angle.

Celebrate Work

Any answers to these two questions could be a trigger for a celebration. 🌳 Has the new employee correctly inserted the *foobar into the goobase?* Celebrate! Did a team member's daring experiment result in a great insight? Yay! Applaud the one who valiantly helped a customer with an important software workaround that saved data, even though it regrettably got 50 other customers disconnected. Perhaps you even want to ring the bell for the person who stupidly deleted all the invoices because it enabled the network administrators to improve their backup procedures.

In some environments, when you start asking these two questions, positive events are harder to find than a Cobol programmer participating in a Miss Universe contest. Maybe that's because there isn't that much good news to share in the first place, or maybe it's because people don't consider their good behaviors and learning outcomes to be worth celebrating. I suggest you don't take what people do for granted. Make every small step worth mentioning.

> Don't take what people do for granted.
>
> Make every small step worth mentioning.

When you celebrate things, keep the following suggestions in mind:

1. **Celebrate frequently.** Every day can be a day to ask these two questions. Every day can be a reason to celebrate. Don't just drool all over the big achievements. Pay attention to the small things too. When everyone is on time for a meeting, celebrate! When the CEO published her first blog post, "Yay!" When Juanita didn't swear for a whole week, "Woohoo!"

2. **Celebrate noticeably.** Make sure celebrations are visible (or loud), so that everyone can see (or hear) what is being celebrated and why. Turn your celebrations into information radiators. With a bit of luck, other parts of the organization will follow your good example. It is hard not to go with the flow when a good vibe washes all over you.

3. **Celebrate remarkably.** Target multiple senses with your celebrations. Be remarkable by introducing your own unique rituals. You can ring a bell, throw confetti, launch balloons, share chocolates, or flash some disco lights and play a song by the Village People. By turning celebrations into little rituals, they will become part of the organizational culture.

When I wrote the first draft of this chapter, I scheduled a visit to my former employer's office. The bell was still there. I was glad to learn they had rung it just a week earlier to celebrate an important product release and the five-year anniversaries of several employees who, unlike me, did *not* leave the company.

From done to celebrate

"We have a kanban board that visualizes our workflow, and periodically our tasks move from *In Work* to *Done*. Sometimes we celebrate getting tasks to Done with a "hurray" and then we move the sticky notes to a big Done area on the whiteboard. But now I am thinking I can draw your celebration grid on the whiteboard in the Done area. When stickies move to Done, we put them into the appropriate region of the celebration grid and let learning and celebration commence."

Geoffrey Lowney, *United States*

Better retrospectives

"I thought that it might be a great idea to use the celebration grid as a framework for organizing team retrospectives. So, I tried it out with a scrum team with which I had been working by drawing the diagram on a whiteboard and discussing the concept of how most learning occurs through experiments. I suggested that we could use the diagram as a way to structure the retrospective to get us in a mode of thinking about what we are actually learning. The team agreed that it looked like a promising approach.

I asked the team to take 10 minutes to write on sticky notes the mistakes, experiments, and good practices they had identified. When time was up, the team members placed the stickies on the grid in the appropriate locations, and we had a conversation on our findings and new ideas. During the team conversation, we identified additional experiments to put on the board, and the team committed to several process improvements.

The retrospective went extremely well. The feedback from the team was very positive. Every person thought it was the best retrospective that they had attended. For me, it was by far the best that I had facilitated. We think the celebration grid provided a great visual framework, and the concepts of experimenting, learning, and celebrating gave real direction, meaning, and purpose to the retrospective."

Robie Wood, *United States*

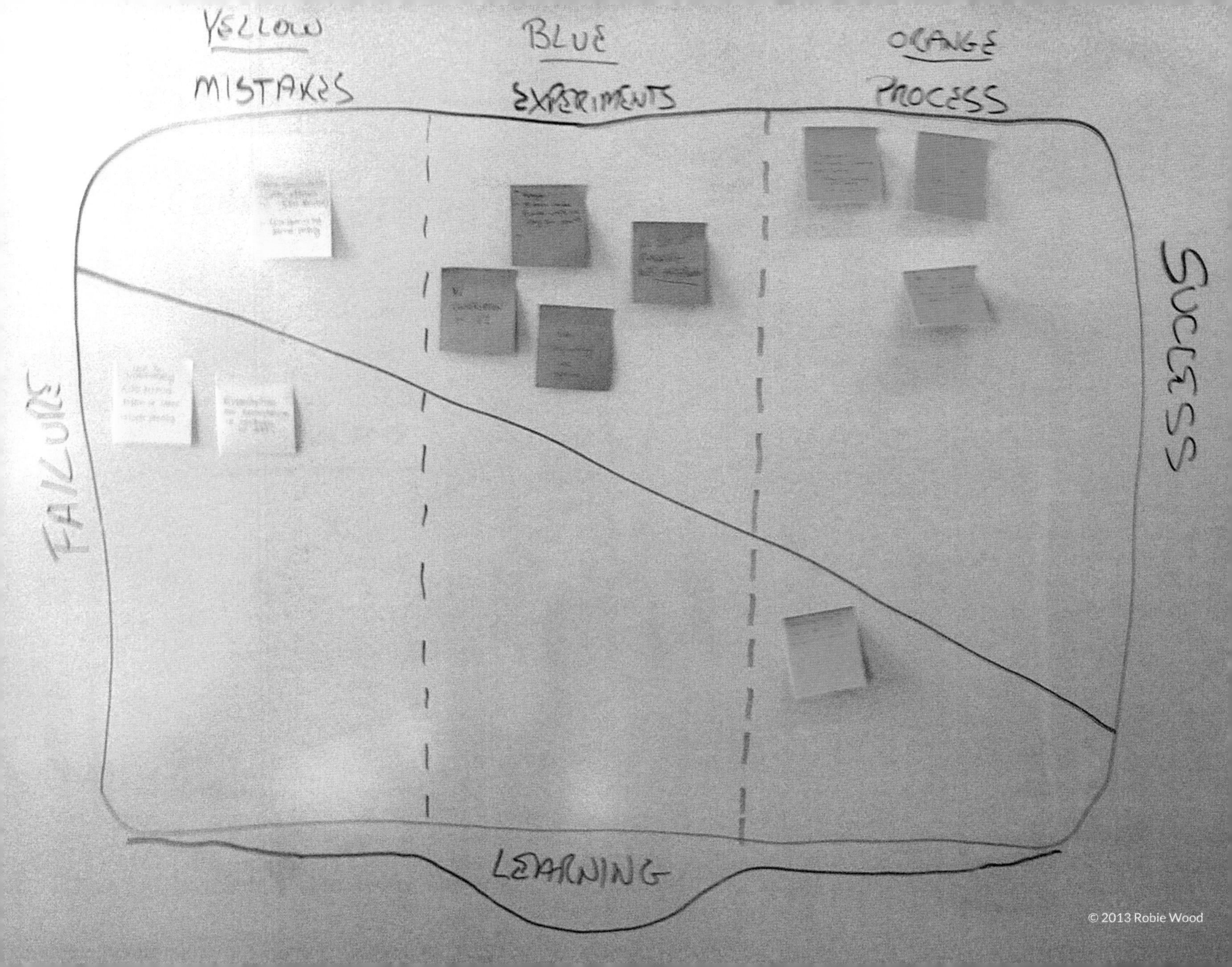

YELLOW
MISTAKES

BLUE
EXPERIMENTS

ORANGE
PROCESS

FAILURE

SUCCESS

LEARNING

© 2013 Robie Wood

How to Get Started

Try this when you want to get started celebrating things:

1. Draw the celebration grid on a whiteboard 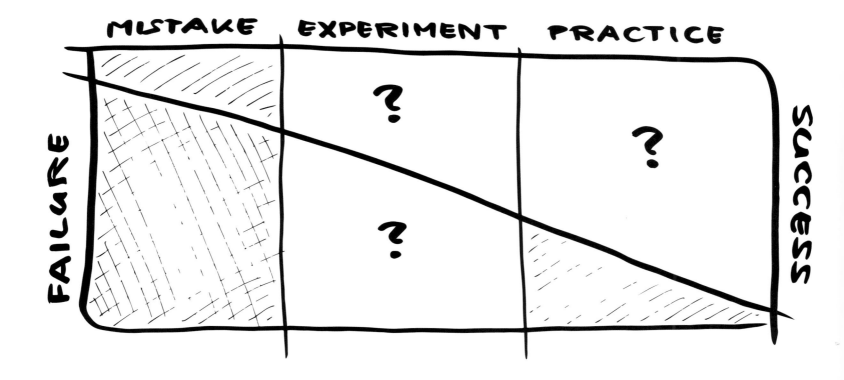 and discuss it.

2. For each of the regions, ask people for a few concrete examples so that you might learn from all mistakes, experiments, and practices, no matter whether you failed or succeeded.

3. At the start or at the end of your meetings, try asking the two questions, "What did we do well?" and "What did we learn?"

4. Decide how you're going to celebrate what you learned and what you practiced in a way that is noticeable, remarkable, and fun.

Tips and Variations

Before you use the celebration grid with a group of people, explain the difference between mistakes (behavior) and failures (outcome). In ordinary language, they are often confused.

Draw a celebration grid on a whiteboard or flip chart so that an entire team can contribute and share learnings.

Get people to interact by handing out sticky notes and getting them to write things on the grid, instead of doing it all yourself.

Try asking the two questions, "What did we learn?" and "What did we do well?" in different ways. For example, "What should we try?" and "What should we repeat?"

You can draw a funnel above the celebration grid to indicate an area where new-experiments-to-try can be placed.

I found that the celebration grid is particularly powerful in change programs. It shows that the hierarchy can support industry best practices while the network will try and experiment.

I always use the celebration grid at the end of a workshop day. It's great to have people stand around a whiteboard and reflect on what they've learned. They love that.

The grid is a reflection tool. But what about using it as a forecast tool? What will you have learned in one week, one month, or one year from your mistakes and practices?

With a remote team, a loud bell obviously won't work. Instead, try a special channel on your communications platform or something that generates a notification for a whole group.

We had to find another way to announce celebrations because, where I come from, people associated a bell too much with school grounds. :-)

Many announcements for celebrations should come from management. And not only for customer sales and product launches. Learning from failure can be celebrated, too!

Find specific tools and more ideas at m30.me/yay-questions and m30.me/celebration-grids.

conclusion

Never Stop Experimenting

> I feel very strongly
> that change is good
> because it stirs up
> the system.
>
> **Ann Richards,**
> **American politician (1933–2006)**

I have collected ideas from many sources and offered them as concrete practices. But copying games and exercises is not enough to change organizations. You must adapt practices to your needs and keep in mind the principles of engaging people, improving the system, and delighting all clients.

We've reached the end of the book, and this makes me feel both happy and sad. I feel happy because you wouldn't believe the amount of work it takes to produce a book like this. It's not just the effort of jamming a hundred thousand words into a text editor. The main challenge is putting them in a sensible order! And then there's the research (fun!), the illustrations (I make them all myself), the formatting (delegated with pleasure), the marketing (*never* delegate this!), and the reviewing, rereading, rewriting, restyling, redrawing, redacting, referring, recycling, and (thank heavens!) also some reclining and rejoicing. And the e-mails. My God, the e-mails! I could bury a pair of horses, with carriage, under the amount of e-mails I get each day. But, to be honest, it's the e-mails that keep me going. The encouragement from readers always makes me happy. However, reaching the end of a big project delights me even more! As I wrote long ago on my blog, I can only enjoy my work when I know it will come to an end.[1]

The end of this book also makes me feel sad because there's still so much I want to discuss with you! We didn't cover collaborative hiring, A3 problem solving, modern recruiting, conflict resolution, competence grids, and many other topics. I haven't told you that story of the boss who woke up in a meeting room with a binder full of performance appraisals wedged in his trousers.

In any case, what I hope I have achieved with the chapters I *did* write is that you believe, as I do, that *everyone* is responsible for management. You shouldn't wait for full-time managers to innovate the way you organize your work. Good management practices are about engaging the workers, improving the system, and delighting the stakeholders. Anyone can do that. Anyone can manage for more happiness in the workplace.

> **The work of managing can be done by just about anyone if they have the right information, incentives, tools, and accountabilities.**
>
> Gary Hamel, *What Matters Now*[2]

The Idea Farmer

Almost everything in this book emerged because I read a lot of books, blogs, websites, and magazines. (And I travel a lot.) I read because I love collecting other people's good ideas. As I often say, "steal and tweak" is the best recipe for innovation. Everything I say is stolen and tweaked, even the concept of "steal and tweak" itself.

If you aim to reach as high as possible, don't limit yourself to the giants. Find the small ones who are standing on their shoulders!

In my search for good ideas, you may have noticed that I don't limit myself to reading the timeless classics of famous gurus. I also refer to many lesser-known books and articles that only a few people have read. The thinking behind this approach is that if you aim to reach as high as possible, don't limit yourself to the giants. Find the small ones who are standing on their shoulders!

I nurture all the big and small ideas that I find. I water them with my attention, and I feed them with my thoughts. After a bit of time and energy, the ideas often start sprouting offspring. 🌳 I allow them to mix and mingle with each other; I let them connect, compete, cooperate, and copulate in the weirdest ways. Sometimes they make me blush. But the offspring are worth the trouble. I care for these new ideas, and I try to make them healthy and strong.

Stories of success and failure consistently exaggerate the impact of leadership style and management practices on firm outcomes, and thus their message is rarely useful.

Daniel Kahneman, *Thinking, Fast and Slow* [3]

I'm an **idea farmer**. I grow new ideas from old ones. When the new ideas are fully grown, I sell them. Or when they're still young and small, I often just give them away for free because that helps them to become better and more experienced.

You've almost finished reading a book full of ideas about concrete management practices that people can implement next Monday morning—not only managers, but *everyone* who is concerned about the management of an organization. Management is too important to leave to the managers! However, just copying ideas and practices from other sources is not enough to change an organization.

Never forget that better *principles*,

not better *practices*,

are what organizations really need.

Never forget that better *principles*, not better *practices*, are what organizations really need. It is far too easy for organizations to let newly adopted good practices evolve into bad principles![4] Most workers, however, don't know how to pursue abstract principles without concrete practices. Creative workers usually appreciate actionable advice. People tell me that they want to experiment with delegation boards, moving motivators, feedback wraps, merit money, and much more. With this book, I have tried to give you exactly that—much more. But these happier practices are just the start. Your goal should not be to merely implement the practices I gave you because this is unlikely to change any outcomes. Your goal is to teach the organization the new principles.

> The world is too complex to give you merely a list of practices to follow. What managers in the twenty-first century need most is insight so that they can develop their own prescriptions for their own particular needs.

Daniel Mintzberg, *Managers, Not MBAs*[5]

But . . . We're Different!

Almost every time I'm in another country (did I tell you I travel a lot?), people ask me, "Is management different elsewhere?"

"Are better management practices more difficult in China?"

"Are problems in eastern Europe different from those in the West?"

"Is it easier to be agile in Scandinavia than in the United States?"

"How does business culture in *Holland* compare with *the Netherlands*?"

My answer is always, "Yes, things are a bit different." But this difference is a lot less than people seem to expect. No matter where I go, people have the same problems with management and leadership; they notice the same challenges with self-organizing teams; and they report the same findings about business transformation and organizational culture. Certainly, some (generalized) cultural differences between countries are real. The Germans are straightforward and the French are sensitive. The British are polite and the Dutch are blunt. But you'd be an idiot—remember, I'm Dutch—to see this as an obstacle.

Business culture trumps geographical culture—always. In my experience as a manager, I noticed that the differences between developers in the Netherlands and developers in Ukraine were insignificant when compared to the differences between *developers* in the Netherlands and *account managers* in the Netherlands. Likewise, the cultural differences between our two offices in the Netherlands and Ukraine were nothing when compared to the differences between our Web development company and . . . oh, let's say an investment bank, a beer manufacturer, or, God help us, a government institute *in our*

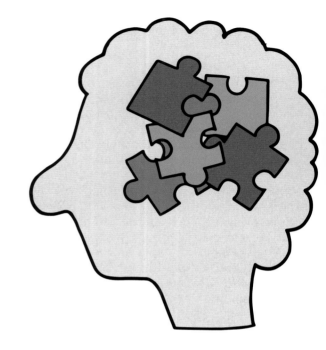

own country! I've noticed, again and again, that cultural differences between geographical areas pale in comparison to the cultural differences between industries, job types, and companies.

Don't get me wrong. I don't mean that we can safely ignore regional cultures. I just mean that, when people are always focusing on the differences between countries, they tend to overlook the much richer diversity in their own backyard. They also overlook the many ways in which different workplaces around the world are actually quite similar. Perhaps we should stop focusing on how people in other countries are different. We can solve more problems 👤 when we realize how much we are actually the same, and how much we can learn from what others are doing on the other side of the world.

But... It Doesn't Work!

Be aware that "learning what others are doing" is not the same as "doing exactly what others are doing." Say that a cook uses a recipe found online, decides to follow it to the letter, and the apple pie doesn't come out as expected. Did the recipe "fail"? What if the cook says, "Apple pies don't work around here. We tried. Nobody liked them." Would that make sense?

You may remember the story of my horse ride in the Andean mountains of Chile, which I shared with you in Chapter 3. The ride started with a four-hour trip. It had been raining all day, and everything was wet, and I had scraped my leg against a rock, and we were tired and cold and grumpy, and my horse was trying to bite the other horses, and basically, everyone in the group was feeling miserable, horses included. That is, until we arrived at our destination, a cabin deep in the forest. The place was lovely, warm, and cozy. And Jane, the American tourist who had arrived a day earlier, had baked an apple pie for everyone. It was deeeeeeliciousss. Jane felt a bit unsure because she had to adapt her recipe due to not having some of her favorite ingredients, having a strange kind of apple to work with, and having to use a simple wood oven that didn't have CoolTouch, FanGrill, or PyroTech features. But she had adapted remarkably well. Her apple pie was the best thing that could have happened to us after four hours of Andean suffering.

> **Great workplaces become great due to their own unique approach. Assuming that there is "one best way" can slip you into an external locus of control pretty quickly.**
>
> Jennifer Robin and Michael Burchell, *No Excuses*[6]

A recipe is just a sequence of suggestions, nothing more. A cook cannot say, "The recipe doesn't work," because the recipe doesn't *do* anything. The one who does all the work is *the cook*. If you don't get what you hoped for, my guess is that you may be inexperienced in the current environment and need some time to learn how to *adapt* the recipe. Maybe you didn't compensate for the bigger-than-average eggs that you used, or the hotter-than-intended oven, or the different brand of flour, or the bland taste of the cheap spices you purchased in the convenience store, or the various culinary preferences of your guests. "The recipe doesn't work" is shorthand for "I haven't yet worked out how to adapt the instructions to local circumstances and *make* a version of the recipe that works."

It's the same for any other useful practice, whether it's a recipe for cooking, a management practice, or a workout exercise. *Of course*, things often don't work exactly as prescribed somewhere else in the world. You have to make an effort to *make* things work. Be like Jane, work with what you have, and learn to be great. Apply the practices in your own unique way.

Management Habits

This book is full of suggestions for happier management, and I'm sure it's just the tip of the iceberg. Many other people have great ideas for concrete practices that can help you to motivate any team. In fact, there is no shortage of ideas. There is a shortage of commitment to making them happen.

> ## There is no shortage of ideas.
> ## There is a shortage of commitment
> ## to making them happen.

The world is too complex to merely give you a list of practices to follow. This is why I started this book describing the principles of Management 3.0. Just giving people a few principles, however, is not enough to improve behaviors. Most people may understand principles intellectually by hearing about them, but they only truly grasp their significance by experiencing them. It's the experience that follows from adopting good practices.

Now it's up to you!

It's your turn to make things happen by implementing practices and experiencing principles. With some practices, this may involve convincing a manager to make time, space, or money available for your experiments. Convincing managers of the benefits of new ideas is best done by delivering on commitment in order to create trust, always trying to solve your manager's problem first, and experimenting with new ideas in safe-to-fail environments.[7]

With other games, you don't need anyone's cooperation and you can just start right away. Usually, the main challenge here is to keep exercising regularly. The benefits of new practices may take a while to reveal themselves. Your efforts should focus on finding the right triggers that make it easy to initiate good behaviors, and finding short feedback loops that reward you and enable you to turn the practices into habits.[8]

For all tools presented here, I can say they have already proved their benefits for other businesses, but you must try them for yourself and make them your own.

> Trying to copy or reproduce another company's tools, techniques, or principles does little to change an organization's culture, its way of doing things. For example, how do you get people to actually live principles? On the other hand, focusing on developing daily behavior patterns is a leverage point because, as the field of psychology shows us, with practice, behavior patterns are changeable, learnable, and reproducible.
>
> Mike Rother, *Toyota Kata*[9]

A project wizard

"If I have to say one thing about your work, it is complexity theory and systems thinking that I have been able to use the most. Knowing that it is all about how the entire system acts on individuals, and how individuals act on the entire system, has made me more confident and systematic as a project manager and as a change manager.

I know that what I need to do is to locally construct just enough boundaries and feedback mechanisms to get going and improve from there. My managers are impressed and I enjoy my work. An identity as 'the project wizard' has stayed with me."

Johan Dahlbäck, *Sweden*

I Love Management

I remember well that I hated management many years ago. I hated checking whether people had done what I told them to do. I hated doing performance appraisals. I hated negotiating individual salaries and bonuses. I hated aligning teams with top management's business-strategy-of-the-week. And I hated wearing a suit and tie while all the nice people were wearing jeans and sweaters.

It took me a while to understand why, but now I know.

It was *bad* management I hated.

It's different now. These days I love giving direction to the Management 3.0 licensing program.  I love discovering the intrinsic motivation of people, inspiring them with storytelling, and discussing constraints with self-organizing teams and facilitators. I love developing courseware and measuring my progress when writing or speaking. I love being one of the founders of both the Agile Lean Europe network and the Stoos movement, and I love developing and nurturing our Happy Melly business. Oh, and I love wearing jeans and sweaters.

Now it's easy to understand why.

I love *good* management, and it seems I'm one of the few people in the world who actually loves his job.

Life is too short to spend in jobs we don't love

"I was in the middle of designing a complex 360-degree evaluation system when I heard about Management 3.0 for the first time. One of my friends told me about a course in Turkey and I decided to take this opportunity. After the course, I returned to work with several ideas, including the merit money practice. It was a much simpler method than the system I originally had in mind. We started it with 20 people in three teams. Nobody argued about its fairness. It was entertaining; it caused many fun discussions among teams; and it gave me a simple metric that was not based on my own subjective opinion.

There was also a little book in my bag called *How to Change the World* that I had received at the course in Turkey. The book started with a simple argument: 'If you are not happy with your job, you have three options: Ignore it, quit your job, or try to change the organization.' It was like hitting a switch and turning on the light! I did my best to convince my boss and the board about the problems people had with their management style. I was sure that something would change: Either management would improve or I would leave.

And indeed, things changed! I left the company along with several people from our teams. We created our own workplace, in the way we wanted, and without burning somebody else's money. ;-) Now we are not employees but initiators. We realized that life is too short to spend our lives in a workplace we don't love."

Alix Moghadam, *Iran*

When I started writing this final chapter of my book, I received the following message from a reader:

> **I find your work not just interesting, but also important, helping people and organizations to cope with the challenges at work every day. I also find that it is very important in efforts to innovate the way we are organizing work today.**

Lazar Todorov, *a kind reader from Germany*

I often maintain a healthy skeptical attitude toward any claims and praise in the e-mails I receive, but for messages like these, I gladly make an exception. ;-)

Hopefully, I have given you enough inspiration to motivate any team and manage the workplace for more happiness. With this book, you now have serious games to help improve organizational culture, simple practices that increase employee engagement, creative stories that inspire teamwork and collaboration, new ways to achieve team accountability and responsibility, concrete steps toward more creativity and innovation, easy exercises to make the business more agile, and modern tools that enable people to enjoy a happy Monday.

Now you can change your organization's culture, step-by-step, by engaging your people, improving your work, and delighting your clients. Manage for happiness and motivate any team.

Have fun!

M3.0

WEB

GieM
MARTA
10

Notes

Introduction

1. Steve Tobak, "Want to Be Successful? Learn How to Manage," *Entrepreneur*, February 19, 2014, http://bit.ly/1m3BFmF.

2. Steve Denning, "Leadership in the Three-Speed Economy," *Forbes*, May 1, 2013, http://onforb.es/1cixHX8.

3. Jurgen Appelo, "Are You a Creative Networker?" noop.nl, January 2, 2014, http://bit.ly/QaDnsp.

4. Josh Bersin, "Why Companies Fail to Engage Today's Workforce: The Overwhelmed Employee," *Forbes*, March 15, 2013, http://onforb.es/1dJMuVW.

5. Mark C. Crowley, "The Sharp Drop-off in Worker Happiness—And What Your Company Can Do About It," *FastCompany*, April 20, 2012, http://bit.ly/1hu5igi.

6. Ryan Scott, "The 7 Ways You're Not Engaging Your Employees," *Forbes*, February 6, 2014, http://onforb.es/1fR54iC.

7. University of Warwick, "We Work Harder When We Are Happy, New Study Shows," *ScienceDaily*, March 20, 2014, http://bit.ly/OV0HZP.

8. Sergei Netessine and Valery Yakubovich, "Get Employees to Compete Against Each Other," *Harvard Business Review* (June 1, 2012), http://bit.ly/1dYsGBF.

9. Matthew Swyers, "What Your Employees Do When You're on Vacation," *Inc.*, June 1, 2012, http://bit.ly/Ni0Zcs.

10. Riva Richmond, "3 Tips for Legally and Ethically Monitoring Employees Online," *Entrepreneur*, May 31, 2012, http://bit.ly/1nTl30o.

11. Lisa Haneberg, "How to Have Great One-on-Ones," *Management Craft* (April 8, 2005), http://bit.ly/1hze8sy

12. Jack Zenger and Joseph Folkman, "Getting 360 Degree Reviews Right," *Harvard Business Review*, September 7, 2012, http://bit.ly/ONhWgs.

13. Robert S. Kaplan and David P. Norton, "Using the Balanced Scorecard as a Strategic Management System," *Harvard Business Review*, July 2007, http://bit.ly/1d6ZpEi.

14. Danny Miller and Jon Hartwick, "Spotting Management Fads," *Harvard Business Review*, October 2002, http://bit.ly/1bVddDm.

15. Stafford Beer, *Designing Freedom* (Concord: House of Anansi Press, 1993).

16. "7th Annual State of Agile Development Survey," VersionOne (2013), https://www.versionone.com/pdf/7th-Annual-State-of-Agile-Development-Survey.pdf.

17. Peter F. Drucker and Joseph A. Maciariello, *Management* rev. ed. (New York: Collins, 2008), loc:1038

18. Gary Hamel, "First, Let's Fire All the Managers," *Harvard Business Review*, December 2011, http://bit.ly/1cEshFS.

19. "The #NoManager Organization and the Manager of One," Happy Melly (blog), September 23, 2013, http://bit.ly/1h4MKmJ.

20. Camille Sweeney and Josh Gosfield, "No Managers Required: How Zappos Ditched the Old Corporate Structure for Something New," *FastCompany*, January 6, 2014, http://bit.ly/1cEsvNe.

Chapter 1: Kudo Boxes and Kudo Cards

1. Nic Fleming, "The Bonus Myth: How Paying for Results Can Backfire," *New Scientist*, April 12, 2011, http://bit.ly/fK7uXJ.

2. Mark Buchanan, "Banking Cheats Will Always Prosper," *New Scientist*, March 23, 2011, http://bit.ly/fbEwIT.

3. Fleming, "The Bonus Myth."

4. Drucker, *Management*, 42.

5. Alfie Kohn, *Punished by Rewards: The Trouble with Gold Stars, Incentive Plans, A's, Praise, and Other Bribes* (Boston: Houghton Mifflin Co., 1993).

6. Kohn, *Punished by Rewards*, 320.

7. Fleming, "The Bonus Myth."

8. Kerry Patterson, Joseph Grenny, David Maxfield, Ron McMillan, and Al Switzler, *Influencer: The Power to Change Anything* (New York: McGraw-Hill, 2008), 194.

9. Daniel Pink, *Drive: The Surprising Truth about What Motivates Us* (New York: Riverhead Books, 2009), loc:524

10. Fleming, "The Bonus Myth."

11. Mitch McCrimmon, "Celebrating Success at Work," Suite, April 9, 2008, http://bit.ly/N1XLrP.

12. Amy Alberg, "How to Celebrate Success Throughout Your Projects," Making Things Happen (blog), May 21, 2008, http://bit.ly/I94FWZ.

13. Fleming, "The Bonus Myth."

14. Pink, *Drive*, loc:2523.

15. Paul Klipp, "How and Why You Should Build a Secret Spy Network to Monitor Employee Behavior," Agile Activist (blog), November 20, 2012, http://bit.ly/1hw15Fx.

16. Eric Markowitz, "3 Weird, Game-Changing Ways to Make Employees Happy," *Inc.* (May 11, 2012), http://bit.ly/Jqa1fj.

17. Mig Pascual, "Four Peer-to-Peer Ways Zappos Employees Reward Each Other," Zappos Insights, September 10, 2012, http://bit.ly/1g3kdJM.

Chapter 2: Personal Maps

1. Alistair Cockburn, *Agile Software Development: The Cooperative Game*, 2nd ed. (Upper Saddle River: Addison-Wesley, 2007).

2. Patterson et al., *Influencer*, loc:3904.

3. Jurgen Appelo, *Management 3.0: Leading Agile Developers, Developing Agile Leaders* (Upper Saddle River: Addison-Wesley, 2011), loc:5155.

4. Daniel Markovitz, "Go to Where the Actual Work Is Being Done," *Harvard Business Review*, March 31, 2014, http://bit.ly/1exOh60.

5. Mark Rosenthal, "Walking the Gemba," The Lean Thinker (blog), January 28, 2009, http://bit.ly/h49DCA.

6. Mike Rother, *Toyota Kata: Managing People for Improvement, Adaptiveness, and Superior Results* (New York: McGraw Hill, 2010), loc:1995.

7. Walter Isaacson, "The Real Leadership Lessons of Steve Jobs," *Harvard Business Review* (April 2012), http://bit.ly/GBedqe.

8. Mike Cohn, *Succeeding with Agile: Software Development Using Scrum* (Upper Saddle River: Addison-Wesley, 2010), 370.

9. Alex Pentland, "The New Science of Building Great Teams," *Harvard Business Review*, April 2012, http://bit.ly/GAC3lk.

10. Tim Harford, *Adapt: Why Success Always Starts with Failure* (New York: Farrar, Straus and Giroux, 2011), loc:3583.

11. Richard Branson, *Like a Virgin: Secrets They Won't Teach You at Business School* (London: Virgin, 2012).

12. Farhad Manjoo, "Marissa Mayer Has Made a Terrible Mistake," *Slate*, February 26, 2013, http://slate.me/17axzlt.

13. Jessica Stillman, "Remote Work Boosts Productivity? Only for Creative Tasks, Says New Research," Gigaom, April 30, 2012, http://bit.ly/17ax0rY.

14. Richard Branson, "Give People the Freedom of Where to Work" Virgin, (May 2013), http://bit.ly/11T0Bni.

15. Sam Grier, "The Gemba Walk—A Tool for IT Management and Leadership," IT Managers Inbox, http://bit.ly/15EZt1.

16. Appelo, *Management 3.0*, loc:2309.

17. "Feedback for Real," *Gallup Business Journal*, March 15, 2001, http://bit.ly/10dWi2b.

18. Appelo, *Management 3.0*, loc:2191.

Chapter 3: Delegation Boards and Delegation Poker

1. Patrick Hoverstadt, *The Fractal Organization: Creating Sustainable Organizations with the Viable System Model* (Hoboken: John Wiley & Sons, 2008). loc:517.

2. Appelo, *Management 3.0*, 108.

3. John Seddon, *Freedom from Command & Control: Rethinking Management for Lean Service* (New York: Productivity Press, 2005), 193.

4. John P. Kotter, *Leading Change* (Boston: Harvard Business School Press, 1996), loc:1775.

5. Kenneth W. Thomas, *Intrinsic Motivation at Work: What Really Drives Employee Engagement* (San Francisco: Berrett-Koehler Publishers, 2009).

6. Roger Lewin and Birute Regine, *Weaving Complexity and Business: Engaging the Soul at Work* (New York: Texere, 2001).

7. D. E. Bowen and E. E. Lawler, "Empowering Service Employees," *Sloan Management Review*, Summer 1995, 73–84.

8. S. Caudron, "Create an Empowering Environment," *Personnel Journal* 74:9 (1995), 28–36.

9. Russell L. Ackoff, *Re-creating the Corporation: A Design of Organizations for the 21st Century* (New York: Oxford University Press, 1999), 180.

10. Ackoff, *Re-creating the Corporation*, 287.

11. Stephanie Vozza, "How to Set Healthy Boundaries in Your Workplace," *Entrepreneur*, December 30, 2013, http://bit.ly/1l9NgRs.

12. Donald G. Reinertsen, *Managing the Design Factory: A Product Developer's Toolkit* (New York: Free Press, 1997), 107.

13. Appelo, *Management 3.0*, loc:2884.

14. Jurgen Appelo, "Delegation Poker (Free Exercise)," noop.nl, updated May 6, 2013, http://bit.ly/16gsgl5.

Chapter 4: Value Stories and Culture Books

1. Hamel, *What Matters Now*, loc:340.

2. James M. Kouzes and Barry Z. Posner, *The Leadership Challenge: How to Make Extraordinary Things Happen in Organizations* (San Francisco: Jossey-Bass, 2012), loc:1173.

3. Ronald N. Ashkenas, *Simply Effective: How to Cut Through Complexity in Your Organization and Get Things Done* (Boston: Harvard Business Press, 2010), loc:242.

4. Rosabeth Moss Kanter, "How Great Companies Think Differently," *Harvard Business Review*, November 2011, http://bit.ly/WIYuNI.

5. Appelo, *Management 3.0* loc:2256.

6. Geert Hofstede, Gert Jan Hofstede and Michael Minkov, *Cultures and Organizations: Software of the Mind*, 3rd ed. (New York: McGraw-Hill, 2010).

7. Kouzes and Posner, *Leadership Challenge*, loc:1207.

8. Appelo, *Management 3.0*, loc:2241.

9. Torben Rick, "Value Statements Can Be Real Business Drivers," *Meliorate*, March 7, 2014, http://bit.ly/1pDX3Rq.

10. Teresa Amabile, Colin M. Fisher, and Julianna Pillemer, "IDEO's Culture of Helping," *Harvard Business Review*, January–February 2014, http://bit.ly/1juZ2po.

11. Tim Brown, "The Little Book of IDEO," SlideShare, December 18, 2013, http://slidesha.re/1i9KFE5.

12. *Valve Handbook for New Employees*, 1st. ed. (Valve Press, March 2012), http://bit.ly/1muZHHj.

13. Susan M. Heathfield, "20 Ways Zappos Reinforces Its Company Culture," About.com, updated August 9, 2015, http://abt.cm/1jTjTFA.

14. "The Zappos Family Culture Book," Zappos Insights, 2012, http://bit.ly/1jTB0Hz.

15. Jennifer Robin and Michael Burchell, *No Excuses: How You Can Turn Any Workplace into a Great One* (San Francisco: Jossey-Bass, 2013), 1120.

16. Drake Baer, "Netflix's Major HR Innovation: Treating Humans Like People," *Fast Company*, March 13, 2014, http://bit.ly/QBLw9y.

17. Reed Hastings, "Netflix Culture: Freedom & Responsibility," SlideShare, August 1, 2009, http://slidesha.re/1s2inSQ.

18. Patty McCord, "How Netflix Reinvented HR," *Harvard Business Review*, January–February 2014, http://bit.ly/1e7yO7o.

19. Peter Senge, *The Fifth Discipline: The Art and Practice of the Learning Organization* (New York: Doubleday/Currency, 2006), loc:6345.

20. Suzanne Lucas, "Culture Comes First. The Rest Is Noise," *Inc.*, December 19, 2013, http://bit.ly/1hYa6Y9.

21. Frédéric Laloux, *Reinventing Organizations: A Guide to Creating Organizations Inspired by the Next Stage in Human Consciousness* (Brussels, Belgium: Nelson Parker, 2014), loc:3368.

Chapter 5: Exploration Days and Internal Crowdfunding

1. Drucker, *Management*, loc:5807.

2. Erin Hayes, "Google's 20 Percent Factor," ABC News, May 12, 2008, http://abcn.ws/Ku53ka.

3. Christopher Mims, "Google's '20% Time,' Which Brought You Gmail and AdSense, Is Now As Good As Dead," Quartz, August 16, 2013, http://bit.ly/1q46QPd.

4. Christopher Mims, "Google Engineers Insist 20% Time Is Not Dead–It's Just Turned Into 120% Time," Quartz, August 16, 2013, http://bit.ly/1dXmI6g.

5. "Danger, If You Read This Story You May Want to Apply at This Company!" Happy Melly (blog), March 12, 2013, http://bit.ly/1jNQWsa.

6. Jurgen Appelo, *How to Change the World: Change Management 3.0* (Rotterdam: Jojo Ventures BV, 2012), 48.

7.   Daniel H. Pink, "How to Deliver Innovation Overnight," DanPink.com, July 5, 2011, http://bit.ly/ipXAE5.

8.   David Zax, "Secrets of Facebook's Legendary Hackathons Revealed," *Fast Company*, November 9, 2012, http://bit.ly/RTPk2H.

9.   Zax, "Secrets of Facebook's Legendary Hackathons Revealed."

10. Dave Brands, "FedEx Day at PAT," Agile Studio, May 7, 2012, http://bit.ly/MQkiXO (no longer available).

11. "ShipIt Day FAQ," Atlassian, January 1, 2013, http://bit.ly/W5O27X.

12. Jon Silvers, "ShipIt Day in the Wild," Atlassian Blogs, November 12, 2010, http://bit.ly/JF5j3d.

13. Christopher Mims, "Google Engineers Insist 20% Time Is Not Dead—It's Just Turned into 120% Time," Quartz, August 16, 2013, http://qz.com/116196/google-engineers-insist-20-time-is-not-dead-its-just-turned-into-120-time.

14. David Burkus, "Why Hierarchy Stifles Creativity" *Psychology Today*, March 23, 2014, http://bit.ly/1gwpJ88.

15. Michael Schrage, "Just How Valuable Is Google's '20% Time'?" *Harvard Business Review*, August 20, 2013, http://bit.ly/1fV4OME.

16. Mims, "20% Time Is Now As Good As Dead."

17. Mims, "20% Time Is Not Dead."

18. Laura Vanderkam, "Why Encouraging Employees to Be Entrepreneurs Can Create an Incredible Place to Work," *Fast Company*, January 16, 2014, http://bit.ly/QOgKKy.

19. Donald G. Reinertsen, *The Principles of Product Development Flow: Second Generation Lean Product Development* (Redondo Beach: Celeritas, 2009).

20. Vanderkam, "Encouraging Employees to Be Entrepreneurs."

21. Hoverstadt, *The Fractal Organization*, loc:161.

22. "Hackathons Aren't Just for Developers," Spotify Developer, February 2, 2012, http://bit.ly/1QVOOQI.

23. Jurgen Appelo, "Innovation Is Not Only in Your Code," noop.nl, February 5, 2014, http://bit.ly/1jf0GuO.

24. William Taylor and Polly G. LaBarre, *Mavericks at Work: Why the Most Original Minds in Business Win* (New York: William Morrow, 2006), loc:3507.

25. Ricardo Semler, *The Seven-Day Weekend: Changing the Way Work Works* (New York: Portfolio, 2004), 133.

Chapter 6: Business Guilds and Corporate Huddles

1.   Sheilagh Ogilvie, "Guilds, Efficiency, and Social Capital: Evidence from German Proto-Industry," CESifo, December 2002, http://bit.ly/Lv8u8I.

2.   Thomas Malone, *The Future of Work: How the New Order of Business Will Shape Your Organization, Your Management Style, and Your Life* (Boston: Harvard Business School Press, 2004), 84.

3.   Craig Brown, "On Community of Practice," Better Projects (blog), March 28, 2012, http://bit.ly/HcQhj7.

4.   Etienne Wenger, *Cultivating Communities of Practice: A Guide to Managing Knowledge* (Boston: Harvard Business School Press, 2002), loc:144.

5.   Gary Hamel, "Moon Shots for Management" *Harvard Business Review*, February 2009, http://bit.ly/UrOjRV.

6.   John Seely Brown, "Complexity and Innovation," in *The Interaction of Complexity and Management*, ed. Michael Lissack (Westport: Quorum Books, 2002).

7.   Wenger, *Cultivating Communities of Practice*, loc:518.

8.   Henrik Kniberg, "Scaling @ Spotify with Tribes, Squads, Chapters & Guilds," Crisp's Blog, November 14, 2012, http://bit.ly/1kzzy95.

9.   Piotr Anioła, "Guilds @ BLStream," BLStream, March 2014. Shared privately.

10. Ronald N. Ashkenas, *The Boundaryless Organization: Breaking the Chains of Organizational Structure* (San Francisco: Jossey-Bass, 2002), 157.

11. Adriana Gardella, "The Verdict on Huddles," *The New York Times*, April 5, 2012, http://nyti.ms/1kdOWwa.

12. *Wenger, Cultivating Communities of Practice*, loc:153.

13. Brian Bozzuto and Dennis Stevens, "Beyond Functional Silos with Communities of Practice," SlideShare, August 18, 2012, http://slidesha.re/1hxsqek.

14. Seth Godin, *Tribes: We Need You to Lead Us* (New York: Portfolio, 2008).

Chapter 7: Feedback Wraps and Unlimited Vacation

1. David G. Javitch, "The Benefits of Flextime," *Entrepreneur*, June 5, 2006, http://bit.ly/18FhwPr.

2. Paul Boag, "The Benefits and Challenges of Remote Working" boagworld (blog), September 17, 2013, http://bit.ly/1h2seSk.

3. James Surowiecki, "Face Time," *The New Yorker*, March 18, 2013, http://nyr.kr/18WkyBp.

4. Amy-Mae Elliott, "4 Important Considerations for Creating a Remote Work Policy," Mashable, September 12, 2011, http://on.mash.to/J9HBfN.

5. Jena McGregor, "Flextime: Honing the Balance," Bloomberg Business, December 10, 2006, http://buswk.co/18Wlg1r.

6. Surowiecki, "Face Time."

7. David Hauser, "What's Wrong with a No-Remote-Work Policy at Yahoo?" davidhauser.com (blog), February 27, 2013, http://bit.ly/18nBP5R.

8. Douglas MacMillan, "To Recruit Techies, Companies Offer Unlimited Vacation," Bloomberg Business, July 19, 2012, http://buswk.co/1iZy1wm.

9. Lotte Bailyn, "Unlimited Vacation Time Is Better in Theory Than in Practice," Quartz, August 27, 2013, http://bit.ly/18DWFJc.

10. Dugald McConnell and Erin McPike, "Unlimited Vacation? Some Workplaces Offer It," CNN, September 2, 2013, http://cnn.it/IHk71C.

11. McConnell and McPike, "Unlimited Vacation?"

12. Bailyn, "Unlimited Vacation Time."

13. Carolyn Gregoire, "Unlimited Vacation Policies Might Be Too Good to Be True," Huffington Post, November 1, 2013, http://huff.to/19jIr3Z.

14. Jena McGregor, "The Catch of Having an Unlimited Vacation Policy," *The Washington Post*, 13 August 13, 2013, http://wapo.st/1dsTNlh.

15. Robert F. Hurley, *The Decision to Trust: How Leaders Create High-Trust Organizations* (San Francisco: Jossey-Bass, 2012), loc:616.

16. Hurley, *The Decision to Trust*, loc:3175.

17. Monique Valcour, "The End of 'Results Only' at Best Buy Is Bad News," *Harvard Business Review*, March 8, 2013, http://bit.ly/18WqGtt.

18. Aubrey Daniels, "Results Only Work Environment? It's a Leadership Problem," Aubrey Daniels' Blog, March 27, 2013, http://bit.ly/1n233HH.

19. Halvor Gregusson, "Creating a Remote Work Policy that Works," Yast (blog), March 28, 2013, http://bit.ly/1bxVMSc.

20. Tom Coens and Mary Jenkins, *Abolishing Performance Appraisals: Why They Backfire and What to Do Instead* (San Francisco: Berrett-Koehler Publishers, 2000), loc:779.

21. Coens and Jenkins, *Abolishing Performance Appraisals*, loc:402.

22. Coens and Jenkins, *Abolishing Performance Appraisals*, loc:457.

23. Gabriella Jozwiak, "Is It Time to Give Up on Performance Appraisals?" *HR Magazine*, October 22, 2012, http://bit.ly/18WsB0Y.

24. Kohn, *Punished by Rewards*, loc:3568.

25. Josh Bersin, "Time to Scrap Performance Appraisals?" *Forbes*, May 6, 2013. http://onforb.es/1f9si1o.

26. Samuel A. Culbert, "Get Rid of the Performance Review!" *The Wall Street Journal*, October 20, 2008, http://on.wsj.com/1bGTSDd.

27. Stephanie Vozza, "10 Reasons to Scrap Year-End Performance Reviews," *Entrepreneur*, December 23, 2013, http://bit.ly/1e80Nco.

28. Ray B. Williams, "Why 'Constructive Feedback' Doesn't Improve Performance," *Psychology Today*, November 26, 2011, http://bit.ly/19jMz3R.

29. Coens and Jenkins, *Abolishing Performance Appraisals*, loc:769.

30. Coens and Jenkins, *Abolishing Performance Appraisals*, loc:72.

31. Bersin, "Time to Scrap Performance Appraisals?"

32. Drake Baer, "Why Jerk Bosses Make People Worse at Their Jobs," *Fast Company*, February 20, 2014, http://bit.ly/R0QA7r.

33. Ron Ashkenas, "Stop Pretending That You Can't Give Candid Feedback," *Harvard Business Review*, February 28, 2014, http://bit.ly/R0RbpM.

34. Ed Batista, "Building a Feedback-Rich Culture," *Harvard Business Review*, December 24, 2014. http://bit.ly/1qgqqK8

35. Alina Tugend, "You've Been Doing a Fantastic Job. Just One Thing . . ." *The New York Times*, April 5, 2013, http://nyti.ms/IHnpSq.

36. Carolyn Kaufman, "Giving Good Constructive Feedback," *Psychology Today*, June 13, 2012, http://bit.ly/18E1CBA.

37. Julius Tarng, "How to Give Constructive Design Feedback over Email," Medium, October 21, 2013, http://bit.ly/1e7Hm2X.

38. Amy Gallo, "Giving a High Performer Productive Feedback," *Harvard Business Review*, December 3, 2009, http://bit.ly/IRablC.

39. Kaufman, "Giving Good Constructive Feedback."

40. Gallo, "Giving a High Performer Productive Feedback."

41. Kaufman, "Giving Good Constructive Feedback."

42. Tarng, "How to Give Constructive Design Feedback over Email."

43. Tugend, "You've Been Doing a Fantastic Job."

44. Bersin, "Time to Scrap Performance Appraisals?"

45. Kaufman, "Giving Good Constructive Feedback."

46. Heidi Grant Halvorson, "Sometimes Negative Feedback Is Best," *Harvard Business Review*, January 28, 2013, http://bit.ly/1e8lh4T.

47. Kaufman, "Giving Good Constructive Feedback."

48. Tugend, "You've Been Doing a Fantastic Job."

49. Williams, "Why 'Constructive Feedback' Doesn't Improve Performance."

50. Grant Halvorson, "Sometimes Negative Feedback Is Best."

51. Bersin, "Time to Scrap Performance Appraisals?"

52. Gregusson, "Creating a Remote Work Policy."

53. Miki Kashtan, "Is Nonviolent Communication Practical?" *Psychology Today*, May 21, 2012, http://bit.ly/18nGswF.

54. Coens and Jenkins, *Abolishing Performance Appraisals*, loc:925.

55. Marshall B. Rosenberg, *Nonviolent Communication: A Language of Life* (Encinitas: PuddleDancer Press, 2003).

Chapter 8: Metrics Ecosystem and Scoreboard Index

1. Sandeep Gautam, "4 Major Goals of Life," *Psychology Today*, February 4, 2014, http://bit.ly/1fdWFSh.

2. Jay Yarow, "This Is the Internal Grading System Google Uses for Its Employees—And You Should Use It Too," *Business Insider*, January 6, 2014, http://read.bi/1hkkNV3.

3. Dean R. Spitzer, *Transforming Performance Measurement: Rethinking the Way We Measure and Drive Organizational Success* (New York: American Management Association, 2007), loc:431.

4. Jamshid Gharajedaghi, *Systems Thinking: Managing Chaos and Complexity: A Platform for Designing Business Architecture*. (Amsterdam: Elsevier, 2006).

5. Gharajedaghi, *Systems Thinking*, 47.

6. Douglas W. Hubbard, *How to Measure Anything: Finding the Value of "Intangibles" in Business* (Hoboken: Wiley, 2010).

7. Drucker, *Management*.

8. Jeffrey Gedmin, "Our Mania for Measuring (and Remeasuring) Well-Being," *Harvard Business Review*, September 2013, http://bit.ly/1iYZzyi.

9. Yarow, "This Is the Internal Grading System Google Uses."

10. W. Edwards Deming, *Out of the Crisis* (Cambridge: Massachusetts Institute of Technology, Center for Advanced Engineering Study, 1986), 121.

11. Hubbard, *How to Measure Anything*, 27.

12. Spitzer, *Transforming Performance Measurement*, loc:784.

13. "Data, Data Everywhere," *The Economist*, February 25, 2010, http://econ.st/1goRsuj.

14. Peter Brownell, "The Most Important New Advanced Soccer Statistics and Why They Matter," Bleacher Report, April 9, 2013, http://bit.ly/1epNTzE.

15. Eric Ries, *The Lean Startup: How Today's Entrepreneurs Use Continuous Innovation to Create Radically Successful Businesses* (New York: Crown Business, 2011), 143.

16. Hoverstadt, *The Fractal Organization*, 102.

17. Ackoff, *Re-Creating the Corporation*, 33.

18. Stephen Denning, *The Leader's Guide to Radical Management: Reinventing the Workplace for the 21st Century* (San Francisco: Jossey-Bass, 2010), loc:1385.

19. Appelo, *Management 3.0*, loc:6604.

20. Spitzer, *Transforming Performance Measurement*, loc:1022.

21. Drucker, *Management*, loc:7160.

22. Drucker, *Management*, loc:6032.

23. Robert D. Austin, *Measuring and Managing Performance in Organizations* (New York: Dorset House Publishing, 1996). loc:1899.

24. Seddon, *Freedom from Command and Control*, 19.

25. Kelly Allan, "3 Deming-Based Alternatives to Management by Objective," Process Excellence Network, April 12, 2012, http://bit.ly/1jwxJww.

26. Hoverstadt, *The Fractal Organization*, 138.

27. Yarow, "This Is the Internal Grading System Google Uses."

28. Michael Schrage, "Team Chemistry Is the New Holy Grail of Performance Analytics," *Harvard Business Review*, March 5, 2014, http://bit.ly/1hJMI5d.

29. Jeffrey K. Liker and Gary L. Convis, *The Toyota Way to Lean Leadership: Achieving and Sustaining Excellence Through Leadership Development* (New York: McGraw-Hill, 2011), loc:4056.

30. Yarow, "This Is the Internal Grading System Google Uses."

31. Spitzer, *Transforming Performance Measurement*, loc:1333.

32. Austin, *Measuring and Managing Performance*, loc:464.

33. G. Lyons, *Social Research and Public Policies* (Hanover: Dartmouth College, The Public Affairs Center, 1975), 35.

34. Liker, *The Toyota Way to Lean Leadership*, loc:592.

35. Drucker, *Management*, loc:6032.

36. Kohn, *Punished by Rewards*, loc:1343.

37. Yarow, "This Is the Internal Grading System Google Uses."

38. Kohn, *Punished by Rewards*, loc:1159.

39. Austin, *Measuring and Managing Performance*, loc:2977.

40. Hoverstadt, *The Fractal Organization*, 109.

41. Spitzer, *Transforming Performance Measurement*, loc:905.

42. Yarow, "This Is the Internal Grading System Google Uses."

43. Liker, *The Toyota Way to Lean Leadership*, loc:3133.

44. Gerald M. Weinberg, *Becoming a Technical Leader: An Organic Problem-Solving Approach* (New York: Dorset House, 1986), loc:659.

45. Patrick Kua, "An Appropriate Use of Metrics" Martin Fowler, February 19, 2013, http://bit.ly/1ooprY6.

46. Robert S. Kaplan and David P. Norton, *The Balanced Scorecard: Translating Strategy into Action* (Boston: Harvard Business Review Press, 1996).

47. Austin, *Measuring and Managing Performance*, loc:750.

48. Mike Rother, *Toyota Kata: Managing People for Improvement, Adaptiveness, and Superior Results* (New York: McGraw Hill, 2010), loc:2428.

49. Spitzer, *Transforming Performance Measurement*, loc:2081.

50. Yarow, "This Is the Internal Grading System Google Uses."

Chapter 9: Merit Money

1. Bjarte Bogsnes, *Implementing Beyond Budgeting: Unlocking the Performance Potential* (Hoboken: John Wiley & Sons, 2009), loc:73.

2. Kohn, *Punished By Rewards*.

3. Pink, *Drive*.

4. Fleming, "The Bonus Myth."

5. Joel Spolsky, "Incentive Pay Considered Harmful," Joel on Software (blog), April 3, 2000, http://bit.ly/11q4Czh.

6. Fleming, "The Bonus Myth."

7. Kohn, *Punished By Rewards*.

8. Pink, *Drive*.

9. Nikolaj Bomann, "Bonus Schemes Should Be Handled with Care," Pointbeing.net, June 27, 2009, http://bit.ly/Roavfl.

10. Jonathan Haidt, *The Happiness Hypothesis: Finding Modern Truth in Ancient Wisdom* (New York: Basic Books, 2006), 67.

11. Dan Ariely, *Predictably Irrational: The Hidden Forces That Shape Our Decisions* (New York: Harper, 2009).

12. E. D. Boyd, "At IGN, Employees Use a 'Viral Pay' System to Determine Each Other's Bonuses," *Fast Company*, December 16, 2011, http://bit.ly/11q83G7.

13. James Surowiecki, *The Wisdom of Crowds: Why the Many Are Smarter Than the Few and How Collective Wisdom Shapes Business, Economies, Societies, and Nations* (New York: Doubleday, 2004).

14. Haidt, *The Happiness Hypothesis*, 66.

15. Daniel Kahneman, *Thinking, Fast and Slow* (New York: Farrar, Straus and Giroux, 2011), 55.

16. Markowitz, "3 Weird, Game-Changing Ways to Make Employees Happy."

17. "Merit Money: A Crazy Idea That Works," Happy Melly, October 7, 2013, http://bit.ly/1eEqph8.

Chapter 10: Moving Motivators

1. Jacob Shriar, "13 Scary Statistics on Employee Engagement," *Digitalist Magazine*, December 1, 2014, http://bit.ly/1Puczzs.

2. John Hollon, "How Important Is Engagement? 87% of Leaders Say a Lack of It Is a Key Issue," *Talent Management and HR*, March 4, 2015, http://bit.ly/1NdBROB.

3. John Roberts, *The Modern Firm: Organizational Design for Performance and Growth* (Oxford, New York: Oxford University Press), 2004.loc:1040.

4. Kohn, *Punished by Rewards*, loc:3528.

5. Jeff Grabmeier, "Intrinsic Motivation Doesn't Exist, Researcher Says," The Ohio State University, September 5, 2005, http://bit.ly/1MuRx0t.

6. Edward L. Deci and Richard M. Ryan, *Handbook of Self-Determination Research* (Rochester, NY: University of Rochester Press, 2002).

7. Pink, *Drive*.

8. Steven Reiss, *Who Am I? The 16 Basic Desires that Motivate Our Behavior and Define Our Personality* (New York: Berkley, 2002).

9. Garth Sundem, "A New Kind of Reward Increases Intrinsic Motivation," *Psychology Today*, March 19, 2014, http://bit.ly/1DcbSAs.

10. David Kelley and Tom Kelley, *Creative Confidence: Unleashing the Creative Potential Within Us All* (New York: Crown Business, 2013).

11. Sylvia Ann Hewlett, Melinda Marshall, and Laura Sherbin, "How Diversity Can Drive Innovation," *Harvard Business Review*, December 2013, http://bit.ly/1zZCruD.

12. Reiss, *Who Am I?*

13. "Power Is the Ultimate High," *New Scientist*, July 4, 2012, http://bit.ly/1Z0TFSr.

14. Fritjof Capra and P. L. Luisi, *The Systems View of Life: A Unifying Vision* (Cambridge: Cambridge University Press, 2014), loc:612.

15. Laloux, *Reinventing Organizations*, loc:5713.

16. Mihaly Csikszentmihalyi, *Creativity: The Psychology of Discovery and Invention* (New York: Harper Perennial Modern Classics, 2013), loc:1887.

17. Les McKeown, "A Very Simple Reason Employee Engagement Programs Don't Work," *Inc.*, September 10, 2013, http://bit.ly/1U6OPR0.

18. McKeown, "A Very Simple Reason."

19. Sebastian Radics, "Advanced Moving Motivators Sessions – Don't Miss These 6 Expert Hints" On the Agile Path, May 22, 2015, http://bit.ly/1M4KhDW.

20. Sander Huijsen, "My Experience Playing Moving Motivators," Medium, August 7, 2015, http://bit.ly/1QgZvNS.

Chapter 11: Happiness Door

1. Steve Crabtree, "Worldwide, 13% of Employees Are Engaged at Work," Gallup, October 8, 2013, http://bit.ly/1aG9kMn.

2. Devi Clark, "Fascinating Facts about Job Satisfaction and Motivation All Over the World," Lifehack, February 16, 2015, http://bit.ly/1vEQJuL.

3. University of Warwick, "We Work Harder When We Are Happy, New Study Shows," Science Daily, March 20, 2014, http://bit.ly/1e1eeuF.

4. Shawn Achor, *The Happiness Advantage: The Seven Principles of Positive Psychology That Fuel Success and Performance at Work* (New York: Crown Business, 2010).

5. Jonathan Haidt, *The Happiness Hypothesis: Finding Modern Truth in Ancient Wisdom* (New York: Basic Books, 2006).

6. Daniel T. Gilbert, *Stumbling on Happiness* (New York: A. A. Knopf, 2006), loc:561.

7. Martin E. Seligman, *Authentic Happiness: Using the New Positive Psychology to Realize Your Potential for Lasting Fulfillment* (New York: Free Press, 2004).

8. Harvey B. Simon, "Giving Thanks Can Make You Happier" Harvard Health Publications, November 22, 2011, http://bit.ly/1s2KuRg.

9. Kelly Fitzpatrick, "Are We Happier When We Give or Receive Gifts?" Greatist, December 20, 2011, http://bit.ly/1PwpqAp.

10. Jenny Santi, "The Secret to Happiness Is Helping Others," *Time*, October 14, 2015, http://ti.me/1ZItBg7.

11. Rachael Moeller Gorman, "New Science Links Food and Happiness," *EatingWell*, May/June 2010, http://bit.ly/1OkkLR1.

12. Leo Widrich, "What Happens to Our Brains When We Exercise and How It Makes Us Happier," Buffer Social, August 23, 2012, http://bit.ly/YKZMQZ.

13. Lindsay Holmes, "All the Ways Sleep Affects Your Happiness, in One Chart," Huffington Post, July 23, 2015, http://huff.to/1g9bdLl.

14. Jay Cassano, "The Science of Why You Should Spend Your Money on Experiences, Not Things," *Co.Exist* (blog), *Fast Company*, March 30, 2015, http://bit.ly/1CoOIlx.

15. "Spending Time in Nature Makes People Feel More Alive, Study Shows," University of Rochester, June 3, 2010, http://bit.ly/UyDdg1.

16. Elise Bialylew, "4 Ways Mindfulness Can Enhance Your Happiness," Huffington Post, April 16, 2015, http://huff.to/1FY1bo1.

17. Kimberly Schaufenbuel, "Why Google, Target, and General Mills Are Investing in Mindfulness," *Harvard Business Review*, December 28, 2015, http://bit.ly/1TmWHgu.

18. Robert Waldinger, "What Makes a Good Life? Lessons from the Longest Study on Happiness," TED, November 2015, http://bit.ly/1QI5o7B.

19. Emily Esfahani Smith, "There's More to Life Than Being Happy," *The Atlantic*, January 9, 2013, http://bit.ly/1QI5o7B.

20. Melinda Wenner, "Smile! It Could Make You Happier," *Scientific American*, September 1, 2009, http://bit.ly/1oxz0pU.

Chapter 12: Yay! Questions and Celebration Grids

1. Robin and Burchell, *No Excuses*, loc:589.

2. "Celebrate Failure," *Fast Company*, November 21, 2005, http://bit.ly/g9d7Ra.

3. Alexander Kjerulf, "Top 5 Reasons to Celebrate Mistakes at Work," The Chief Happiness Officer Blog, June 3, 2010, http://bit.ly/1gUfL4Q.

4. Leigh Buchanan, "Welcome to the Church of Fail," *Inc.*, November 2013, http://bit.ly/1lk6abG.

5. Jason Fried, "Failure Is Overrated, a Redux," *Signal vs. Noise*, March 23, 2009, http://bit.ly/41Ffok.

6. Donald G. Reinertsen, *The Principles of Product Development Flow: Second Generation Lean Product Development* (Redondo Beach: Celeritas, 2009), loc:1512.

7. Reinertsen, *The Principles of Product Development Flow*, loc:1512.

8. Deming, *Out of the Crisis*, 128.

9. Alberg, "How to Celebrate Success Throughout Your Projects."

10. Bruce Eckel, "You Get What You Measure," Reinventing Business (blog), August 2, 2011, http://bit.ly/pc0CwQ.

11. Atul Gawande, *The Checklist Manifesto: How to Get Things Right* (New York: Metropolitan Books, 2010).

12. Grant Halvorson, "Sometimes Negative Feedback Is Best."

13. McCrimmon, "Celebrating Success at Work," http://bit.ly/N1XLrP.

14. Jurgen Appelo, *How to Change the World: Change Management 3.0* (Rotterdam: Jojo Ventures BV, 2012).

15. Jim McCarthy, *Software for Your Head: Core Protocols for Creating and Maintaining Shared Vision* (Boston: Addison-Wesley, 2002).

16. Pascal Van Cauwenberghe, "We Expect Nothing Less Than Perfection," Thinking for a Change (blog), August 12, 2006, http://bit.ly/I9i0ih.

Conclusion

1. Jurgen Appelo, "Where's the End?" noop.nl, December 13, 2012, http://bit.ly/1fGScHv.

2. Gary Hamel, *What Matters Now: How to Win in a World of Relentless Change, Ferocious Competition, and Unstoppable Innovation* (San Francisco: Jossey-Bass, 2012), loc:4123.

3. Kahneman, *Thinking, Fast and Slow*, loc:3473.

4. Jim Highsmith, "Agile Bureaucracy: When Practices Become Principles," Jim Highsmith (blog), July 10, 2012, http://bit.ly/1njD8bV.

5. Henry Mintzberg, *Managers, Not MBAs: A Hard Look at the Soft Practice of Managing and Management Development* (San Francisco: Berrett-Koehler Publishers, 2004), 252.

6. Robin and Burchell, *No Excuses*, loc:702.

7. Scott Berkun, "How to Convince Your Boss to Try New Things," Scott Berkun (blog), March 26, 2014, http://bit.ly/1gMMc1I.

8. Charles Duhigg, *The Power of Habit: Why We Do What We Do in Life and Business* (New York: Random House, 2012).

9. Rother, *Toyota Kata*, loc:171.

Index

Wait, there's more!

work expo
Explain Purpose by Collecting Artifacts

identity symbols
Invite Workers to Create a Shared Identity

improvement dialogues and copilot programs

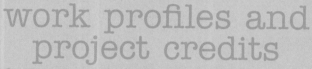
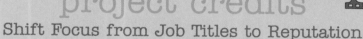

Improve Performance through Collaboration

problem time
Keep Solving Problems and Deliver Value

work profiles and project credits

Shift Focus from Job Titles to Reputation

$$S = \left\{ \frac{\sqrt{\sum_{i=1}^{C} \frac{(T^2 \cdot L)^3}{(A \cdot P)} \times \sqrt{\frac{E \cdot G^2}{\int_s^2 t^n \, dt \cdot S}{M \cdot e^x \cdot N}}}}{\sum_{i=0}^{\infty} \left[\frac{\int f(E) \, dx \, H}{f(G) \, dx \, T} \right]} \right\}$$

salary formula
Keep People's Trust with Fair Compensation

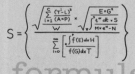

champfrogs checklist
Understand How to Be a Better Influencer

m30.me/morehappiness

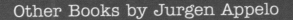

It is one of the questions we get most often: How do I deal with my crappy organization? I like my work but I don't like what our management is doing. How do I deal with it? Well, that's easy. You have three options: (1) Ignore it; (2) quit your job; or (3) learn about change management. This booklet for those who choose option 3.

m30.me/hcw

Agile management is an often overlooked part of agile. There are at least a hundred books for agile developers and project managers, but very few for agile managers and leaders. However, when organizations adopt agile software development, not only developers and project managers need to learn new practices. Development managers and team leaders must also learn a different approach to leading and managing organizations.

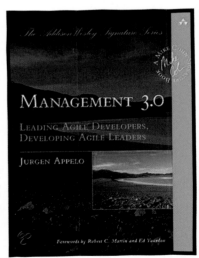

m30.me/m30

Please review this book!

You finished the book.
Thank you.

I worked on this book for **three years.**
Therefore, may I ask you for a favor? : -)

Please **leave your review** on Amazon: **m30.me/amazon**
Or on GoodReads if you prefer: **m30.me/goodreads**
I would really appreciate that.

The law of writing says that **reviews sell books.**
Even better, you can **blog about the book!**
I will happily share your article.

That's all for now,
Thanks!

Jurgen

About the Author

Jurgen Appelo is pioneering management to help creative organizations survive and thrive in the twenty-first century. He offers concrete games, tools, and practices, so you can introduce better management, with fewer managers.

Jurgen calls himself a creative networker. But sometimes he's a writer, speaker, trainer, entrepreneur, illustrator, manager, blogger, reader, dreamer, leader, freethinker, or . . . Dutch guy. Inc.com has called him a Top 50 Leadership Expert, a Top 50 Leadership Innovator, and a Top 100 Great Leadership Speaker. Since 2008, Jurgen writes a popular blog at NOOP.NL, offering ideas on the creative economy, agile management, organizational change, and personal development. He is the author of the book *Management 3.0*, which describes the role of the manager in agile organizations, and he wrote the little book *How to Change the World*, which describes a supermodel for change management (management30.com). Jurgen is founder of the business network Happy Melly (happymelly.com). He is also a speaker who is regularly invited to talk at business seminars and conferences around the world (jurgenappelo.com).

After studying software engineering at the Delft University of Technology, and earning his master's degree in 1994, Jurgen has busied himself starting up and leading a variety of Dutch businesses, always in the position of team leader, manager, or executive. Jurgen has experience in leading a horde of 100 software developers, development managers, project managers, business consultants, quality managers, service managers, and kangaroos, some of which he hired accidentally.

Nowadays he works full-time developing innovative courseware, books, and other types of original content. But sometimes Jurgen puts it all aside to do some programming himself, or to spend time on his ever-growing collection of science fiction and fantasy literature, which he stacks in a self-designed bookcase. It is 4 meters high. Jurgen lives in Rotterdam (The Netherlands)—and in Brussels (Belgium)—with his partner Raoul and a Wi-Fi network called Scooby.

 twitter.com
/jurgenappelo

 youtube.com
/user/jurgenappelo

 linkedin.com
/in/jurgenappelo

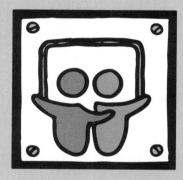 slideshare.net
/jurgenappelo

 facebook.com
/jurgenappelo

 www.noop.nl

Co-Creators

It is impossible to write a book like the one you've just read without the help of a supportive community of friends, partners, professionals, and readers. Many people have assisted in the creation of this book—sometimes even without realizing it.

The book was copyedited—and my nonnative English was significantly grammatically improved—by Betsy Goolsby, David Gregory, and Wayne Purdin.

The design edition of this book was beautifully formatted thanks to the amazing design skills of Linda Hirzmann. Some early drafts and late adaptations of individual chapters were created by Erik Gille.

Useful photos were graciously offered by Anthony Claverie, Dave Brands, Gary Shepherd, José Ignacio de Juan, Jürgen Dittmar, Kamil Sowa, Koen van Wijk, Mateusz Gajdzik, Omar C. Bermudez, and Robie Wood.

It would have been a boring book without the wonderful stories and contributions offered by Agnieszka Zimończyk, Alix Moghadam, Anders Ivarsson, Cláudio Pires, Flavius Ştef, Florian Hoffmann, Gary Shepherd, Geoffrey Lowney, Gerardo Barcia Palacios, Inga-Lill Holmqvist, Ivo van Halen, Ivo Velitchkov, Jason Little, Johan Dahlbäck, Juhani Lind, Lazar Todorov, Paul Bowler, Paul Holden, Patrick Verdonk, Peter Rubarth, Riccardo Bua, Robie Wood, Sebastian Radics, and Stefan Wunder.

Inspiring company visits were organized by Anders Ivarsson, Ivo van Halen, Jesper Richter-Reichhelm, Jordi Ascolies, Kees de Koning, Leighton Gao, Olve Maudal, Paweł Pustelnik, Rory Abbott, and Volker Dusch.

The book would have been a pain to read without the many improvements offered by my proofreaders Adrian Lupei, Alexandros Philopoulos, Andrej Ruckij, Angelo Anolin, Caspar Below, Craig Brown, Dan Woodward, Derek Graham, Eduardo Scudeler Fernandes, Erik Weber, Inga-Lill Holmqvist, Jan Pastwa, Janka Haderkova, Jorge Ronchese, Ken Weir, Koen van Wijk, Matthias Wolf, Max Heywood, Maxim Krizhanovsky, Mike Griffiths, Mike Leber, Nilesh Kulkarni, Paul Immerzeel, Paweł Pustelnik, Pierre Fauvel, Preeti Gholap, Rafael Cichini, Rainer Grau, Ramkumar KB, Riccardo Bua, Scott Duncan, Sergiu Damian, Sigrid Smeele, Stefan Haas, Stefano Leli, Thomas Kuryura, Tomasz Skubisz, Tony Navarro, Vibhu Srinivasan, Vijay Bandaru, Voranc Kutnik, Wim Heemskerk, Yehonathan Sharvit, and Yves Charreire.

Finally, my team at Happy Melly has always been very supportive. Thank you all!

I offer my apologies for the deplorable quality of all the illustrations. I made them myself.

In fact, you can start by downloading all illustrations that I made for my first three books, including this one! Yes, it is all free. And yes, you may use them in your own work, commercial or not. I would just appreciate it if you would you credit me, with a link to one of my websites.

• • • • • • • • • • • • • • •

However, what I really hope is that you start drawing yourself. The world already has too much stock photography!

M30.ME/
ILLUSTRATIONS
→

The Management 3.0 events aim at leaders and knowledge workers who are trying to be more agile and lean in their approach to management. The courses and workshops typically draw a mix of team leaders, development managers, directors, agile coaches, HR managers, project managers, and creative workers.

The most important goal for Management 3.0 events is for people to take action to improve their organizations. All events adhere to the following principles: theory and practice in small chunks; clear and effective visuals; inspiring stories and metaphors; fun games and exercises; focused group discussions; and concrete practices with tangible results.

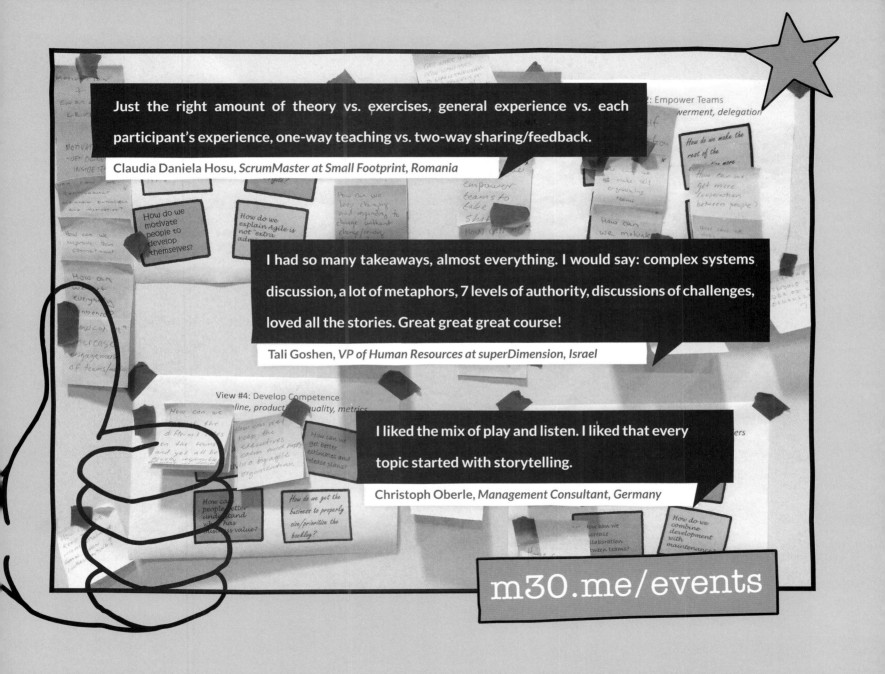

Just the right amount of theory vs. exercises, general experience vs. each participant's experience, one-way teaching vs. two-way sharing/feedback.

Claudia Daniela Hosu, *ScrumMaster at Small Footprint, Romania*

I had so many takeaways, almost everything. I would say: complex systems discussion, a lot of metaphors, 7 levels of authority, discussions of challenges, loved all the stories. Great great great course!

Tali Goshen, *VP of Human Resources at superDimension, Israel*

I liked the mix of play and listen. I liked that every topic started with storytelling.

Christoph Oberle, *Management Consultant, Germany*

m30.me/events

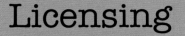

Licensing

Would you like to teach people the Management 3.0 principles and practices?

Do you want to use delegation poker, moving motivators, and all the other cool games, exercises, slides, and illustrations in your classes?

Join a growing global community of Management 3.0 facilitators!

m30.me/licensing

As a licensed facilitator you can give Management 3.0 courses and workshops anywhere in the world, in your own company, or as public events.

And many more . . .

m30.me/facilitators